PROSPECTS FOR
GREEN LIBERAL DEMOCRACY

Sverker C. Jagers

University Press of America,® Inc.
Lanham · Boulder · New York · Toronto · Plymouth, UK

Copyright © 2007 by
University Press of America,® Inc.
4501 Forbes Boulevard
Suite 200
Lanham, Maryland 20706
UPA Acquisitions Department (301) 459-3366

Estover Road
Plymouth PL6 7PY
United Kingdom

Library of Congress Control Number: 2006935154
ISBN-13: 978-0-7618-3610-0 (paperback : alk. paper)
ISBN-10: 0-7618-3610-1 (paperback : alk. paper)

To Lisa

Table of Contents

Acknowledgements

Plenty of people have been involved in the completion of this study and they all deserve the sincerest acknowledgement.

I am forever grateful to my homebase during these years: The Department of Political Science at Göteborg University. This is a splendid place of work, combining a leading research environment with an immense scope for individual initiatives, comradeship leavened with a large dollop of humour.

In preparing the final manuscript, Lennart J. Lundqvist, Gunnar Falkemark, Bo Rothstein and Bengt-Ove Boström gave me valuable comments, as did Jonas Hinnfors, Urban Strandberg and Marie Uhrwing at earlier stages of the process.

At the Department of Physical Resource Theory at Chalmers University of Technology, Stefan Wirsenius deserves an acknowledgement. His patience with my poor knowledge of science and his impressive modelling of the global biomass system made this book realisable in the first place.

At the Keele and Open Universities I am indebted to Andy Dobson.

At Melbourne University I wish to thank Nicholas Low for his invitation and Robyn Eckersley for thoughtful comments on Chapters 4 and 8.

Just as there are no free lunches there are no free research projects. Besides Forskningsrådsnämnden (FRN), I am most grateful to Adlerbertska forskningsfonden, Göteborgs Universitets Jubileumsfond, STINT, Kungl. och Hvitfeldska Stiftelsen, Kungliga Vetenskapsakademien and finally The Swedish Environmental Protection Agency.

I have an infinite number of reasons to be grateful to my wife Lisa whose support in everything I do is very valuable and to my three wonderful children Klara, Petter and Lukas, who were all three 'delivered' during these years.

Göteborg, April 2006

Sverker C. Jagers

Chapter 1

Compatibility Between Sustainable Development and Liberal Democracy

"No great improvements in the lot of mankind are possible, until a great change takes place in the fundamental constitution of their modes of thought."
(J. S. Mill 1873: Autobiography)

Sustainable development is a political goal with a scope that exceeds most objectives experienced in our political history. Unquestionably it is also a global project.[1] Only when there is global balance between society and the ecological system can it be said that there is real sustainable development. But that is just half the story. Sustainable development also requires a global fulfillment of human needs. It must meet the needs of both present and future generations. Into the concept of sustainable development is built a moral decree that requires present generations to share global resources equitably both among themselves, and with future generations. For this to be realised, according to one of the inventors, The Brundtland Commission, "painful choices have to be made" (WCED 1987:9).

It is easy to agree with this. Implementation of sustainable development would be an arduous task for any political system. There are no examples today of countries that have jointly applied a common 'distribution policy' aimed at reaching a goal such as global need satisfaction. To carry this through with simultaneous control for bio-physical limits certainly complicates the issue further. When adding the concern for future generations to the web of challenges (whose needs cannot be defined, and whose interests can hardly be politically represented), adopting such a goal could almost be seen as committing political suicide.

Implementation would, however, be particularly difficult for liberal democracies. Their citizens make use of the greatest part of all resources and goods being produced annually and practically 'must' do so in order to uphold the great variety of (individually chosen) lifestyles. If some of these resources are suddenly to be distributed differently, for example according to human needs (rather than purchasing power)—not to speak of future human needs— this means that people in the 'free world' must change their lifestyles. This is easier said than done, because liberal democracy is usually considered a political system that has elevated the individual's liberty to choose a lifestyle to the highest priority. Obviously, the relationship between liberal democracy and sustainable development is far from straightforward, and there are strong arguments for asking whether we have any reasons to believe that liberal democracy can realise sustainable development.

For the last thirty years, several environmentally concerned political theorists have analysed the relationship between liberal democracy and sustainable development (and similar visions). In these studies it has been suggested that there are 'features' within liberal democracies which make sustainable development unattainable, or incompatible with liberal democracy. For example, some theorists have argued that liberal democracy presupposes nation-bound political institutions that can never produce the kind of border-crossing policies needed to implement sustainable development. Others have pointed at normative tensions; liberal democracy emphasises individual liberty, while sustainable development would rather deprive individuals of it. I am particularly interested in this latter assertion and the major concern in this book is the following:

> Can policies aimed at realising sustainable development be considered compatible with upholding of the normative values constituting liberal democracy?

I have four major theoretical and methodological motives for raising this particular question. These motives will be further developed throughout this first chapter.

In Section 1.1, I examine the weaknesses that have been pointed out as explanations as to why liberal democracy cannot cope with sustainable development. This criticism comes from both eco-authoritarian and democratic theorists. I claim that these explanations and contra-arguments have to be systematised as 'philosophical' and 'institutional' arguments to become intelligible, particularly if we wish to perform a stringent compatibility analysis. In Section 1.2 I analyse how distinguished critical scholars have defined liberal democracy, and I conclude that we ought to strive to attain distinct definitions in the form of liberal-democratic ideal-types. In Section 1.3 I examine how liberal theorists have responded to the critique, and how they have shown that at least certain aspects of the complex idea of sustainable development can be given due attention in a liberal democracy. I claim that the different pro-arguments are both of an institutional and/or philosophical nature. In Section 1.4, I discuss what liberal democracy should be compatible with and suggest two alternatives: (i) environmental values, or (ii) environmental policies. Following this I summarise the possible compatibility analyses in a matrix. From that specification I conclude that one category of compatibility analyses (what I then call 'type-four analysis') has been poorly performed. Consequently I am ready to establish the objectives of my book, and the specific research questions to be answered. This I do in the last Section 1.5.

1.1 Liberal-Democratic Practice and Its Philosophical Foundation Ought to Be Kept Apart

1.1.1 Liberal Democracy Can Not Prevent Ecological Destruction; The Eco-Authoritarian Arguments

The 1960s and 1970s are sometimes characterised as the era of the "apocalypse" (cf. Barry 1999a:195). Scientists and political theorists delivered a straightforward message: without significant changes in human behaviour, in industrial metabolism, agriculture, individuals' day-to-day life, and global birth rates, the earth would collapse within the near future.[2] The larger the world population, and the more extensive its consumption, the greater the risk that nature strikes back on society and humanity in the form of resource scarcity. These predictions also raised questions on how to deal politically with these challenges. One of the main solutions was a centrally orchestrated redirection of humanity towards a more environmentally sound way of living. Enormous forces had to be mobilised, which would not possibly arise as a result of individuals' free will.

In his classic article ' The Tragedy of the Commons', Garreth Hardin (1968) outlines what happens when self-interested actors enjoy open access to, or unlimited use of, for example, natural resources. Each individual gains or benefits fully from additional exploitation while the costs would be shared with all other users of the resource. Thus, the tendency would be over-exploitation; what is most logical and rational for the individual results in a disaster for the collective, which in the long run also strikes back at the individual. Hardin's solution to this dilemma was not necessarily a liberal democracy, but either to replace open access to the current resource with enforceable private property rights, or to impose governmental restrictions via a centralised political system.

The neo-Malthusian[3] ecologist Paul Ehrlich (1968) argued that the only way to get a serious grip on the accelerating extinction of resources was through population control, which must be imposed at any cost:

> "We must have population control at home, hopefully through a system of incentives and penalties, but by compulsion if voluntary methods fail . . . We [i.e. United States] must use our political power to push other countries into programs which continue agricultural development and population control."
> (Ehrlich cited in Hayward 1995:147)

The American economist Robert Heilbronner pessimistically predicted severe social disputes as a result of the onset of resource scarcity, and therefore recommended political measures far beyond the limits of liberal democracy:

> "The likelihood that there are obdurate limits to the reformist reach of democratic institutions within the class bound body of capitalist society leads us to expect that the government of these societies, faced with extreme internal strife or with potentially disastrous social polarisation, would resort to authoritarian measures." (Heilbronner 1974:90)

Ophuls (1977, 1992), who also outlined an authoritarian system, saw this more as a transitional state on the way towards a less strenuous world— decentralised we may assume. Nevertheless, at least the short-term development of society was certainly of a less democratic kind:

> ". . . We have been living in an age of rampant individualism that arose historically from circumstances of abnormal abundance. It seems predictable, therefore, that on our way toward the steady state we shall move from individualism toward communalism. The self-interest that individualistic political, economic and social philosophies have justified as being in the overall best interests of the community . . . will begin to seem more and more reprehensible and illegitimate as pollution and other aspects of scarcity grow. And the traditional primacy of the community over the individual that has characterised virtually every other period of history will be restored." (Ophuls&Boyan 1992:285)

More recently, the English historian and political scientist Paul Kennedy (1993) has argued that to deal with environmental problems, politicians must make radical decisions today whose beneficial consequences will occur 40 years, or even more, into the future (Kennedy 1993:336). Thus, there is an intrinsic antagonism between environmental demands and the democratic capacity to meet them. The public and their representatives are unwilling to accept the trade-off of incurring significant short-term personal cost, in return for (uncertain) long-term improvements. Accordingly, sustainable development is always dependent on political will. Among other things, Kennedy suggests that mandate periods ought to be considerably lengthened so that politicians are encouraged to disregard other (often more powerful) interests that work contrary to long-term environmental concerns.

Defenders of democratic rule have criticised these 'eco-authoritarian' approaches for many reasons.[4] They question the limits to growth and the tragedy of the commons paradigms, as well as the effectiveness of authoritarian solutions compared to democratic ones. Rather, it is only by democratic means and democratically accepted regulations that the environmental problems can be dealt with, i.e., centralist control is one of the major elements causing the environmental crisis (Radcliffe 2000:29). That does not mean that all "green democratic" responses have defended liberal democracy as an appropriate political system—rather the opposite.

1.1.2   *Liberal Democracy Can Not Prevent Ecological Destruction; The 'Strong' Democratic Arguments*

Instead of defending, or proceeding from, liberal democracy as a democratic response to eco-authoritarianism, green democratic theorists have commonly suggested varying forms of de-centralised, 'participatory' and 'deliberative' democracy (Eckersley 1995:171)[5]—popularly called 'strong' democracy.[6] One argues that the whole foundation of liberal democracy is incompatible with environmental concern or sustainable development (cf. Dobson 2000:164ff). However, what 'compatibility' means is not obvious.[7] One leading green theorist, John Dryzek, summarises much of the critique by suggesting that "there are features intrinsic to liberal democracy which prevent the generation of truly effective solutions to ecological problems" (Dryzek 1996:112f). De Geus correspondingly talkings about the "inherent" weaknesses of liberal democracy (2001:20ff).[8]

Speaking in terms of 'intrinsic' or 'inherent' features is partly misleading because the arguments against liberal democracy do not only refer to intrinsic aspects of liberal democracy. In my view, an intrinsic feature of a political system, or of a political theory, essentially refers to something non-exclusive, i.e., a necessary component, and which is for that political system so fundamental that if dismissed, or unjustifiably complemented with other values or features, abrogates the original idea. Otherwise what would be the point in attributing a feature as 'intrinsic'? I contend that besides pure philosophical or political-theoretical features (which I take to be equivalent to 'intrinsic' features), arguments of a more practical-political character are common, and in my view these different kinds of arguments ought to be kept separate if we wish to conduct a stringent compatibility analysis. Let me clarify by examining some often quoted theorists.

Dobson (2000:167) argues that liberal democracy cannot be consistent with ecological concerns because liberalism's "thorough-going focus on the means rather than the ends of political association makes it even less compatible than some other political ideologies with an end-oriented concept of political and social life such as ecologism."[9] A similar explanation is offered by Mathews who asserts that to claim a compulsory concern for environmental issues would violate the whole foundation of liberal democracy, i.e., autonomy and individual self-rule (1995b:69). Furthermore, liberalism seeks to deal with the problem of environmental protection by treating nature as a set of resources only for human use. Even if the often referred to liberal 'harm principle'[10] is said to range over not only individuals now living but future generations as well (1995a:5), there is a lack of an intrinsic or definitive concern for others in liberalism (1995b:71). The emphasis on individual freedom and autonomy characteristic of liberal regimes simply works against the emergence of ecological identity and consciousness (1995b:94).

While Dobson consistently sticks to political-theoretical arguments, such as liberalism's emphasis on means rather than ends, Matthews both refers to values, such as autonomy and individual self-rule, and at the same time also discusses institutional factors such as liberal regimes.

Others criticise liberal democracy for lacking the means to act beyond its national borders. "At present the regulation of the distribution of environmental quality falls on national governments and their subsidiary (regional and local) states" (Low & Gleeson 1998:104). Yet, for environmental action to be truly effective on a global scale, it requires a global (cosmopolitical) regulatory system, spanning the whole sphere within which the environmental problem 'resides' (cf. Held 1995; Thompson 1995; O'Neill 2000). In my view, Low and Gleeson discuss both institutional aspects of present liberal democracies, but also the way liberal democracies function in a wider context.

Yet another critique is that that there are limits to the problem-solving capacity of liberal democracy. For example, the distribution of power in liberal democratic systems is inevitably skewed, and business always has a "privileged" position due to the financial resources available to it (Dryzek 1992:22ff). Liberal democracies also identify and disaggregate environmental problems based on the particular interests of affected parties. The time horizon in a liberal democracy is often no longer than that of the market.[11] Furthermore, liberal democracy is addicted to economic growth because if growth ceases, then distributional inequalities become more apparent. This fear of economic downturn means that liberal democracies are imprisoned by the market's growth imperative (cf. Hayward 1998:162).

In addition, much of politics today consists of an uneasy juxtaposition of liberal democracy and the administrative state. There is also some sort of mutuality between capitalism and liberal democracy, which makes it difficult to view them separately. Elsewhere Dryzek argues that the structure of liberal democracy itself is ultimately incapable of responding effectively to ecological problems and is incapable of incorporating 'negative feedback' to citizens when the ecological environment so demands. It is also incapable of 'co-ordinating' action in a multi-actor setting(Dryzek 1995:15f).

Dryzek's critique is comprehensive and certainly not only ranges over liberal democratic institutions, but also covers temporal issues and the way in which liberal democracies are related to, and function, in their surrounding societal environment.

By some, liberal democracy is considered a particularly restricted form of democracy. It represents a compromise between liberalism's primary concern with individualistically conceived property rights on the one hand, and a vision of democratic representation, participation and accountability on the other (Barns 1995:102). As far as I understand, this compromise prevents the state from regulating individuals to the benefit of the environment. As a final example, Hayward's (1995:216) explanation as to why liberal democracy is incompatible with environmental concern moves in the same direction. She maintains that a majority of liberal democratic initiatives fail to respond adequately to complex environmental problems because they are committed to competitive elections as well as individual liberty and private property. Barns as well as Hayward present both theoretical and practical arguments against liberal democracy.

1.1.3 Examining the Arguments

Obviously, a large number of factors from rather different proceeding points have been proposed as explanations as to why liberal democracy and sustainable development are incompatible with each other. It may very well be that each and every single objection points at weaknesses and limitations in the liberal-democratic construction. Still, I doubt whether all these objections can be summarised into one consistent portfolio of arguments to be characterised as "intrinsic features". For example, can we argue that the liberal democratic addiction to economic growth is an intrinsic feature?[12] Furthermore, is the inability of liberal democracies to co-ordinate across diverse interest groups, and the limitations of liberal democratic bargaining processes, sufficient justification to place them in a category referred to as liberal democracy's core philosophical base? Provided that 'intrinsic' refers to something inherent or unconditional, I cannot see how features such as these can be considered intrinsic. Additionally, and most importantly, they are so strikingly different that if put together they hardly make any sense at all.

Rather, I suggest that all these different objections point towards at least two, but probably four different kinds of 'feature categories'. If we set out the objections as shown below, I think it becomes rather clear which feature categories are intrinsic and which are not.

(1) The philosophical foundations of liberal democracy. For example, liberalism's denial of specific ends as legitimate to pursue, its lack of a moral concept of peoples' appropriate relation to nature, the emphasis on autonomy, individual self-rule, liberty, private property and lack of intrinsic concern for others.

(2) Present liberal democratic institutions (and their functioning). Under this category fall objections like the lack of a moral basis in liberal political organisations, the nation-centred government, the skewed distribution of power, the favouring of particular interests, the inability to co-ordinate and the fact that its bargaining processes work poorly and with uncertainty.

(3) The context within which liberal democracies function.[13] Liberal democracy is dependent on capitalism. It has an uneasy juxtaposition with the administrative state, it is addicted to economic growth and suffers limitations in the international (cosmo)political arena.

(4) The temporal dimension of liberal democracies. If societal transition into a sustainable society is an urgent task, then democracy, and liberal democracy

in particular, is a slow and inappropriate political system. But also, and perhaps even more important, the time horizon of liberal democracy is limited by the mandate periods.

I consider that only the philosophical dimension of liberal democracy is a genuine intrinsic feature of liberal democracy. If this liberal foundation were taken away, it would not only change the liberal democratic outlook, but would actually change the system into something non-liberal.[14] We cannot dismiss this by arguing that current liberal democracies differ so much that they hardly have anything in common. How liberal democracies are actually operating has little to do with the normative foundation of liberal democracy.[15] Rather, the causality chain goes the other way around. That is, it is not the liberal democratic institutions that decide and influence the philosophical foundation, but it is the foundation that decides the shape of the institutions.

The second category, liberal-democratic institutions and their functioning, is a product of ongoing historical processes whose final result is unpredictable. Thus, as far as the objections within this category point at intrinsic features, these are empirical and (at least might be) temporary, since they refer to present institutions which by their very nature will not exist indefinitely. This means that if we wish to make a compatibility analysis between sustainable development and liberal democratic institutions, the research question has to be whether the demands set by sustainable development can be met within the institutions of liberal democracies as they are today.[16]

The third category, the context, to a certain degree constitutes a product of liberal democracy. However, it primarily consists of an environment in which liberal democracy functions (e.g., the market existed long before the idea of liberal democracy was invented although today's liberal democracies and the market are tightly connected), and is therefore not necessarily a prerequisite for, and thus not an intrinsic feature of, liberal democracy.[17] In so far as the context has anything to do with compatibility between liberal democracy and sustainable development, this is because the success of a present liberal democracy is partly dependent on this context, i.e., the context influences the design of today's liberal democracies.[18] Again, however, we are dealing with an empirical issue: How well do liberal democracies cope with sustainable development in a context that is influenced by other factors?

The fourth temporal category can hardly be intrinsic, although present liberal democracies do have short mandate periods. This is because we cannot establish that the present design is a perpetual feature of and a prerequisite for liberal democracy (although I would be most surprised if it changed). Thus, for this category to represent an intrinsic feature we have to prove that a short time horizon is a necessary condition for the existence of liberal democracy.

To sum up, I conclude that compatibility between liberal democracy and sustainable development can be analysed as either a theoretical or an empirical issue. This also means that both theoretical (intrinsic) and factual features can explain (in)compatibility or can be used in order to show (in)compatibility.[19]

While the former feature category (1) is quite straightforward and refers to the philosophical foundations or the core values of liberal democracy, the latter feature categories (2-4) can either be packaged as a broad category of empirical/factual features, or be dealt with individually.

For reasons of relevance, stringency and specification, I advocate the latter approach. This allows us to focus on present liberal-democratic institutions, and how well they are designed to meet environmental concerns.[20] However, we must not forget that the value of such a study is limited in time, since we can only say to what extent present institutions can be expected to produce a topical policy, or uphold a current environmental value. This is because we cannot forecast the nature of future liberal-democratic institutions. We can only determine whether the topical value will (can be expected to) be paid due attention at present.

This brings us to the following conclusion. To analyse compatibility between liberal democracy and environmental concern, we either ought to proceed from liberal democracy's philosophical foundation, or the performance of its present institutions. To mix the two has been commonplace in the academic debate, something that makes a stringent compatibility analysis difficult.[21]

1.2   Is There a Uniform Liberal Democracy?

1.2.1   Determine the Philosophical Foundation of Liberal Democracy

In this section I focus on the philosophical feature category identified in the previous section and I assert that the arguments found in the green literature about the main philosophical core values of liberal democracy do not provide us with an appropriate set of value premises. They only lead to a list of inconsistent (interpretations of) concepts, which originate in liberal political philosophy in general.

It does not take long to notice this shortcoming. Let me start this argument by briefly studying some of the concepts that have been nominated as being either typical liberal-democratic, and/or most incompatible with environmental concerns.

One argument maintains that many features in liberal political theory run counter to radical ecology, like individualism, the pursuit of private gain, limited government and market freedom (for example Martell 1994). Others claim that liberal freedom ought to be understood as freedom of choice, opportunities or capacities (Sen 1982, 1988, 1993b). Another common objection is the argument that liberal democracy is a political system that upholds and defends liberty and neutrality between different conceptions of the good (O'Neill 1993:90-98). Therefore, it is argued, liberal democracy cannot pay particular attention to the good of environmental concern. Wissenburg (1998:11) characterises liberal democracy as a particular type of input-output machine, which transforms the preferences of individuals into rights for individuals. Furthermore he discusses the classical distinction[22] between negative and positive liberty (1998:33-42),[23] where he seems to be more committed to the former. Despite this, he claims elsewhere that liberal democracy is a political system that uses principles of justice, liberty and equality[24] to order conflicting claims and perhaps judge them as illiberal.

De-Shalit views liberal democracy as a system based on liberty, but also as an "egalitarian democracy"(2000:71). He claims that "If we want to see (liberal democratic) policies protecting the environment, but at the same time do not wish to retreat into totalitarian regimes, we must take the opportunity that liberalism as a philosophy offers us" (2000:92). That is, to look for a theory that is more socially oriented.

To these examples can be added the other philosophical characteristics that were presented in the former section.[25] In doing so, we are confronted with a characterisation of a political system that is said to be incompatible with sustainable development because it emphasises as disparate values as: autonomy, individual self-rule, liberty, freedom, freedom of opportunity, negative and positive liberty, neutrality, private property, private gain, limited government, market freedom, justice, equality, egalitarian democracy, rights, means—rather than ends, and which is also a political system that lacks moral conceptions and an intrinsic concern with others.

1.2.2 Examining the Arguments

No one would call into question that most (or even all) of these features belong to liberal political theory. Nonetheless, if the above list is what guides scholars when analysing compatibility between liberal democracy and environmental concern, it is not surprising that most theorists conclude that liberal democracy and sustainable development are incompatible.[26] If we summarise all the features mentioned, we end up with a list of concepts, and especially interpretations of concepts, some of which have a rather uneasy relationship to each other. In this list we obviously find various definitions of liberal democracy, including highly central concepts such as equality, liberty and rights, the precise meanings of which are extraordinarily important to determine if we wish to use these concepts in a stringent compatibility analysis. Because, in my view, without clearly defining these concepts one cannot establish the normative framework within which sustainable development must 'stay' in order to be considered compatible with liberal democracy, i.e., establishing criteria for judging compatibility.

According to several green theorists,[27] we can hardly speak of one liberal democracy, or liberalism. In the light of the above list, this assertion seems reasonable. Ideally all objections against liberal democracy (as well as each compatibility study) should be based on one general definition of liberal democracy. Clearly, this is impossible. It is, however, possible to construct liberal-democratic ideal-types, which together cover at least the most elementary conceptions (or features) of liberal democracy. Partly different versions of such ideal-types have been suggested (notably Sagoff 1988;

Eckersley 1995; Wissenburg 1998; Barry 1999b, 2001; Mason 1999; Dobson 2000; de Geus 2001) Common to all of them is the differentiation between 'classical' or 'protective' and 'social' or 'developmental' liberal democracy, where the former mainly emphasises individuals' negative liberty from state intervention and the latter (to various degrees) advocates state intervention in order for individuals to enjoy liberty.[28]

Although these theorists have pointed to the advantages of working with such ideal-types, and have hinted at the different outcomes we can expect from them, I have not found any completed compatibility analysis based on the two. Thus, de Geus (2001:35) thoroughly points out the weaknesses of classical liberalism, but only recommends theorists to take a closer look at the social liberalism descended from John Stuart Mill. So does Barry (2001:59-80). In my view, it is not enough to clarify the differences between the ideal-types when conducting such an analysis. One also has to specify testable frameworks or restrictions that each ideal-type constitutes, and which sustainable development must not contradict if it is ever to be considered 'compatible', i.e., derive compatibility criteria.[29]

1.3   In Search for a Green Liberal Democratic Theory

It is fair to say that mostly alternative variants of democracy have had a dominant share of the green political theoretical arena ever since the eco-authoritarian heydays. Although surprisingly few, there are, however, some examples of liberal democratic theorists who have discussed potential compatibility between liberal democracy and largely ecological values, or have shown how the ecological political project can be expressed within the "liberal idiom" (Dobson 2000:165). Those theorists have proceeded from either the institutional and/or the philosophical aspect of liberal democracy that we discussed in Section 1.1. Most of their attempts have been focused on rather specific issues, such as whether the liberal list of rights can be extended to include future generations, or if the ideas of a particular liberal theorist can be extended to cope with environmental issues.[30] I argue that more thorough analyses are required before anyone can dismiss or support liberal democracy because of its (non)conflicting relationship to sustainable development, and even more so before any consistent theory of green liberal democracy is to be formulated.

1.3.1   Institutional Arguments

Already in the early 1970s, Passmore (1974) suggested that governments in Western democratic states could pass preventive legislation against environmental degradation and exhaustion that directly harms present and future human beings. He also maintained that parliamentary democracy provides opportunities for people with special environmental interests to have their case heard and their claims weighed by their political representatives. After Passmore there was a huge gap of more than ten years before Sagoff

(1988:146-170) brought up the issue of liberal democracy's compatibility with environmental concerns (cf. Dobson 2000:164).

Eckersley (1995) discusses whether an extension of the liberal rights discourse and the liberal principle of autonomy can connect green values to liberal democratic theory. This point of view has received scant attention from green theorists. While the utilitarian branch of liberalism emphasises aggregation of individual human preferences (running the risk of abusing certain minorities for the benefit of the majority), the deontological tradition of liberalism insists that there are certain inviolable rights of individuals which may not be bargained away by simple majorities. These rights are not derived from any law or any utilitarian calculation, but from a set of moral principles which rest on a respect for the "inherent dignity and value of each and every individual" (1995:176), i.e., each individual's autonomy. The strongest practical expression for such thinking is the UN Declaration of Human Rights. Now, claims Eckersley, while there is no necessary connection between the principles and procedures of green politics: ". . . if green values were to be grounded in a critique of domination (of humans and other species) and a general defence of autonomy (the freedom of human and non-human beings to unfold in their own way and live according to their species life)" (1995:79), then procedures and outcomes might be linked.

Remaining to be decided is how to incorporate—as many Greens insist—non-humans in the principle of autonomy. Eckersley 'solves' this by borrowing the concept of "vital needs" from deep ecology (Naess 1989), which refers to the requirement that human beings do not have the right to reduce the richness and diversity of life-forms, unless it is for satisfying vital human needs. This principle brings forth a demand for justification. That is, any such interference has to be justified. This gives birth to the view that where humans have a range of alternatives, they ought to choose the course of action producing the least interference with richness and diversity. From this, according to Eckersley, a case could be made that "certain fundamental rights of non-human species should be incorporated and entrenched alongside fundamental rights in a constitutional bill of rights to ensure that they are not 'bargained away' by a simple majority. This would seem to be the only way in which non-human interests can be incorporated into the ground rules of democratic decision-making"(1995:181).[31]

Obviously, both Passmore and Eckersley hint at potential compatibility between liberal democracy and sustainable development, but their analyses are hardly comprehensive enough to show that they actually are compatible.

1.3.2 Philosophical Arguments

Saward (1993) analyses whether Greens should be regarded as undemocratic. He claims that ecological value-sets often contain a considerable tension between advocating certain essential policy outcomes and valuing democratic procedures (1993:64): "If democracy is understood as a responsive rule meaning that rulers are responsive to the felt wishes of [a majority of] citizens, then there is a natural compatibility between liberalism and democracy which does not obtain between ecology and democracy"(1993:69). The main problem for Greens, according to Saward, is that they tend to see nature as an intrinsic value, and as long as they do so their goal can never be compatible with democracy of whatever kind. According to Saward, however, there are a few ways to get around this. Above all, Greens should not think in terms of overriding principles and imperatives, since that is unjustifiable from a liberal-democratic perspective. Greens instead ought to view democracy and ecology on an equal footing. Most classic definitions do not see democracy as a value in itself, but rather as something that is justified as a means to some separate, valued end. Thus, green values ought to be seen as one goal out of many, and perhaps even environmental quality as a means, rather than an end.

This is similar to Dobson's (1990) ideas. Environmental values and beliefs may persist, but "political change will only occur once people think differently or, more particularly, that sustainable living must be prefaced by sustainable thinking" (1990:140). Only if ecological matters become significant political issues will they gain respect in a democracy. Thus, if Greens stop considering environmental values as intrinsic, then there is, at least theoretically, no more tension between ecology and democracy than there is between liberalism and democracy.

Achterberg (1993) approach the issue of liberal democracy and environmental concern from a different but interesting angle. Instead of confronting liberal democracy with environmental values (the way many other green liberal theorists have), he proceeds from The Netherlands National Environmental Policy Plan (NEPP) and investigates to what extent this plan, with its implied policies, can be considered compatible with liberal democracy. This approach can be criticised for many reasons, such as the national scope of the plan, while sustainable development is a global project.[32] Still, Achterberg paves the way for a, so far, quite unexplored compatibility analysis. He compares policies for (auto)mobility and economic growth with Rawls (1972 and 1987) theorising about liberal neutrality and 'overlapping consensus'. In his study of the environmental plan, Achterberg concludes that the implementation of sustainable development requires regulation, planning and market restrictions that would have to be justified, in relation to liberal theory. This justification is, however, difficult from a liberal perspective, unless the idea of overlapping consensus (i.e., consensus about a political concept of justice where the aim is to ensure a minimal but stable social unity over generations) is supplemented with a 'Transmission principle':

> "We should not hand the world that we have used and exploited on to our successors in a substantially worse shape than we received it."[33] (Routley & Routley 1982:123 cited in Achterberg 1993:97)

If this principle is added to the liberal foundation and taken in a non-anthropocentric sense, Achterberg argues that Rawls argumentation "is at least heuristically useful" (1993:155). This is because one can then develop a 'thin theory of the good' into the concept of a more broadly conceived (non-moral) good. This means, as I understand it that Greens (and others) can demand certain sacrifices for the benefit of the environment without jeopardising the moral neutrality so important to them.

I agree that proceeding from Rawls is 'heuristically useful'. However, more thorough analyses are required before Achterberg's conclusions can be considered valid for liberal-democratic theory in general.

1.3.3   The Use of both Institutional and Philosophical Arguments

One of the pioneering liberals who argued that environmentalists can be liberals was Sagoff (1988). According to him, this statement is valid, even if environmentalists "may be said to constitute a moral lobby, if not a moral majority, of a sort, insofar as they advocate laws that embody ethical and perhaps even religious ideals concerning the way we ought to treat our natural surroundings." (1988:150). Sagoff puts forth two arguments to prove that environmentalists can be liberals even if "the laws and policies supported by the environmental lobby are not neutral../..but express a moral conception of people's appropriate relation to nature." (1988:ibid). One argument is typically institutional, and one is philosophical.

Sagoff's first argument is that liberals make a distinction between the structure of institutions and the social policies that emerge from them (1988:166). Secondly, liberals have a great tolerance for competing views (1988:167).[34] As long as the liberal democratic procedures are neutral, then the content of environmental policy rarely becomes relevant from a liberal perspective. Each and every one is welcome to advance and defend views of the good life—including a good environment.[35]

Perhaps it cannot be said that Sagoff proved that sustainable development is compatible with liberal democracy, but he certainly provides us with additional reasons for further investigating the relationship between the two. For example, what if some variants of liberal democracy suggest that its citizens ought to have guaranteed access to certain basic goods in order to actually enjoy a good life and a decent environment. And, can it be argued that the liberal democratic state is obliged to provide these goods, then would not that be an entry to compatibility?[36]

1.3.4   Examining the Arguments

All these examples should be viewed at least as minor contributions to a conceivable coherent liberal theory of a green society. By way of introduction, Sagoff does not really see any conflict between ecological projects and liberal values or institutions. Both Saward and Dobson suggest that the environmental goals be 'played down' a bit in order to be compatible with liberal democracy.[37]

Eckersley elaborates on the liberal institutions in order to find mutual ground between liberal democracy and environmental concerns. Like many of the others, Achterberg proceeds from liberal values, but instead of confronting them with environmental values, he brings them face to face with suggested policies for sustainable development, and manages to conclude that some kind of compatibility may exist by adding an (acceptable) principle to Rawls liberal theory.

However, it is uncertain if any of these attempts show convincingly that liberal democracy and environmental concerns can be compatible. In my view, the analyses are far too fragmented for that. If anything they imply that we should investigate the issue further, since we cannot conclude unconditionally that liberal democracy and sustainable development are incompatible.

1.3.5   Approaching Green Liberalism

The first really comprehensive attempt to analyse the relationship between liberal democracy and environmental concern and to formulate a theory of green liberalism is the one made by Wissenburg (1998).[38] He reinterprets (from a fairly 'thin' and protective view of liberty)[39] Rawls (1993:274) "saving principle" into a restraint principle which says:[40]

> ". . . no goods shall be destroyed unless unavoidable and unless they are replaced by perfectly identical goods; if that is physically impossible, they should be replaced by equivalent goods, resembling the original as closely as possible; and if this is also impossible, a proper compensation should be provided." (Wissenburg 1998:123)

With this principle, he formulates a fairly strong protection of environmental resources—at least for being within the liberal paradigm. However, this principle may not be enough if we view it from, e.g., a deep ecologist's perspective arguing that all living creatures have the same rights and that human beings ought to obey these at any price. For example, how much of a protection does "unless unavoidable" offer? This may be a problem. Liberal democracy can never guarantee that all animals and other species will be completely safe. On the other hand, anyone demanding such guarantees must seriously reflect upon whether any other system could actually offer that. Nevertheless, even if other political systems would be able to do that, Wissenburg dismisses them as unrealistic options: "Green communitarianism would be the nightmare of Utopia come true." (1998:224).

What Wissenburg manages to show is that a liberal democracy can, with legitimacy, do quite a lot to benefit the environment, although perhaps not save every individual life form on earth. He concludes that:

> ". . . if the worst possible futures of our present society are held against liberal democracy, it is only fair that we compare these to the worst possible futures under alternative circumstances . . . if we feel that a 'greened' liberal

> democracy is insufficient to warrant sustainability, if we feel that with or
> without a free market, there is still danger because the presence of ecology-
> conscious citizens is a necessary condition for the ecologically balanced
> society. . . [then] either we choose to try to get a grip on the minds and
> opinions of humans, taking the first steps on the road to serfdom, or we take
> up the challenge." (Wissenburg 1998:225)

Even if Wissenburg's analysis of liberal democracy's compatibility with
environmental concerns is the most comprehensive work that I have found,
much research remains before the relationship between liberal democracy and
sustainable development has been fully explored.[41]

Besides using ideal-types and compatibility criteria (cf. Section 1.2), one
supplement I would like to suggest is a deeper investigation of what liberal
democracy should be compatible with, i.e., the features of environmental
concern or 'sustainable development'. Throughout this chapter I have indicated
that the compatibility debate has circled mostly around environmental values.
That is, liberal democratic values or institutions have been analysed in relation
to typical environmental values such as concern for future generations and
other species. An exception in this respect is Achterberg (1993) who we saw
confronted liberal democracy with environmental policies instead of values. De
Geus (2001) is another. Even if none of them explores the policy track very
thoroughly,[42] they indicate that this would be a fruitful way to take the debate
further.

1.4   Sustainable Development as Values or Policies

1.4.1 Liberal-Democratic Compatibility with What?

The main focus of the early debate on compatibility between democracy and
ecology was on specific environmental problems, such as discharges of toxic
substances (Carson 1962), population growth (Ehrlich 1968) and the overuse of
global resources (Hardin 1968). This was also linked to fairly precise policy
recommendations. The problems should be solved by substantial and, if needed,
enforceable changes in individual life patterns and behaviour. The core matter
was whether such changes and policies could be produced in a democracy.
Since then, the 'original' challenges for democracies have been reformulated
into theoretically more sophisticated, but also more ideological/philosophical,
challenges such as ecologism (Dobson 2000), ecocentrism (Eckersley 1992) as
well as 'weaker' and 'stronger' interpretations of sustainable development (cf.
Baker et al. 1997:9,13-16; Dobson 1998:33-61).

Thus, the debate once started as a comparison largely between environmental
policies and democratic institutions but has since transformed into mostly
comparisons of values. One reason for this may be that the original policy
challenges to democracy drew scientific criticism for being based on unreliable
scenarios and predictions. Succeeding Greens therefore spoke in terms of

easily be condemned as non-neutral. Finally, the number of possible policy combinations meant to produce sustainable development is simply overwhelming (cf. Wissenburg 1998:63).

These objections are all totally legitimate. However, we must not forget that a (re)introduction of environmental policies brings us closer to the environmental political realm. That is relevant for several reasons.

First, it is probably important that our political theoretical studies are in touch with both environmental and political realities if we wish to see a healthier environment in the future. One way to achieve this is to make the compatibility debate accessible and publicly intelligible by taking practical cases into the analyses.

Second, such studies might have positive informative and psychological affects on the individuals who, according to current environmental policy suggestions, are supposed to change their behaviour. If people think the environment is doomed, and there is nothing to do about it since any effort would be 'undemocratic', or unattainable, then what incentive do they have to actually change their behaviour?

Third, compatibility may be more successful in practice than in theory. Dryzek has suggested that "greening is far less ambiguous when it comes to real-world cases than it is at the level of philosophical reflection." (1996:109). For two philosophical values or concepts to be compatible, it is tempting to argue that they have to be fully compatible. Even a minimal contradiction would then overturn compatibility between them. This way of reasoning might be philosophically interesting, but at the same time means that many environmental political projects are 'impossible', even if they actually take place.[43] Another possible position when it comes to environmental policy versus democracy and its institutions is that (at least roughly speaking) it is enough that a majority of the people agree to the particular policy. If so, then whether liberal democracy and an environmental policy are compatible is entirely an empirical question. To go that far is quite uninteresting from a political theory point of view, and not even necessary. This is because, by bringing in environmental policies (instead of yet another environmental value) and putting them against liberal democratic values, we pave a way in-between the pure philosophical and empirical investigations. We can add nuances to the political theoretical analyses of compatibility, while at the same time also get closer to the political realm.

Fourth, even if some scholars claim to have shown that ecological values might be compatible with either liberal values, or liberal institutions (notably Sagoff 1998, Saward 1993; Eckersley 1995; Wissenburg 1998), most of the studies are relatively shallow. For example, we still have little evidence that the compatibility established would be valid when moving towards practical policies for global sustainable development.

Figure 1.1   Matrix over plausible compatibility studies

Sustainable development	Liberal democracy	
	Institutions	Philosophical foundation
Values	1	2
Policies	3	4

Commentary: Besides the two dimensions in the matrix, we must keep in mind the ideal-types, discussed in Section 1.2. It is most important to clarify to what particular liberal democratic philosophy (classic/protective or social/developmental) we are referring when we examine the results of any of the compatibility analyses we find especially in 2 and 4. The studies implied in 1 and 3 are also subject to the same demand for clarification, i.e., to which institutions do we refer? However, these institutions can either be found in political theory (and can then be captured by the 'classical' and the 'social' ideal-types), or they can be derived from real cases, i.e., based on the systems in different liberal-democratic countries.

In the matrix above, it is illustrated what I consider to be the possible ways to analyse compatibility between liberal democracy and ecological concern. In Section 1.1 we discussed the first dimension of this matrix, namely the one specifying liberal democracy either as the philosophical foundation, or the political institutions. From the discussion on what liberal democracy ought to be compatible with, we now also have the second dimension that constitutes this matrix. This dimension is the concern for the environment (read sustainable development), which can either be expressed as environmental values, or as environmental policy. The foregoing analysis thus leads me to suggest the following four variants of compatibility studies:

The first study (square 1) is a common approach in the green literature. This is when environmental values are put against liberal-democratic institutions. Important examples referred to throughout this chapter are Eckersley (1995), Dobson (1996, and Goodin (1996).

The second type of study (square 2) is a typical political theoretical compatibility analysis, where liberal values are compared with environmental values. Examples that have been given here are Dobson (2000), Barry (1999), Wissenburg (1998), Saward (1993) and Goodin (1992).

At issue in square 3 is whether environmental policies can be produced and fulfilled by present liberal democratic institutions. This is another way of analysing compatibility—based less on a green political theoretical starting point, and more on empirical observation.[44] Examples of research in this category are many of the eco-authoritarian scholars such as Heilbronner (1974) and Ophuls (1977), and the literature on the redesigning of global environmental politics, notably scholars like Altvater (1999), Low & Gleeson (1998) and Held (1995). Also the school of so-called 'Ecological modernisation' may be placed under this category (cf. Langhelle 2000b).

The fourth study (square 4) is a far less known and developed category. A typical research question here would be: "Can environmental policy X be considered justifiable seen from the viewpoint of liberal democratic value (set) Y, i.e., can we argue that policy X falls within the policy restrictions (frames) set by the value structure of liberal democracy?[45] I earlier mentioned Achterberg (1993) as an (yet quite undeveloped) example. De Geus's (2001) analysis of how far liberal political theory can constitute a basis for solving the environmental issue by comparing the political goals of Dutch green parties with (mainly) John Locke´s political philosophy should be considered another.

1.4.2 *Proceeding from Sustainable Development Policies*

As I pointed out earlier, there are several reasons for complementing the democracy-vs-environment debate by adding a policy dimension to environmental concern, or sustainable development, which is the most prevalent concept today. Such a supplement is, however, afflicted with difficulties.[46]

First, there is no such thing as 'a sustainable development', or a global state called 'sustainability'. To design policies from an image of what sustainability looks like is thus doomed to failure, because the end is solely a normative image. At the same time, it is probably not possible to suggest any policies at all, unless we have information about the present environmental conditions and what needs to be changed. What can be done, it has been suggested, is to outline a less unsustainable society and investigate what transitions and thus what policies (or policy directions) are required for the implementation of such a society (e.g., O'Riordan 1996).[47] To design a study like that is of course an arduous task.

Second, another problem is the question, how extensive should the transition be? Not least this depends on whether we start from an anthropocentric (human-centred) starting point or if we choose to proceed from a biocentric (nature-based) viewpoint.[48] I do not think it is—other than perhaps normatively—possible to argue that one starting point is more adequate than another. We can be certain that the more anthropocentric our point of departure is, the more likely that the transition will be compatible with liberal democratic values. And also, the less biocentric our point of departure is, the less nature and environment will probably be saved for, e.g., future generations. The only way to overcome this problem, as far as I can see, is to proceed from an as honest, transparent and 'objectionable' interpretation as possible of a 'less unsustainable' state, and to carry through a distinct and well structured analysis; all this in order to make both the approach and the conclusions worthy of serious and informed debate.

Third, the most challenging aspect of the third (and consequently the fourth) study of compatibility is not so much of a theoretical kind. It is instead the fact that political theorists can hardly accomplish the implied studies solely by themselves. To find out what policies would be required for society to become less unsustainable requires co-operation with science and technology, as well as interdisciplinary work with other more closely related disciplines such as economics, sociology and psychology. Nevertheless, if green political theorists are willing to accept this challenge, they will be able to add an interesting dimension to the debate regarding compatibility between liberal democracy and sustainable development. That is, they are willing to accept the challenge of carrying through the 'type four' analysis we find in the matrix.

1.5   Aim

Obviously, the environmental issues are challenging for liberal democracies.[49] Problems like climate change, ozone layer depletion, resource scarcity and nuclear waste, threaten both the political systems and their citizens today, and will for many generations ahead. However, the environmental issue is also theoretically an awkward challenge. Both eco-authoritarian and strong democratic scholars have claimed that a liberal democracy cannot pay due attention to the environment. These accusations are often expressed in terms of 'sustainable development is incompatible with liberal democracy'. This may very well be true. However, to draw such conclusions makes great demands upon the analysis. From what we have learned in this chapter, there is much in the debate on liberal democracy and environmental concern that can be performed more stringently. I have pointed mainly at four aspects that I found problematic in the studies I have examined.

First, there has been a tendency in the green literature to compound philosophical and institutional objections, which makes any stringent analysis of compatibility between liberal democracy and sustainable development difficult. This discovery gave me the impetus to suggest that we should differentiate between arguments derived from the philosophy of liberal democracy and liberal democratic institutions.

Second, in several cases it is unclear what many critical voices actually mean when they refer to liberal democracy (cf. Section 1.2). Any attempt to summarise the different characterisation ends up in an unintelligibly complex web of thoughts. To find a cure for this problem, I suggested that we distinguish between liberal democratic ideal-types, which allow us to cover systematically different liberal democratic interpretations of central concepts and ideas, and also to define frameworks within which sustainable development ought to stay if it is to be considered compatible with liberal democracy.

Third, the issue of compatibility between the specific liberal democracy (not any of the alternatives) and sustainable development has not yet been thoroughly investigated. Thus, additional studies can make important contributions to the overall understanding of this complicated relationship.

Finally, most compatibility studies have been accomplished by comparing liberal and ecological values, or ecological values and liberal institutions (cf. Section 1.4). A less fully explored line of analysis is the issue of compatibility between environmental policies and liberal values. There are a few examples where scholars have based their analysis on possible sustainability policies. Yet, they either have a one country focus, or it is unclear how the policies derived have been determined, selected, and why.

To bring some order into these 'imperfections' would not only be of importance for the green theoretical debate, but would also make possible an alternative compatibility analysis, the 'type-four' analysis in the above matrix, which could make a worthwhile contribution to the debate. This is what I intend to do in this book. More precisely, my objective is twofold:

(1) To bring some order into the compatibility debate by:

(a) Defining two different ideal-types of liberal democracy by chiselling out and interpreting a set of core liberal democratic values, and then determining the restrictions that each value and combination of values impose on policy;[50] that is, establishing criteria for judging compatibility.

(b) Suggesting environmental policies based on scenario-analysis—an approach that clearly shows how the policy suggestions have been developed, and why.

(2) Based on the results in aim 1a and 1b, I will also carry out a 'type-four' compatibility analysis in order to investigate if, or under which conditions it can be concluded that environmental policies cannot be considered compatible since they violate liberal-democratic policy restrictions and core values.

To analyse compatibility is, as we have learned, either an empirical or a theoretical issue. I am heading for the latter. Thus, I am obviously not going to investigate if a certain policy will, or even can, be implemented under present conditions, but *I shall confine myself to examining whether a policy for sustainable development must violate the normative foundation of liberal democracy.* In the next chapter, I develop this line of reasoning further by making my compatibility analysis operational.

Notes:

1 That is not to say that all solutions ought to be handled on a global scale.

2 "If the present growth trends in world population, industrialization, pollution, food production, and resource depletion continue unchanged, the limits to growth on this planet will be reached sometime within the next hundred years. The most probable result will be a rather sudden and uncontrollable decline in both population and industrial capacity". (Meadows et al. 1972:23)

3 See further on neo-Malthusianism in Chapter 4.3.

4According to Paelke (1995:140), the authoritarian perspective can be criticised from at least three angles: 1) Authoritarian rulers are unlikely to be sensitive to, or informed about, ecological matters. 2) Authoritarian regimes are not necessarily good at inducing positive behaviour, especially in the long term. 3) Democracy provides a good climate for social and economic mobilisation. Paelke's notes can be elaborated somewhat further. First, there is no empirical support for an authoritarian regime's success in solving environmental problems, while environmental improvements have been fairly significant in many democracies. Second (which is a matter that can be related to the issue of political decisions permanency), even if an eco-authoritarian political regime were to be established, there are no guarantees that the eco-focus would be kept over time. What will happen the day the ecological king dies? See also Paelke (1996) and not the least Barry (1999a: 194-202) for a short but illuminating critique of the idea of an authoritarian political system, and Lafferty & Meadowcraft (1996:3) on whether authoritarian political systems have been proved more eco-efficient than democratic ones. Ostrom (1990) discusses self-organising environmental management as an empirical (and theoretical) response to the tragedy-paradigm. See also Radcliffe´s (2000) examination of Ophuls and Heilbronner.

5 The most popular variant of strong democracy discussed among Greens today is the 'discursive' or (the somewhat milder variant) 'deliberative' model of democracy (notably Dryzek, 1990; Saward 1993; Eckersley 1997; Jacobs 1996; Hayward 1998; Barry 1999a; De Shalit 2000 [cf the Swedish official reports on democracy "A Sustainable Democracy" SOU 2000:1]). Such democracy refers to a form of collective decision-making that stresses the community over the market or the state as the location for first-order decisions concerning social-environmental relations. This means that such a democracy makes the state and the market instrumental to the democratic decisions of the community. In theory this means that the deliberative 'speech situation' reduces former power relations in such a way that each and every interest speaks and argues on an equal footing, i.e., the best argument wins, no matter whose argument it is. Some even claim that in situations where the good arguments outdo the bad ones, individuals' opinions can be changed in such a way that different opinions are not only modified, but also rectified, i.e., a former controversy ends up in 'consensus' (cf. Habermas 1996; Cohen 1997:75ff).

6 'Strong' should be distinguished here from those who differ between 'classic' and 'social' liberal democracy and sometimes attribute the latter as 'strong' (see Barber 1984).

7 Within philosophy, and especially in Aristotelian logic and semantics, compatibility is usually regarded as (near-)synonymous with 'consistency', i.e., two or more propositions are consistent if they could all be true together (Blackburn 1994:78; Edwards 1967:61). When we discuss the matter of compatibility between sustainable development and liberal democracy, however, compatibility refers to intellectual or real phenomena, rather than true propositions. I discuss the particular kind of compatibility found within the green debate more thoroughly in Chapter 2.1.

8 When I review the literature on the relationship between sustainable development and liberal democracy, it becomes obvious that liberalism and liberal democracy sometimes coincide. When, e.g., Dobson (2000) speaks about liberalism, he consistently refers to the ideology called liberalism, and it is compared with the ideology of "ecologism". When Dryzek (1996, 1992) speaks about liberal democracy, he largely refers to liberal-democratic procedures, i.e., the functions and institutions of liberal democracies. However, several of the other authors I am referring to here are said to analyse, e.g., liberal democracy, but actually discuss liberalism, or the other way around. This is in order, but calls for a specification. A key to the understanding of this 'confusion' is to be found in the distinction between the philosophical foundation of liberal democracy and its practice/institutions (cf. the discussion further below in Section 1.1.3). Liberalism is the philosophical or ideological foundation of liberal democracy. It is inconceivable to think of liberal democracy without liberalism. Liberalism must not, however, presuppose democracy (as democracy must not presuppose liberalism). For example, many of the early liberals were far from democrats, but rather free market capitalists

(Macpherson 1977:20ff; cf. also my discussion especially in Shapter 3.1.1). As long as we compare liberalism with liberal democracy (understood as institutions or procedures), the differences are obvious. Liberal democracy then means a practical political expression of liberalism, i.e., the shape of liberalism when applied in a democratic political form. When we study the philosophical foundation of liberal democracy, however, the differences between liberalism and liberal democracy fade away. This is because we are then actually studying liberalism and more specifically the normative instructions that liberalism imposes on the democratic political authority. I discuss these matters more thoroughly in Chapter 2.2 and in the introductory pages of Chapter 3.

9 He furthermore claims that "Environmental sustainability by definition raises questions regarding the Good life, and so if liberalism is to have a 'take' on environmental sustainability then it must also have a definitive moral conception of people's appropriate relation to nature. If this is a pill that liberalism cannot swallow— as I suspect it cannot—then this may be where liberalism and ecologism finally part company". (Dobson 2000:168 *my italics*) Also see Goodin (1992) who early distinguished between a "green theory of value" (end/goal-oriented) and a"green theory of agency" (means/procedure-oriented) and argued that as long as Greens stick to green values, a greening of politics will never take place. Ideally, according to Goodin, Greens ought to collaborate with a stable socialist (democratic) party—cf. Sweden anno 2006 (also see Eckersley 2004).

10 which is derived from J.S. Mills theorising on how to avoid the production of unnecessary harm to other individuals (and in particular animals) (cf. Barry 1999b 72-77).

11 Eckersley (1995) agrees with Dryzek on liberal democracy's narrow time frames." Liberal democracies generally operate on the basis of very short time horizons (corresponding, at the most, with election periods) Furthermore, she claims that existing "liberal democratic bargaining processes also deal very poorly with uncertainties and complexities of ecological problems." (Eckersley 1995:170).

12 We probably can, but that requires that we understand liberal democracy as economic liberalism. But economic liberalism is hardly the only liberalism available. How could we otherwise make sense of, for example, John Stuart Mill's (obviously) liberal reasoning about a 'steady state economy'—the complete contrast to economic growth (Mill 1848)?

13 "The context within which LD's are working." This is (partly) an odd objection. To a certain extent the international political system has been formed by liberal democracies, but one can hardly argue that the Westphalian Peace Treaty in 1648 (which has formed the international political system to a large extent) was an agreement suggested and implemented by liberal democracies, or by liberal democrats. Rather it was a pact settled by small European kings tired of ruling in a system characterised by constant changes. In addition, according to some observers, this is a system about to change (Weaver 1995; Low & Gleeson 1998).

14 It may, however, be possible to only slightly adjust, or differently interpret a liberal intrinsic feature, or value. For example, the understanding of liberty and the extent to which individuals have the right to hold property may vary, depending on which liberal theorist one focuses on. I discuss this thoroughly in the whole of Chapter 3.

15 That is not to say they have nothing to do with it, because, depending on how the philosophical foundation is interpreted, only a limited amount of designs are possible. My point is that while the philosophical foundation is stable, or given, existing liberal

democracies, although perhaps based on the same foundation, may vary in design (cf. the second feature category called 'Present liberal democratic institutions').

16 If the answer is negative, then we can always speculate on how the institutions ought to be changed in order to meet this value. See my further discussion on the latter approach in Section 1.4.

17 Cf. the discussion in Barry (1999b: 72-77).

18 For example: Since the international economy is becoming more and more globalised, the liberal democracies must partly change in order to keep control over the economy. Analogously, if the environmental problems become global, then perhaps the liberal democracies have to be redesigned in order to cope with the new environmental problems, or perhaps meet the new environmental values.

19 Either theoretically/logically by (1) questioning whether environmental values or policies can be legitimised by (or 'fit' with) liberal-democratic values, or more empirically by asking (2) whether environmental values, or policies can be upheld or sustained in a liberal democracy.

20 I do not mean that context and time are unimportant categories, but they come later in an empirical compatibility analysis, because first we have to analyse whether present institutions can do the job. If they cannot, then can that be explained by either inference from context, or by short time horizons?

21 In Section 1.4 I construct a matrix illustrating the possible ways to analyse compatibility between liberal democracy and sustainable development. The discussion of liberal-democratic features provides the first dimension in this matrix. For reasons I specify in the rest of this chapter, this book mainly focuses on the first category, i.e., the core value premises, or the philosophical foundations of liberal democracy.

22 Cf. the well-known MacCullum (1967) vs. Berlin (1969) debate.

23 "In no respect can liberal democracy and environmental concern be so much at odds as where liberty is concerned//. . . .The environment puts limits to what people can do. . .//. . . .What is really at stake here is a difference of opinion on the 'true' meaning of liberty or freedom: freedom as having access to the valuable things in life, or liberty as having more choices". (Wissenburg 1998:33)

24 Wissenburg starts by giving the following characterisation: "Equality, liberal democracies' second pillar, seems to be the most simple idea of all. One equals one, one and one equals two. Beyond a certain point, though, controversies of medieval subtlety arise". (Wissenburg 1998:30) This is because liberty and equality do not necessarily cope with each other very well.

25 The objections I covered under "the philosophical foundation".

26 Such a political system would probably be incompatible with just about everything.

27 As well as a wide range of more traditional political theorists (e.g., Hayek 1960; Macpherson 1977; Dunn 1979; Eccleshall 1986; Gray 1989; Lukes 1991; Arblaster 1994; Holden 1995; Held 1997).

28 I discuss these two ideal types in length in Chapter 3.

29 For example: That sustainable development cannot be considered compatible with one liberal concept, or interpretation of a concept, such as liberty, does not prove that sustainable development is incompatible with any liberal understanding of liberty. For this to be shown, each liberal interpretation of liberty has to be examined—something for which the ideal-type approach paves the way, since it requires us to find more than one understanding of the topical concept. (Such testable criteria are discussed in Chapters 2.1-2.2 and developed in Chapter 3.)

30 Cf. many of the contributions in the volume edited by Barry and Wissenburg (2001).

31 Cf. Goodin (1996) and Dobson (1996) however, who, independent of each other, published articles on the same theme, in the same year, and with significantly different conclusions, especially regarding how to represent non-human interests in the political process.

32 Issues Achterberg has discussed elsewhere however (cf. Achterberg 2001).

33 This is not exactly a new idea within liberal thinking. John Locke formulated an almost identical reservation (the so-called 'Lockean proviso').

34 Here Sagoff refers to the philosophical foundation of liberal democracy.

35 Dobson (2000) has argued that Sagoff's view would be fine, if it were not for the fact that environmentalists (and in particular political ecologists) also want to know "whether liberalism will bring about their objectives" (p.167). This is certainly a tricky objection. However, I doubt that political ecologists can find any political system that can guarantee a political outcome, whether 'green', red or blue.

36 I discuss this entry in Chapter 8.2-8.4.

37 The same idea influenced most of the contributions in Barry & Wissenburg (2001).

38 It is impossible to give justice to his work in this chapter, thus I only refer to one of the most important contributions in his book, namely 'the restraint principle'. In Chapter 8.4 I return to and discuss more thoroughly his green theory.

39 Although Wissenburg himself is claiming to combine negative and positive liberty, I consider his ideal scope of liberty to be far less positive than, for instance, those of Sen (1982, 1988, 1993b), Dworkin (1977) and Raz (1986) who are usually considered as theorists who successfully combine the two concepts.

40 This principle has similarities with the above-mentioned "Transmission principle", but when comparing them, the restraint principle turns out to be considerably more demanding and far-reaching.

41 If that is at all conceivable. These 'eternal questions' will never be fully discussed and analysed. However, sometimes they can be further elaborated.

42 Only in short book chapters.

43 There are numerous examples of such (cruelly speaking) 'hair-splitting' in the green theoretical literature. For instance, environmental concern, sustainable development or whatever we like to call it, is usually understood as an 'end', and since any end-oriented objective contradicts the 'exclusively means-oriented liberalism', they have to be incompatible. For this to be a complete contradiction, liberalism must be understood as a political theory that cannot allow any ends whatsoever, and/or environmental concern be understood as an end with almost universal proportions. Another example is that since respect for future generations demands a restrictive use of natural resources, while liberalism often is assumed to emphasise private property rights more than anything else, any concern shown for future generations can be 'proved' to be a violation of liberalism, since a restricted use of natural resources, unless based on free will, violates the idea of property rights. With this I do not mean to force philosophers to formulate empirically testable hypotheses. However, it further underlines the importance of clearly defining the concepts that are used in the compatibility debate, i.e., to fulfil the demands expressed in Section 1.2 of this chapter.

44 Yet, a caricature of such a project can be outlined by the research question: 'In case an environmental policy is not compatible with present institutions, then how must we redesign our institutions, or make different political decisions in order to fulfil the demands raised by the environmental policy?' Such approaches are not always considered as social science, but rather as social engineering an anathema among the more staunch defenders of liberalism.

45 Or, if we want to be consistent with what I argued for in Section 1.2 on different liberal democracies: whether a policy X does fall within the policy restrictions set by a particular liberal-democratic ideal-type (notably 'protective', or 'developmental').

46 See also the more thorough discussion on methodological considerations in Chapter 2.

47 I discuss this more closely in Chapter 2, and also in the introduction to Chapter 4 on sustainable development.

48 An example of a typical anthropocentric-based transition is O'Riordan (1996:140) who suggests the following rough categories of transition: 1) to utilise renewable resources up to the point of replenishability, or to apply the precautionary principle where thresholds of renewal are in doubt, 2) to direct an increasing amount of the profit from the use of non-renewable resources to the effort of discovering renewable substitutes, or to ensure an orderly succession of non-renewable alternatives, 3) to safeguard those critical life support processes, species and habitats whose existence and functioning are essential to the survival of life on earth—again applying precaution where scientific knowledge is limited, 4) to redistribute essential liveability requirements to all people so that each and every one has an entitlement to minimum conditions of health, wealth and natural beauty, 5) to guarantee basic rights of civil liberty, education, self-expression and political freedom and 6) to monitor environmental and social change as the transition proceeds, to ensure that the economy, polity and ecology evolve in symbiosis.

49 And every other political system, of course.

50 I thus leave out the institutional aspects of liberal democracy.

Chapter 2

Operationalising a Type-Four Compatibility Analysis

In this chapter I lay out the design of my investigation.

The concept of *compatibility*, which is of great importance in my analysis, calls for specification. In Section 2.1 I (a) provide a definition of compatibility to be used in my analysis. I then (b) introduce my analytical framework (which will be dealt with in greater detail throughout the following chapters). Finally I (c) establish a principal criterion for judging whether compatibility is present or not.

To make this compatibility criterion applicable and functional, the specific restrictions that liberal-democratic core values impose on the choice of policies must be determined. In Section 2.2 I describe how these policy restrictions are derived.

Furthermore, to carry out the compatibility analysis I specify what is required to procure policies that would realise sustainable development. This is done by way of science based scenarios. In Section 2.3 I describe the major steps required to establish these policies.

These first three steps make up my analytical framework. I then carry out my analysis of compatibility between liberal-democratic core values and policies for sustainable development. In Section 2.4 I describe the major steps to be taken to realise that analysis.

2.1 Deriving Criteria

Compatibility is usually defined as two (or more) phenomena that are "capable of existing together in harmony" or are "capable of orderly, efficient integration with other elements in a system".[1] Examples abound in political theory where compatibility between two concepts (e.g., liberty and equality) is frequently analysed (e.g., Halldenius 2000; Sen 1988; Lukes 1991; Hayek 1961). At issue is whether these concepts can co-exist, i.e., be simultaneously emphasised or maintained without contradiction, or if giving space to one must lead to decreased space for the other.[2] Within legal science, compatibility between two (or several) laws is commonly analysed. The question there is whether adherence to one (inferior) law, rule, principle or norm would violate another (superior) law, rule, principle or norm (cf. Peczenik 1995:444-466; Hart 1961:84-100).

In such analyses, determining compatibility is rather straightforward. In the *first* example, we are dealing with two phenomena that are principally found on *the same level*, e.g., two concepts or *values*.[3] By establishing *criteria* for how much space each concept requires so that it is not compromised, i.e. *weighing*, we can judge whether or not the two concepts conflict. In the *second* example the two laws, rules or norms are not at the same level, but are still within *the same system*, e.g., *environmental* legislation. Here also criteria or weighing principles can be used for judging whether the inferior law or principle will violate the superior one (Peczenik 1995:486).

Are liberal democracy and sustainable development compatible? Can they exist 'harmoniously'? And, perhaps more importantly, what criteria are there for judging whether they are compatible or not? In Chapter 1, I presented four partly different compatibility questions. Let us compare them with the two examples from political theory and law.

(1) Liberal-democratic institutions vs. sustainability values. Here we have different *levels of analysis* (institutions and values). Yet, they are largely within the *same system* or subject field (concern for the environment). This variant clearly differs from both the conceptual and legal examples. Compatibility now refers to *capacity*, i.e., something *practical* and *empirical*. For example, *can* the Swedish environmental administration maintain or defend the needs of future generations? Clearly, compatibility is at hand if protection for future generations is actually built into those institutions. The *criterion* for judging compatibility is empirical, i.e., do we find this protection within the institutions?

(2) Liberal-democratic values vs. sustainability values. This category should be identical with the concept example. The question is whether maintenance of one value (e.g., concern for future generations) would violate or interfere with simultaneously maintaining a liberal-democratic value such as individual liberty. The analysis is at the *same level* (two *values*) but within *different subject fields* (liberalism and sustainability). Compatibility is at hand if introducing the value of sustainability does not violate the liberal-democratic value or vice versa. Reasonably, to determine compatibility requires rigorous theoretical criteria and analysis. We need to know both *when* violations occur, and perhaps also what *degree* of violation is acceptable.

(3) Liberal-democratic institutions vs. sustainability policies. This question ranges over both the *same level* (a political body or institution that implements a policy) and more or less the *same subject field* (environmental institutions and

sustainability policies). It refers to practical and empirical compatibility. One example is the literature on "global democracy" (e.g., Held 1995) and how democracy must develop in order to cope with trans-boundary environmental problems and/or ethical concerns (cf. Low and Gleeson 1998 ch. 6-7). *Empirical* compatibility criteria are required. Compatibility is at hand if one can demonstrate that current liberal-democratic institutions can or would be able to decide and implement the policies needed to realise sustainable development.

(4) Liberal-democratic values vs. sustainability policies. This concerns the, I dare to say, most peculiar form of compatibility in our matrix, i.e., one that ranges over both *different levels of analysis* (values and policies) and *different subject fields* (liberalism and the environment). It deals with whether policies aimed at realising sustainable development can be decided upon and implemented by the state without violating the core values of liberal democracy. The *criterion* for judging whether or not a policy is compatible with these values must be one that specifies *the proper scope of action of the liberal- democratic state.* Now, does this make sense?

To illustrate why we can speak of compatibility under the conditions found in the fourth variant, and why such an analysis of compatibility certainly makes sense, I will use an analogy from jurisprudence.

2.1.1   The Particular Type-Four Compatibility

Let us start with the *different levels of analysis*. The overarching environmental legislation can schematically be illustrated as in Figure 2.1. There is a lexical order between the different levels, i.e., "the question of compatibility concerns the entire course from the international objective to the various means of national implementation" (Ebbeson 1995:30). The subordinated levels ought to be compatible with every *superior* level. Although Ebbeson analyses compatibility of international (2) and national (3) environmental law, the analysis of compatibility can be extended to also range over e.g., (1) and (3a). Thus, it is appropriate to speak of and analyse compatibility between levels as disparate as *values* (objectives or norms) and *policies*.

The second question about *different subject fields* is also not problematic. Let us assume that an environmental policy (any of 3a-3d in our example) is considered compatible with overarching international environmental objectives. This does not mean that the policy is compatible with every conceivable objective. For example, an environmental policy that prevents land owners from recklessly cutting their forests may be compatible with the environmental objectives, but yet be in violation of a country's business objectives, or be considered incompatible with the value of possessing and individually managing private property.

Figure 2.1   Schematic survey of environmental legislation

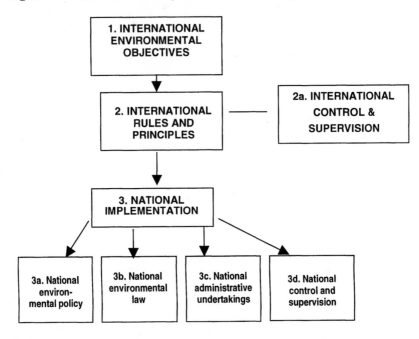

Source: Ebbeson (1995:29)

The same is true when we speak of compatibility in our type-four case. The sustainable development policies (equivalent with 3a-3d in the above scheme) might be compatible with international environmental objectives, i.e., sustainable development. Still, that does not mean that these policies are also compatible with liberal-democratic core values or any *other* objectives. That is a matter for further analysis.

Thus we face a compatibility analysis that confronts two phenomena found on *different levels* and within *different subject fields*: liberal-democratic *values* and sustainable development *policies*. This provides the basis for the following *analytical framework*.

Liberal-democratic core values constitute the first dimension. In line with the discussions in Chapter 1, these values ought to be specified for each liberal-democratic *ideal-type* (cf. Section 1.2). Sustainable development *policies* constitute the second dimension (cf. Section 1.4). These ought to be judged as either *compatible* (+) or *incompatible* (-) with the core values specified in the first dimension.

Figure 2.2   Analytical framework

Sustainable Development Policies	Core values of Liberal democracy *ideal-type 1*	Core values of Liberal democracy *ideal-type 2*
Policy$_x$	Compatible (+) /incompatible (-)?	Compatible (+) /incompatible (-)?
Policy$_y$	Compatible (+) /incompatible (-)?	Compatible (+) /incompatible (-)?

To *judge* whether these policies can be considered compatible or not, they must meet specific compatibility *criteria*. The following principal compatibility criterion can be introduced.

Principal compatibility criterion
Any sustainable development policy presupposing a violation of liberal-democratic policy restrictions is to be considered incompatible with the core values of liberal democracy

Before this criterion can be operational, we must determine the specific *policy restrictions* that the core values of each liberal-democratic ideal-type give rise to.

2.2   To Determinate Policy Restrictions

In Chapter 3, I explore the two liberal-democratic ideal-types that I introduced in Chapter 1. I call them *Protective liberal democracy* (PLD) and *Developmental liberal democracy* (DLD). For each ideal-type I establish what can be seen as the *common denominator*. This means that several typical liberal democratic values and issues are left out of my characterisation.[4] In defining the ideal-types and delimiting their range, I proceed from Holden's analysis in *Understanding Liberal Democracy* (1995). The focus is on what Holden, along with several other theorists, considers the *main components* of liberal democracy and which are found to be the common denominators in practically every theory about liberal democracy. Another reason for proceeding from Holden's analysis is that the procedural and practical aspects of liberal democracy can be omitted. These are less crucial for my specific objectives (cf. Chapter 1.1 and 1.4).

Holden's work suggests that democracy, liberty and equality constitute liberal democracy. All three have a more or less uncomfortable and tense relationship with each other. The way I understand Holden, 'democracy' both refers to the classic 'rule by the people' and the executive body of a liberal democracy, i.e., the state. It is mainly the latter understanding that is of importance for this study. The objective of the state is to execute the will of the people. The state is thus *regulated* by the people's will and instructions (constitutional rules), which are mainly exercised through elections. These regulations largely belong to the institutional side of liberal democracy and I pay relatively little attention to them in my analysis.

Figure 2.3   The Crucial Relationship in Liberal Democracy

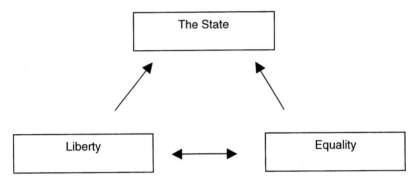

Comments: In Figure 2.3 the (for this book) most important relationship between the liberal-democratic state and the two values of liberty and equality is illustrated. The figure should be interpreted as follows: First of all, liberty and equality regulate the liberal-democratic state and its action (the arrows from the two values to the state). These arrows correspond with the policy restrictions discussed earlier in this chapter. Second, liberty and equality mutually affect each other: full maintenance of, e.g., liberty, may obstruct full maintenance of equality—and the other way around (therefore a two-way arrow). Most certainly the state and its functions also affect liberty and equality, intimating that there is in fact a two-way relationship there also (e.g., for the state to be in force it requires certain authority, something that may be possible only if individuals' liberty is limited). However, the issue of how much liberty and equality can be allowed while at the same time sustaining an active state or one practising the "rule of the people" is largely beyond the scope of this book. Instead the prime target is how comprehensive state activity (policy) is allowed from a liberty and equality perspective.

The liberal-democratic state is, however, also regulated by the values of liberty and equality, i.e., the two other constituents of liberal democracy. This means that whenever a liberal-democratic state acts, it must make sure that these two values are properly considered and adequately maintained. There is thus a tense relationship between what the state can do and these two values. In addition, liberty and equality also have a complicated relationship to each other; some even argue that they cannot be fully maintained simultaneously (Lukes 1991). This threefold relationship can be illustrated as in Figure 2.3.

In the above Figure 2.3, the concepts of *democracy* (the state), *liberty* and *equality* constitute the liberal-democratic core values. Liberty and equality are assumed to restrict state action and thus also policies. To be able to determine the scope and direction of policy restrictions, I analyse how these three components are related to each other within each ideal-type. The following steps are to be conducted.[5]

First, I characterise the liberal-democratic state. This I do by establishing the essential state-assignments for each ideal-type, i.e., what are the principal functions of the state, and within which areas should or should not the state be involved? In this part, I mainly work with literature originating from the history of ideas, notably Held (1997), Eccershall (1986), Dunn (1979, 1969) and Macpherson (1977). By reviewing how the concept of the state has developed over time I try to define the role of the state specifically and intelligibly for each ideal-type.

Second, I determine what can be labelled the typical view of liberty within each ideal-type. Here I focus more directly on individual liberal theorists linked to the two positions. I contend that 'protective' theorists have a 'negative' view of liberty, i.e., the state ought mainly to protect the people *from* each other and from the state. What I call 'developmental' theorists are more difficult to categorise. I ascribe to them a more 'positive' view of liberty. However, there are great differences in *degree*; there is no unanimity as to which liberties (besides negative ones) individuals really ought to enjoy.

Third, I explore the meaning of equality within each ideal-type. What implications does this have for state action? How should we understand the relationship between equality and liberty in the two ideal-types? The 'protective' view of equality will be described as 'thin'. If the state is not to jeopardise individual liberty, it ought to legislate for equal rights only for a very limited set of mainly political and jurisdictional goods. It may prove harder to determine the boundaries of and define the 'developmental' directions to equality, since the set and scope of the goods that ought to be equally available to all citizens are different for practically every developmental liberal theorist. I will thus concentrate on the general principle of equality of opportunity, and will contend that the precise set of opportunities cannot be *theoretically* derived. This is principally a personal and ideological matter.

Having completed these sections, I go on to specify the policy restrictions for each ideal-type, and thus also the compatibility criteria. In the last section of Chapter 3, I connect the policy restrictions to my overarching objectives and establish my precise compatibility criteria. This completes the first part required to accomplish a type-four compatibility analysis. Thereafter remains the work of determining sustainability policies.

2.3 To Determinate Sustainable Development Policies[6]

To determine sustainable development policies is a rather circumstantial and long-winded procedure. One is inevitably forced to conduct studies beyond social science. Several major decisions have to be made and procedures adopted. At least four successive steps are necessary:

(1) Conceptual delimitation. The interpretation of sustainable development is limited to the use found in the Brundtland Commission Report 'Our Common Future' (WCED 1987). Thereby I establish how sustainable development is to be understood in this book. However, I reformulate the commission's definition into instructions (an 'operational guide') on how to realise sustainable development, as a necessary prelude to step 4.

(2) Scenario calculation. Scenarios are formulated to correspond as much as possible with the instructions identified in step 1. One scenario is selected as an 'ideal scenario'and is the main focus throughout the following chapters. However, the other scenarios are important as references.

(3) Scenario comparison. Given the present physical, technological and socio-economic conditions, I identify a range of (societal) changes required for a particular scenario to be implemented, and also other political *challenges* that may arise largely as an effect of our (theoretical) attempt to realise the scenario, e.g., giving priorities to certain interests.

(4) Policy specification: Finally I outline the content of the *policies* that would be required for realising a scenario, i.e., the policies needed to deal with and bring about the societal changes and challenges identified in step 3.

The second step is the most startling part of this 'thought experiment', and I therefore spend particular effort in clarifying how it is accomplished (Section 2.3.2- 2.3.5).

2.3.1   Converting Sustainable Development into Operational Goals and Measures

Sustainable development is a 'contested concept' (Dryzek 1997:125), meaning there is no complete agreement on its definition. Economists, physicians, ecologists, social scientists, ecocentrists and representatives of the rich and the poor world, all have their own understanding. My choice of proceeding from the interpretation made in the Brundtland Commission Report, 'Our Common Future' (WCED 1987), is thus not self-evident. However, two arguments favour making this choice. *First*, of all interpretations of sustainable development, the one in 'Our Common Future' is by far the most quoted and politically accepted one. *Second*, while the *definition* of sustainable development may be disputable, i.e., what is comprised and who is included in the transition towards the goal, the elaborated *conception* of it is rather clear and well defined in the report (cf. Langhelle 2000a:59). This means that the goals and suggested means are sufficiently well specified to permit the derivation of more *operational* goals and measures. Throughout my analysis of the report, I strive to substantiate my conclusions by working extensively with quotations I view as central to the Brundtland Commission's conception. This leads to the following 'operational guide':

Operational Guide for Calculating Scenarios

(1) Each and everyone, within and across generations, should be ensured the opportunity to:
   (a) Be spared from poverty by having basic needs fulfilled
   (b) Have their aspirations for a decent/good life ensured and fulfilled
(2) Equitably distributed economic development is a prerequisite for combating poverty, for ensuring human beings the opportunity to fulfil aspirations, and for financing the development and global distribution of new and efficient technology
(3) Economic development must stay within biophysical limits, today and in the future
(4) Biophysical limits are variable, and when the limits are reached depends on
   (a) Quality of technology
   (b) Access to technology
   (c) Institutional design
   (d) Lifestyle patterns

2.3.2   Realising Sustainable Development by Way of Scenarios—A Thought Experiment

In the second part of Chapter 4, a rather qualified thought experiment is carried out. Adhering to the above Operational Guide, scenarios are postulated which *as much as possible* can be said to meet the goals recommended by the Brundtland Commission. This approach can be seen as a highly 'theoretical' attempt to realise sustainable development.[7] The calculations stem from an inter-disciplinary research project involving political and environmental science, where the above guide was applied to the specific case of global animal food consumption.[8]

The case of global animal food consumption is adequate for both theoretical and practical reasons. *First*, the confrontation of liberal democracy and sustainable development requires a case that affects all the social, economic and ecological aspects of sustainable development. The food sector is among the most discussed issues within the sustainable development debate. *Second*, food is a basic good, which makes it theoretically more interesting than most other commodities. *Third*, animal food production is more resource demanding than practically any other food production, making it environmentally challenging. *Fourth*, animal food consumption is a recognised problem in the Brundtland report, making it particularly interesting.[9] Yet, the Brundtland

Commission practically requires increased animal food consumption at least in some parts of the world.

Admittedly, a major shortcoming of the idea of picking out one particular case when analysing sustainable development is that 'everything' is interconnected. In reality we can isolate neither animal food production nor general food production from the rest of the global ecological system. Thus, when we assume adjustments in our specific sector (the elaboration of different scenarios), we must be aware that these changes will have repercussions in the grander system which we cannot fully control.[10]

Based on the above Operational Guide, two questions influence the construction of scenarios to illustrate sustainable animal food production:

(1) *What would happen, in terms of resource demands, if we assumed an equitably and globally distributed increase in social and economic development (growth) resulting in global increases of animal food consumption* (i.e., a fulfilment of mainly the first two guidelines suggested by the Brundtland Commission)?

Quite obviously, since animal food production is very resource demanding, the resource requirements would be enormous.[11] At first sight, therefore, the social and economic objectives seem to be in conflict with the objective of staying within ecological limits, i.e., the third target in 'Our Common Future'. However, although social, economic and ecological sustainable development are the three core objectives in the report, these goals are *conditioned* by the four measures of quality of (and access to) technological and organisational development and by changes in lifestyle patterns, according to the Operational Guide. Thus, another question must guide the scenario analysis:

(2) *Is it possible to meet an increased demand for animal food by improving production efficiency through any of the measures suggested in the Brundtland Report?* Can we attain the social and economic goals without jeopardising the ecological ones?

To answer the second question, different scenarios are created. One of them, called scenario SD-4, has been deemed to imply resource demands that are not unreasonable and unmanageable.[12]

2.3.3 Backcasting—Not a Conventional Way of Calculating and Using Scenarios

Scenario methodology is frequently used within science, but has had scant interest and has even been profoundly criticised, within social science. The main reason is that the longer the projected time span (together with the kind of data available within social science), the more will factors change over time and thus change the future image that the scenario once predicted (Patton & Sawichi 1993:422ff; Premfors 1989:29f; Ascher 1979, Ezekiel & Fox 1967:318-324,344ff). That is, society is a highly complex phenomenon and social variables are not law-bound. However, the way in which scenarios are used in this study means that precise predictions are not of central importance.

Robinson (1990;1988) discusses 'backcasting' as an alternative way of using scenarios (cf. Steen et al. 1997; Dreborg 1996; Biesiot & Mulder 1994; Steen & Åkerman 1994). Instead of projecting historical data into the future, backcasting proceeds from a goal and then works *backward* in time to catch all the challenges that may arise and that will have to be dealt with on the way towards achieving that goal. The objective of the backcasting scenario is thus completely different from the forecasting approach: "It offers a method for exploring the implications of alternative development paths and the values that underlie them" (Robinson 1990:823). For a backcasting analysis to be complete, seven steps must be considered (ibid 1990:824).[13] These steps are applied in this study in the following order:

(1) Establish the aim of the analysis. In my case this means to illustrate sustainable development as defined in the Brundtland Commission's Report.

(2) Specify the goal that ought to be reached to realise our sustainable development assumption in the case of animal food consumption.

(3) Carry out the scenario. Make the scenarios calculation (in co-operation with environmental science) and present the outcomes in the form of diagrams.

(4) Establish exogenous variables. In our case this means identify *what* and *who* will be affected by a realisation of the scenario.

(5) Describe present conditions that must change if the goal is to be realised. This is done in Chapters 5-6 when I analyse 'challenges' such as *increased use of resources* (e.g., water and phosphorus), *technological development, changes in dietary patterns* and *production conditions.* Other challenges concern how farmers will be affected by the changes and how public opinion might affect the comprehensive use of biotechnology.

(6) Accomplish a consequence analysis. That is, analyse the challenges, e.g. why might there be a problem with our assumptions about global improvements in agricultural technology?

(7) Establish recommended implementation. I do not actually recommend any policies in Chapter 7, yet I point out policies that may be required to effectively cope with the challenges.

2.3.4   *The Calculation of Scenarios*

Comprehensive data collection underlies the scenario calculations. These data have been fed into a computer model that describes global agriculture for the years 1992-1994.[14] The model elaborates a number of variables (largely productivity levels and consumption patterns) required to satisfy the different scenarios. A range of *assumptions* and *interpretations* constitute initial values for the scenario calculations:

Major scenario assumptions

- A world population of 9.4 billion people.
- A global economic standard equivalent to that of Western Europe today.
- An average animal food consumption of 30% of the daily food intake.
- A high technological standard within agriculture across the globe.
- Use of biotechnology both in crops and animals (especially in the ideal scenario SD-4).[15]
- Dietary changes (reduced consumption of cattle and beef and increased consumption of pork and chicken)

As with all such exercises, our assumptions can be questioned for being either *unrealistic* or *unattainable*. Perhaps the most *unrealistic* assumption concerns global animal food consumption. Nowhere does the Brundtland Report mention the 30 per cent figure, and no one can justifiably claim that people *need* 30 per cent animal food in their diet. This level is, however, based on people's *aspirations* and *wants*. If today's poor people experience an increase in economic development (expressed as *desirable* in the Brundtland Report), then we have good reason (cf. Chapter 4.3.2) to assume that their animal food consumption will increase. Furthermore, the commission *does* support a certain increase in animal food consumption although no level is specified.[16]

Also the assumed *economic standard* can be questioned. However, if everyone's needs and (legitimate) aspirations are to be met without making use of too many resources (read: using more efficient technology), then a relatively high economic standard is required both for people to afford what they *want* and to afford using the *best available technology*. The major propelling force behind this economic development is assumed to come from industry (WCED 1987), so why not assume the economic level we find in today's industrialised world? This is not to say that these countries ought to go through *the same* industrial development as Europe:

> "Our ecological movement is not against industry, but we must think of the social function of industries and that pollution and progress are not the same thing. Pollution is not the synonym of progress and therefore time has come for new development concepts to come." (WCED 1987:256)

Admittedly, the technological development assumed here can be considered *unattainable*. The same holds for the comprehensive use of biotechnology, especially in light of the present public opinion in the Western World (cf. Section 6.1). However, for scenario SD-4 to be realised (in terms of resource demands), these productivity levels are required. In addition, practically every technology that I discuss in Chapter 5.2 does exist today, so those technologies are *technically* attainable. They may, however, be *economically unattainable* with today's measures, but that is one of the *challenges* to which the idea of sustainable development gives birth.

2.3.5 An Astronaut's Perspective: A Critical Examination[17]

I have used a global perspective. I thus do not study specific conditions in a region or a local area, and I do not point out more down-to-earth needs and requirements.[18] Nonetheless, for both *theoretical* and *practical* reasons I consider this perspective to strengthen my book.

By viewing sustainable development from an entirely global perspective,[19] I have *first* of all been able to examine more closely one of the most commonly cited reasons why sustainable development is a challenge for liberal democracy: the fact that sustainable development is a global project that requires *border-crossing solutions*. This challenge can hardly be captured if we view sustainable development solely from a national or a local perspective.

Second, by trying to fulfil *all* the Brundtland Commission's recommendations for social, economic and ecological development, I manage to capture more of the total *complexity* associated with sustainable development than if I only focus on either *local* conditions, or merely on *one* of the ecological, social or economic aspects of sustainable development. Thus, what I might lose in precision and specificity by not applying a local perspective, I more than compensate for by the overall understanding and information I get by adopting the global perspective.

Third, the scenario exercise is based on inter-disciplinary research co-operation involving *political science* and *environmental science*. These two disciplines employ quite different worldviews and languages. Illuminating sustainable development with the grander brushwork of the global perspective has been challenging enough.[20] Were one to go into the ecological and biophysical conditions in such detail as to analyse local energy flows and entropy, difficulties to control for 'external' conditions might prove insurmountable, or at the least make the resulting outcomes inaccessible to me as a political scientist.

2.3.6 Scenario Comparison: The Identification of "Challenges"

The scenarios are based on expected demand, i.e., they illustrate how much biomass will be demanded depending on what assumptions we proceed from. Thus, they say nothing explicit or substantial about (1) the conceivable inputs needed for a scenario to be realised, (2) the social consequences arising should the scenario be implemented or (3) what happens if these inputs run short. These factors constitute the basis for my search for challenges in Chapters 5 and 6. Certainly, to actually realise any of the scenarios described in Chapter 4 would involve enormous societal transitions and difficult decisions, which cannot be fully encompassed and illustrated in a thought experiment like this. To cover as many of these challenges as possible I work with broad (partly overlapping) categories, which I exemplify by discussing cases that I consider to be particularly problematic in a particular scenario. These categories stem from the Operational Guide.

In principal, three inputs are required for scenario SD-4 to be realised: physical, technological, as well as economic and social resources. Physical resources must be supplied to produce the amount of biomass implied in the scenario. The development of new technology is an important means for producing the required biomass within estimated resource limits. Social and economic resources are required both for people to afford new technology and for securing welfare.

Besides different inputs, scenario SD-4 also generates conflicting interests. This is for two reasons. First, for the scenario to be realised, we assume dietary changes. Unless these changes take place voluntarily, they will give rise to disapproval among many interest groups. Second, the scenario requires major changes in agriculture, implying comprehensive social changes. Contrary to many ecological modernists, I thus argue that a state-led (i.e., government-led) implementation of the scenario produces both winners and losers. This is politically challenging, especially when viewed from a liberal-democratic point of view.[21]

In Chapter 5 I discuss challenges connected to the first two categories, i.e., the supply of physical resources and technological development. To supply enough resources without jeopardising the needs of present and future generations presupposes a cautious and optimal use of these resources on a global scale. The demand for technological development is also challenging, not least because it implies active government support for such development, and because technology must be accessible for those who need it.

In Chapter 6 I continue by discussing challenges connected to the third supply category, i.e., demand for social and economic inputs. This category partly coincides with technological development. Unless the developing countries independently manage to generate enough social and economic means to obtain the technological standard assumed in the scenario, as well as the welfare to which they are entitled, implementation of scenario SD-4 implies redistribution of a range of goods. Thereafter I focus on particular *interests* that may be affected by an implementation of scenario SD-4. The scenario is based on assumptions and it calls for actions that give cause to social changes that may not be appreciated by all groups in society. The more powerful the groups are, the more difficult it will be to implement these changes. Thus, unless these changes take place on a voluntary basis, a realisation of scenario SD-4 implies priorities and ranking of interests. It follows that some interests must be overturned with political force.

My objective in Chapters 5 and 6 is to outline as many as possible of the principal challenges that the political sphere may have to cope with and form policies for if scenario SD-4 is to be realised. Thus, even if the categories of challenges may be valid, it is difficult to specify the range of them. The problems I discuss in Chapters 5 and 6 may, but do not necessarily, occur if attempts are made to realise scenario SD-4. Yet, to investigate if sustainable development policies can be regarded as legitimate and compatible from a liberal-democratic viewpoint, I consider it more useful to exaggerate rather than to avoid or neglect challenges that may not arise.

2.3.7 Policy Specification

After I have identified changes and challenges that society has to manage to achieve the goals expressed in scenario SD-4, I develop the last piece needed to accomplish a type-four compatibility analysis in Chapter 7. That last piece is to outline the policies required for the social changes to take place. Even if much of what I discuss there has been touched upon already in Chapters 5 and 6, it is only when the challenges are specified that I can outline and suggest any policies. For obvious reasons I cannot tell exactly what measures and policies are required and desirable for our scenario to be achieved. This is largely a political matter. My objectives are therefore more moderate: I emphasise what I consider to be the most likely direction of policies needed to meet the challenges implied in our scenario.

First I outline policies required to deal with the challenges of global co-ordination and resource logistics identified in Chapter 5. Thereafter I outline policies required to meet the challenges of technological development. After I have discussed these biophysically and technologically related policies, I proceed to determine what policies are implied by the socio-economic challenges established in Chapter 6. I start with the economic and distributional challenges. Finally I discuss what may be required if certain interests do not voluntarily change their current behaviour and/or attitudes in accordance with the requirements set by scenario SD-4. When all the policies are outlined, my analytical framework is complete and ready to be used for conducting my compatibility analysis.

2.4   The Type-Four Compatibility Analysis

Together with the compatibility criteria elaborated in Chapter 3, I turn to an analysis of whether the hypothetically state-imposed policies can be considered compatible with the policy restrictions that each of the two liberal democratic models contains.

In the first part of Chapter 8 the relationship between protective liberal democracy (PLD) and the suggested policies is examined. The guiding question is whether any of the implied policies would violate the policy restriction of PLD, i.e., be in violation of any of this model's core premises.

In the succeeding part, the sustainable development policies are compared with the policy restriction specified for the developmental liberal-democratic ideal-type (DLD). Since the DLD model originally is *nation-state bound* and the policies have both a global and an intergenerational reach, this calls for a specific examination conducted in three steps.

First, a comparison between the policies and the policy restrictions in general is carried out. *Second*, the global aspects of the policies are analysed. To investigate this issue, two different approaches are used. I start by adopting a Rawlsian 'Veil of Ignorance' perspective to see if there are any principal[22] differences between the national and the global level of scenario SD-4. Thereafter the three DLD premises are re-examined to see if any of them may presuppose a specifically limited geographical territory. Finally I examine my own conclusions by asking if the 'asymmetrical relationship', identified by O'Neill (2000) between rights and obligations may make liberal-democratic action crossing the boundaries of the nation-state impossible, and thus constitute an argument for why the policies ought to be considered incompatible with DLD. *Third*, I analyse the *intergenerational* aspects of the policies. This I do by first proceeding from Rawls' (1972) 'Saving Principle' and Wissenburg's (1998) 'Restraint Principle', and I continue by adding the idea of *equal opportunities* to the analysis.

In the final Chapter 9, I discuss the main insights from the book. First I re-examine the conclusions from our particular type-four analysis. What are the major lessons from approaching the compatibility issue from this angle? Thereafter I focus on the theoretical and methodological outcomes from the book, i.e., I return to the four motives with which I criticised the current debate.

Notes:

1 The Macquarie Dictionary, Second Edition, p367. Recall that in Semantics and Logic, 'compatibility' and 'consistency' are near-synonymous concepts, where both refer to whether two (or potentially more if 'consistency') statements can be (logically or empirically) maintained at the same time without contradiction (Mautner 1996:76,82). For example, the two statements 'It is forty degrees Celsius' and 'It is snowing' are logically but hardly empirically compatible. The kinds of compatibility referred to in the green political-theoretical debate are different and largely coincide with the above quotations.

2 A similar problem arises when compatibility between different interpretations of *one* concept, such as positive and negative liberty (cf. Berlin 1969; MacCullum 1967), is on the agenda.

3 One value can certainly be considered superior to the other. This depends on what the topical research question is as well as the normative proceeding point.

4 This can be considered a shortcoming. On the other hand, by keeping down the number of components, I am able to characterise and investigate the two ideal-types in considerable depth (as distinct from many other compatibility analyses proceeding from the ideal-type approach—cf. my discussion in Chapter 1).

5 My effort suffers from at least two weaknesses. The historical part is an overview and mostly borrowed from other sources. Since the two liberal traditions seem to be commonplace within the history of philosophy, I have spent little effort in finding support for them. The ideal-type approach (two traditions expressed with three concepts), inevitably deals more cursorily with other important concepts of liberal political philosophy such as rights, toleration, universalism and impartiality. However, rights, impartiality, as well as universalism are at least referred to throughout the chapter, especially in relation to state neutrality.

6 In this section I mainly introduce the essential methodological considerations and procedures. The construction of scenarios and the assumptions behind them are further discussed in Chapter 4. The model that has been used for modelling the scenarios, and which I only touch upon in this chapter as well as in Chapter 4, is described at length in Wirsenius (2000).

7 As hinted at already in Chapter 1.4, I do not believe that sustainable development can be fully illustrated and substantiated in advance. Thus, if anything, our scenario should be seen as one that is *less unsustainable*, and which meets *as much as possible* the goals recommended by the commission.

8 In this study, 'animal food' includes meat, milk and eggs but not fish. With few regional exceptions, fish constitutes a relatively small share of total animal food consumption (less than 10 per cent) (Wirsenius 2000).

9 The problems surrounding animal food consumption also proved to be socially challenging (and interesting). When a country's economy is strengthened, animal food consumption tends to increase immediately, implying that if we assume global economic development then we should assume, everything else being equal, an increase in animal food consumption.

10 I, at least, *reflect* upon this problem in Chapter 6, e.g., when I discuss the real complexity behind competition for land (cf. Chapter 6.1.1).

11 It was also (partly) illustrated by a scenario where we assumed a continued increase in animal food consumption at the rate we have experienced since the beginning of the 1960s (i.e., the 'BAU-scenario'). A global population of 9.4 billion, increased animal food consumption and an average productivity similar to what we have today would increase the total biomass demand by approx. 300%.

12 For example, the average global productivity level and efficiency level are assumed to be only 17 per cent higher than today, a goal that, seen from a technological point of view, should not be considered unattainable at least in the longer term. Furthermore, the assumed dietary changes only change the composition of food (more chicken and pork and less beef) but do not affect the total intake of animal food.

13 According to Robinson (1990:824) there are only six steps, but he excluded (in his list, not in the paper) the seventh step which he calls "determine implementation requirements". Thus there are actually seven steps.

14 For a full description of the model, see Wirsenius (2000).

15 This assumption is 'implicit', meaning that we do not calculate the immediate effects of using biotechnology, but we assume that for the agricultural productivity levels to be reached, biotechnology will be required. Alternatively, the productivity figures we are using do not make sense without the (intellectual) introduction of biotechnology.

16 Further, sustainable development, according to the Brundtland Report, is not only about basic needs, i.e., *the bare necessities of life* (cf. the above 'instructions').

17 Cf. Sachs (1999: 31ff).

18 I.e., I have not concentrated on pointing out transitions and societal changes at the micro level, e.g., local *resource conditions*, specified *technologies*, specific *legislation*, *land reforms*, *economic* and *social* needs and so forth—something that is certainly demanded by the Brundtland Commission.

19 To view sustainable development from *both* a local and a global perspective would have been impossible with the time and resources that were at my disposal.

20 Ideally, scholars from a range of disciplines should have collaborated on the work that I have accomplished. Not only ecologists, geographers and biologists are required but also social, economic and behavioural scientists.

21 I cannot discuss the fourth measure in the Operational Guide, i.e., *organisational changes*, until I have identified what other social changes are required and what the organisational changes aim at realising.

22 Recall that I say *principal*. In political reality there are a wide range of differences between the national and the international level, for example there is only enabling legislation on the national level.

Chapter 3

Determining Compatibility Criteria

The concept of liberal democracy is often referred to as if it was the most obvious thing in the world. Liberal democracy is, however, an ambiguous concept and there is no general accepted definition of one liberal democracy or any theory about it. As I argued in Chapter 1, this becomes obvious within green political theory where liberal democracy is given attributes such as concern for liberty, equality, rights, justice and neutrality, but the concepts are often understood in quite different ways. So, is there really a core of liberal democracy? In view of what I said then, it would seem futile to define a liberal democracy as distinct from defining the core values that underlie liberal democracies.

The objective of this chapter is to establish policy restrictions, i.e., criteria for judging whether sustainable development policies can be considered compatible with liberal-democratic core values. To do this, I develop core values that constitute liberal democracy and that restrict the power of the state. These core values are democracy, liberty and equality, of which I will pay particular attention to the latter two.

The ideal-type framework within which I do this is a result of a theoretical cross-fertilisation between two partly different approaches. The first one is based on Holden (1995), who establishes the meaning of liberal democracy by analysing what he argues are its three 'core elements'(1995:19), i.e., democracy, liberty and equality. The second approach is largely based on the history of philosophy, where several theorists have pointed out two different traditions within liberalism.

According to Holden, democracy is essentially a contested concept. With this he means "There is in fact agreement on the concept but there are seemingly endless disputes about the merits of rival conceptions" (1995:4). Seen from this perspective, liberal democracy is thus one conception of democracy. It is not a uniform version, however. While liberal philosophy covers a spectrum of ideas ranging from the border of anarchy to egalitarianism close to socialism, so does liberal democracy. Yet, there are some foundations that most liberal democratic theories share. The most significant is that democracy ought to be limited (Holden 1995:16).

Liberalism is an attempt to develop a theory that accepts the idea that there are fundamental and unsolvable differences of opinion regarding what is good for individuals and what their inner spirit is (Holden 1995:16-18). This idea certainly produces important political implications: the liberal state ought to be neutral to individuals' life plans. If the state is not neutral—that is, if it suggests or offers a political community or a common objective rather than promotes a plurality of political thelos/goals (Avnon & De-Shalit 1999:12f) then the theory falls victim to perfectionism (Hurka 1998) or paternalism (Manning 1976:20f, 129f; Jones 1994:132ff), and thus denies the core of liberalism.

Instead of focusing on the good life as the objective of politics, liberals therefore emphasise specific rules that allow individuals the greatest possible liberty to seek for themselves what they see as their preferred lifestyle. Citizens must be free to decide the rules of how, and how much, the government should govern. In terms of democracy the essential objective of the state thus is to make decisions in accordance with rules decided by the people (cf. Holden 1995:15-19). Therefore, liberal democracy should be understood as limited democracy: 'democracy' refers to the location of state power, which ought to be fully in the hands of the people, while 'liberal' refers to limitations of this state power. Ergo, liberal democracy is a political system where the people make the decisions, but where there are (constitutional) limits on what they can decide and impose on others through state action and in the name of democracy.[1] This way of understanding liberal democracy largely belongs to what I named the institutional part of liberal democracy (cf. Chapter 1.1), and thus mainly falls beyond the scope of this study.[2]

What about the other core values that restrict policies, i.e., what I designated the philosophical part of liberal democracy in Chapter 1? Besides being limited by the will of the people and by constitutional rules, the liberal-democratic state is also limited by normative elements. According to Holden, the most common denominators are liberty and equality.[3] The two have a tense relationship both with public authority (the state) and with each other: "The central idea within liberal political thought concerning why public authority should be limited, is that it is necessary to ensure individual freedom or liberty (Holden 1995:17). The relationship between equality and the state is somewhat more complicated: "Equality is closely associated with democracy; and tensions discerned between liberty and democracy may be viewed as tensions between liberty and equality" (Holden 1995:19).

Simply put,[4] whenever the (liberal-democratic) state acts, it must make sure that liberty and equality are properly considered and maintained. Furthermore, it is uncertain whether liberty and equality can be fully maintained at the same time (cf. Lukes 1991:48-53). Thus, liberty and equality are the two core values that I focus upon when I determine principal restrictions on policies, i.e., my compatibility criteria. The framework I proceed from can be illustrated as follows:

Figure 3.1   The Crucial Relationship in Liberal Democracy

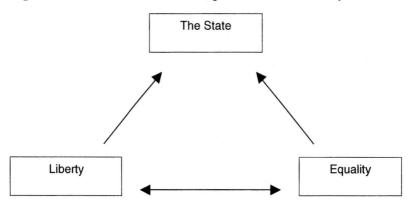

Comments: In Figure 2.3 the, for this book, most important relationship between the liberal democratic state and the two values of liberty and equality is illustrated. The figure should be interpreted as follows: First of all, liberty and equality regulate the liberal democratic state and its action (the arrows from the two values to the state). These arrows correspond with the policy restrictions discussed earlier in this chapter. Second, liberty and equality mutually affect each other: full maintenance of, e.g., liberty, may obstruct full maintenance of equality—and the other way around (therefore a two-way arrow). Most certainly the state and its functions also affects liberty and equality, intimating that there is in fact a two-way relationship there also (e.g., for the state to be in force it requires a certain authority, something that may be possible only if individual liberty is limited). However, the issue of how much liberty and equality can be allowed while at the same time sustaining an active state or one practising the 'rule of the people' is largely beyond the scope of this book. Instead the prime target is how comprehensive state activity (policy) is allowed from a liberty and equality perspective.

Authors as disparate as Held (1997), Eccleshall (1986), Dunn (1979, 1969) and Macpherson (1977) represent the second approach required to determine compatibility criteria (as was outlined in Section 2.2). They all argue that to make sense of liberal democracy and particularly the liberal view of the state, we have to go back to its philosophical roots. Furthermore, to make the idea of liberal democracy comprehensible, it ought to be divided into two different traditions, one protective and one developmental, whose views of government and the state differ in several respects.[5]

Thus, in this chapter I establish what restrictions and limitations each ideal-type (protective liberal democracy and developmental liberal democracy) imposes on policy. I do this by exploring the meaning of, and the relationship between each of the three elements in Figure 3.1, which are to be specified for each ideal-type.

In Section 3.1, I discuss the protective and the developmental liberal view of the state. I argue that the protective liberal tradition lays claim for an autonomous civil society where the state must remain passive to meet demands for liberty and neutrality. The objectives of the developmental state, however, are (or may be) more far-reaching. In Section 3.2 the typical view of liberty is analysed for each ideal-type. I also establish what limitations the different views of liberty impose on the state and contend that the protective liberal view of liberty limits the scope of policies considerably more than the developmental understanding of liberty. In Section 3.3, I continue by discussing the view of equality within each ideal-type. In this context I also relate equality to liberty and the state. I argue that for the developmental liberal state to maintain liberty and equality, it has to take a more active role in policy making than the (largely passive) protective liberal state. In the final Section 3.4, I conclude the chapter by first summarising the principal relationship between the state and liberty and equality within each ideal-type. Thereafter I establish compatibility criteria based on my conclusions in the earlier sections.

3.1   The Liberal Democratic State

Thomas Hobbes' (1588-1679) political theorising deliberately challenged the then existing political philosophy with its idea of a common 'thelos' that was either religiously legitimised, and/or based on a predestined right reason (cf. Ewin 1991:27ff). Ever since, one of the key issues in (European) political philosophy has been how a government can be legitimised and sustained when society ultimately consists of self-interested individuals, who ought to enjoy an adequate degree of freedom from governmental interference. According to Held (1997:75),[6] the idea of liberal democracy historically developed two fairly different answers, i.e., "protective" and "developmental" democracy.[7] The protective idea has its roots in the philosophy of John Locke, and particularly in Locke's response to Hobbes. The main ideas behind developmental liberal democracy can be derived from John Stuart Mill's theoretical contributions.

3.1.1   The Protective Liberal Democratic State

Hobbes argued that individuals can find a peaceful and spacious life only if they are governed by the dictates of an indivisible authority, the Leviathan (1651). John Locke countered that 'government' should be considered an instrument for the defence of life, liberty and estate of its citizens (Dunn 1969: part 3). Locke's political philosophy is built on the notion of natural rights. The formation of a governmental apparatus does not signal the transfer of all subjects' rights to the political realm. The government is therefore only supposed to preserve individual life, liberty and property. Furthermore, its legitimacy is sustained and decided by individual 'consent' (Held 1997:81). The sacrifices that individuals have to make (e.g., individual responsibilities and rights, duties and powers, constraints and liberties) in the creation of a political government are necessary if their ends are to be secured over time.

Locke thereby laid the foundation of modern liberal philosophy. It emphasises the separation between government and individuals and imposes governmental duties for the purpose of facilitating individual lifestyles, whatever that may mean for each individual. As Held puts it:

> . . . /. . . Government exists to safeguard the rights and liberties of citizens who are ultimately the best judges of their own interests; and that accordingly government must be restricted in scope and constrained in practice in order to ensure the maximum possible freedom of every citizen. (Held 1997:81)

Perhaps Locke´s most important contribution is his negative view of government as an entity to which individuals should have as little connection as possible. The liberal idea of individual freedom from governmental intervention and the liberal view of the state as a provider of means for individuals to fulfil their ends are indeed ideas with roots in Locke's political philosophy. He recognised the necessity of sovereign power remaining in the hands of the people, and that the power of legislation and that of the executive should be kept separated.

The need to separate elements of governmental power was developed further by Montesquieu (1689-1755) who distinguished between executive, legislative and judiciary power. He claimed that there is no freedom if it "were the same man or the same body, whether of the nobles or of the people, to exercise those three powers, that of enacting laws, that of executing public resolutions, and of trying the causes of individuals" (Montesquieu 1952:70). However, in exploring the relationship between state and civil society, Montesquieu did not manage to resolve two central matters: 1) how to protect the individual's private sphere from governmental intervention and 2) how freedom could be understood as something else than 'the right to do what the law permits'.[8]

Only when it was realised that protecting individual liberty requires some kind of (political) equality among all mature individuals could the protective theory of democracy be fully expressed. Political equality here refers to an equal capacity to protect the individual's interests from the arbitrary acts of either the state or other individuals. According to Macpherson (1977), there are two sets of contributions to this problem that are more important than any others: those from James Madison, and those from the two early spokesmen for utilitarianism, Jeremy Bentham and James Mill.

Madison's philosophy mostly concerned the problems of factions. The basic source for antagonism and factions was the range of unequal distribution of property. This forms classes in society, which threaten political stability, and may lead to highly unjust outcomes (Macpherson 1977:15-16). Madison was convinced that solving this problem required a popular government—with a federal structure—in which power was divided. The larger the size (but with precisely defined scope, and subject to challenge by other common institutions) of the state, with an economy based on private requirements, the more likely that a greater social diversity exists, and therefore the less chance that majoritarian tyrannies get a grip of the electorate or the elected (Manning 1976:69-70). Such a system would not only ameliorate the worst consequences of factions, but it would also involve citizens in the political process of protecting their own interests. Madison focused on individuals' legitimate pursuit of these interests and on government as a means for the enhancement of them. Put simply, a federal representative state has the scope to aggregate individuals' interests and also to protect their rights—not just purely political ones, but also their rights to hold private property (Held 1997:89-94).

Like James Mill, Bentham stressed that the driving force behind human behaviour was fulfilment of desires—to maximise pleasure and minimise pain. Society consists of individuals who have this 'nature' (Macpherson 1977:31). By necessity this leads to clashes between individuals, in social as well as political life. This means that those who govern act in the same way as individuals in general. Therefore, to avoid governmental encroachments on the governed a system where the government is held accountable for its actions is required. Bentham's design was such that government was directly accountable to an electorate called upon frequently to decide whether its objectives had been met. Another important provision was that individuals should be able to pursue their interests without risk of arbitrary political interference, and thus, to participate freely in economic transactions and to accumulate resources privately. The state may be seen as some kind of referee, while individuals should be able to pursue their own private goals within a society, according to their interests (Macpherson 1977:34-43). Maximum benefit for citizens requires "periodic elections, the abolition of the powers of the monarchy, the division of powers within the state, plus a free market" (Held 1997:95).

Where does all this leave us?

Figure 3.2a The Protective State

> The idea of protective democracy particularly emphasises the separation of people and state. There is a highly restrictive view of the state in relation to individuals. State power is tightly restricted to the creation and protection of a sphere, in which individuals pursue their private lives, without risk of violation, unacceptable social behaviour of others or political interference. Those who govern ought to pursue policies that are commensurate with citizen's interests as a whole. Sovereignty ultimately lies in the people, but is vested in representatives who can legitimately exercise state functions. Freedom from arbitrary treatment is central, as is equality before the law (in terms of political rights or liberties—especially freedom of speech, expression, association, voting and belief). Furthermore, protective liberalism strongly defends the right to hold private property.[1] All this produces a politically autonomous civil society, in which the state is neutral to individual life plans (i.e., the good life), where property and the means of production are privately owned and goods are distributed within a competitive market economy.

3.1.2   The Developmental Liberal Democratic State

The term 'developmental' liberal democracy indicates that something can be advanced or developed in the idea of liberal democracy. As I will show below, it is not only the view of the state and its functions that can vary, but also the view of liberty and equality. This variation depends on how developmental liberals have come to view the relationship between people and the state.

The liberal idea that individuals should be protected from government was based on a suspicion of the state, and was nursed by the historic experience of 'strong' states such as authoritarian monarchies. This restricted view of the state was also complementary to the growing market economy/society, since it would leave the circumstances of peoples' lives to be decided by private initiatives, whether in production, distribution or exchange. However, negative freedom is also linked to another notion of freedom, i.e., the individual capacity to act and to have different options for action. Such a view implies an understanding of freedom as something that can be provided and enhanced through political (read state) action. This idea had, for good reason, been poorly developed among those first liberals. It took quite a radical change in thinking to prompt such reasoning.

John Stuart Mill saw democratic politics as a prime mechanism of moral self-development (Held 1997:111). While he had a sceptical view of individuals' current capabilities, he thought that they could be developed under conditions that were best supplied in a democratic system that lives up to certain demands. For Mill, individual liberty was of utmost importance for individual self-development, and such liberty could only be fully provided if political life was marked by more accountable government, and an efficient governmental administration (free from corruption and with a slim bureaucracy). But Mill did not defend the restricted state as strongly as earlier liberals. He recognised several areas in which governmental intervention was legitimately serving two interrelated purposes: to secure individual self-development, and to ensure society's observance of the no-harm principle. Mill wrote:

> "The only freedom which deserves the name is that of pursuing our own good
> in our own way, so long as we do not attempt to deprive others of theirs or
> impede their efforts to obtain it." (Mill 1859:72)

Furthermore, Mill strongly believed in public participation in political life. Active involvement in political affairs determining the conditions of one's existence is the prime mechanism for the cultivation of human reason and moral development. Such individual development is good for both the individual and society as a whole, and will diminish the risks of a 'static' society. By emphasising the opportunity to enjoy 'human dignity' and 'self-development', both connected to his 'no-harm principle', Mill diverges from earlier protective liberals (Held 1997:102f). According to Held, those implications can be derived from his principle of 'no harm':

> "If we take Mill's principle of liberty seriously, that is, explore those instances in which it would be justified to intervene politically to prevent 'harm' to others, we have at the very least, an argument for a fully fledged 'social democratic' conception of politics." (Held 1997:118)

Things such as education and the distribution of wealth according to need can be woven into a rather extensive interpretation of 'no harm'. The importance of this extension will be clearer when we discuss liberty in the next section. There is also another part of Mills' thinking that deviates from earlier liberal thought, relating to his idea about individual improvements. Self-development was not only good for the individual, but also for society as a whole. After Mill, this idea has been slightly adjusted and has become a particular form of liberty, i.e., autonomy.[9]

Most of the early protective liberals stressed that liberty would flourish in a free-enterprise economy, where as few restrictions as possible are imposed on the accumulation of private property. In that respect, Mill did not differ from his precursors. Still, although his ideal was a free-market economy, it was one in which "self-seeking had yielded to a co-operation adventure in activities which led to self-development" (Eccleshall 1986:34). Interestingly enough, Mill therefore suggested a political economy based on no-growth[10] combined with an inheritance tax to ensure an equitable distribution of available wealth.[11] A certain amount of material goods are, according to Mill, a prerequisite for individuals to enjoy liberty and the independence in choosing the lives they prefer.[12]

By bringing the concept of liberty closer to an interpretation in accordance with individuals having the opportunity to something (e.g. realistic choice), Mill definitively directed his thinking onto a new track. Yet, he continued to defend the idea of a restricted state, and the right of individuals to enjoy the fruits of their labour and to own property. Presumably, this would restrict the actual range of material and economic redistribution that could take place legitimately.

From the end of the 19th century, liberals began to call into question the ideal of the strongly restricted state as well as the sanctity of property rights. It was recognised that too much inequality in wealth and income tends to decrease people's possibilities to exploit their inherent capacities. Ideas about governmental provision of social welfare therefore started to flourish, although on a modest scale. The Cambridge professor A. Marshall, for instance, was strongly influenced by Mill's political economy, although he did not agree with Mill's idea about a stationary state. In Marshall's view, it took a dynamic capitalist economy to provide individuals with the economic means to obtain a decent existence and to make self-improvements (Eccleshall 1986). Like John Stuart Mill, Marshall considered that one of the most important duties for a government was to provide a compulsory education system in order to prepare the masses for this 'higher' life.

H. Samuel argued that it is the duty of the government to make sure that social progress takes place. Such social progress should be understood as enhancing opportunities for individuals 'to lead the best of life' (Ecceshall 1986:42). The obvious fear of government, which early liberals had recognised, was according to Samuel exaggerated and based on an idea of an aristocratic government. Since then, however, the reasons for this suspicion have eroded, mostly because a 'real' democratic parliament was far more likely to secure the interests of the public. The main purpose of legislation, Samuel argued, was to encourage self-reliance throughout society.[13]

The philosopher and journalist L.T. Hobhouse went further than any liberal philosopher before him in his allowance of governmental action.[14] Even if he explicitly defended the idea of "a liberal government", when outlining "the future of liberalism", this government was given an extended licence not only to educate citizens to be able to recognise their view of the good life but also to implement social and fiscal programmes (Hobhouse 1974:110-127). For example, Hobhouse strongly supported the idea of a guaranteed minimum standard of living.

This must be seen as a real blow to the idea of ownership of private property as sacred. Still, the purpose of both the fiscal program, and the minimum standard of living, seems to have been to provide individuals with the means necessary for self-realisation, or development; not for all individuals to reach a common good or a standard imposed by the state. In that particular respect, developmental liberal democracy does not differ from the protective tradition. The liberal claim for 'open-endedness' prevails also when it comes to such extreme expressions as are found in the writings of Hobhouse.[15]

Figure 3.2b The Developmental State

A developmental democracy emphasises a limited state, although the degree of limitation is variable. Participation in political life is necessary not only to protect the individual's interests, but also for individual self-development, expansion of personal capacities and the creation of a well-informed citizenry. State power is limited through the affirmation of individual rights (at least for Mill, especially freedom of thought, feeling, taste, discussion and publication). Mill and later theorists interpret this as 'having the opportunity to fulfil life plans', which gives the state an active role in the provision of those opportunities. Yet, the framework of state neutrality (to the good life) remains and state action ought to be judged according to aim, not range. The right to hold private property becomes less important to post-Mill developmentalists. There is a continued emphasis on market based distribution of goods, but regulations must be permitted since the market does not provide equal opportunities for individuals.

3.2 Liberty

3.2.1 Protective Liberty

In his essay on "Two Concepts of Freedom" (1969), Isaiah Berlin emphasised negative liberty, and argued that positive liberty tends to lead to tyranny. Since then, much of the argument in liberal philosophy has been focused on those two concepts of freedom. Negative freedom contains two components: (1) absence of constraints and (2) doing what one wishes. Absence of constraints refers to the idea that there ought not to be any impediment to the individual's self-determination, which is understood as doing what he or she wishes. "Doing what one wishes is supposed to involve 'simply acting to fulfil one's desires" (Holden 1995:32), whatever desires one may have. Negative liberty is thus considered neutral to what an individual is free to do. That is up to him or her to decide and must not be included in the concept of freedom. The negative conception not only implies absence of governmental restrictions, but also absence of obstruction from other individuals.

The negative conception of liberty is by many theorists regarded as the essential 'liberal' liberty (e.g. Gray 1995:56f) and the protective liberty in particular. To think in terms of 'absence' brings analytical stringency to the discussion. Negative liberty presupposes a distinction between freedom and ability or capacity. Liberty ought to be understood as the absence of constraints and coercion, and consequently has nothing to do with any resources required to fulfil whatever one may be free from external hindrances to do (Plant 1991:223, 226). A strictly negative view of liberty implies that there are no capabilities that can be logically or conceptually connected to liberty. As long as there are no imposed obstacles blocking an individual from doing X, then that individual is free to do X even if he or she, for reasons of individual capacity, cannot do X. Thus, neither intellectual nor social resources have anything to do with freedom; nor have economic and other resources that create 'opportunities' or powers to do certain things.

In fact, if capacity or power were included in the definition of liberty, then we would be confronted by a morality-based concept of freedom.[16] According to protective liberals, however, such a moralising concept of liberty would contradict the liberal idea of moral pluralism, and thus challenge the idea of a neutral state. Therefore, Berlin argues:

> "I am normally said to be free to the degree to which no man or body of men interferes with my activity. Political liberty in this sense is simply the area within which a man can act unobstructed by others..//..Coercion implies the deliberate interference of other human beings within the area in which I could otherwise act." (Berlin 1969:122)

In a similar vein, Steiner claims that:

"An individual is unfree if and only if, his doing of action is rendered impossible by the action of other individuals. That is, the unfree individual is so because the particular action in question is prevented by another." (Steiner 1974:33)

According to the negative view, state neutrality presupposes an objective understanding of liberty, and this can only occur if liberty is understood as freedom from external coercion. There are two different kinds of coercion. The first kind of coercion is irrelevant in this context. It is of a 'natural' kind and refers to the fact that an individual is, for particular reasons, unable to do things, i.e., an unyielding inability.[17] No coercion created by forces outside of personal control can be regarded when we speak of negative liberty. The second form of coercion presupposes intentional and organised hindrance from others, individually, or collectively. Only then can we talk about an actual limitation of individuals' negative liberty (Plant 1991:228ff).

It is quite obvious that negative liberty is a protective liberal expression. The fear of governmental intervention (which we explored in the previous section) is a fear of the loss of individual freedom, caused mostly by the state, although negative freedom not only refers to coercion brought about by the state but also to all kinds of coercion created by other people. The same understanding of negative liberty can also be connected with developmental theorists. John Stuart Mill's 'harm principle' can probably (under certain circumstances) be argued as an expression of negative liberty. For example, if I am intentionally coerced by someone, this may cause me harm. This means that I am harmed if I do not enjoy enough negative liberty. Yet, the harm principle should, as far as I understand it, largely be connected with a positive understanding of liberty (or could most certainly be extended to such a form of liberty) because making sure that no harm is caused to someone else implies not only physical harm, but all sorts of harm—such as the dissatisfaction of not being able to develop one's inherent individual capacities, or to eat properly, or to enjoy a proper education. At the least, this kind of harm cannot be lightly excluded.[18]

Figure 3.3a Protective Liberty

Liberty is understood negatively, i.e., individuals enjoy the absence of constraints to do what they wish unless this produces lack of liberty for others. No capabilities can be connected to liberty. Thus, there is a strong distinction between liberty and capacity. The reason why liberty cannot be connected to any substantial resources is that this contradicts the idea of moral pluralism and state neutrality (passive), and it may confine the almost absolute freedom/right to hold private property. Such an understanding of liberty implies or presupposes no individual or governmental obligations other than to leave other people alone. Consequently, the primary objective of the state is to maintain negative liberty, i.e., to make sure that individuals are guaranteed a sphere in which they are free from coercion (from both the state and other individuals).

While negative liberty refers to individual freedom from constraints on action, positive liberty refers to conditions that enable action. Positive liberty contains two key components, (1) some form of self-determination and (2) the ability to do what one wants (Holden 1995:32f). According to one of the most salient advocates of positive liberty in modern times, the German philosopher G.W.F. Hegel, liberty means that people have the opportunity for self-realisation (Flathman 1987:35).[19] Politically, this implies that if certain resources, powers or abilities are needed for self-realisation, then having these resources should be considered part of freedom itself. In this section I argue that the developmental liberal view of liberty ought to be understood as both positive and negative (not positive in Hegel's version, however, but in the form of autonomy).

The idea of enabling state action to promote liberty and equating liberty with self-realisation is problematic from any liberal point of view. Therefore I elaborate on the idea of positive liberty fairly thoroughly in order to show that such an understanding of liberty can be intelligible and consistent even if viewed from a (developmental) liberal viewpoint.

It is easily pointed out that self-realisation and freedom are not the same thing. An individual may freely choose to sacrifice his or her chances of self-realisation for the sake of a goal valued even higher (Berlin 1969:125). Further, it is unclear what self-realisation is actually about, and it is not difficult to imagine situations in which one individual's self-realisation is in conflict with somebody else's—even if they are striving for the same overall goal. Modern protective liberals, such as Hayek (1960) and Nozick (1974), reject the Hegelian version of positive freedom because, as Hayek points out, such an understanding of liberty must end in the equation of liberty with the power to act (1960:85ff). That is problematic for protective liberals because such power cannot, by its nature, be distributed equally and can thus be used by some to constrain the freedom of others (cf. Section 3.1).

There is thus an inherent conflict between a Hegelian concept of freedom and the liberal ideas of diversity/pluralism and equality. The protective concept of liberty implies the absence of governmental restraints, i.e., minimal governmental interference in the various desires of individuals.[20] Positive liberty emphasises individuals being enabled, or empowered to achieve what they want, which implies quite comprehensive state action in order to secure the provision of such powers.[21]

To be self-determining, therefore, indicates a set of resources (indeterminable I suggest)[22] that are required for individuals to be qualified and to have the powers and possibilities to fulfil whatever they determine is best for them. When supporters of the positive stand argue that liberty and ability are related, or perhaps are even the same things (cf. Plant 1991:243f), then difficult issues arise. The most striking is that if ability and freedom are interchangeable, then it can be argued that a person is only free, if he or she is actually able to do all the things he or she aspires to do. Such reasoning easily becomes absurd: 'I am not free to go to Costa Rica because I cannot afford it'.

Another difficulty with positive liberty is that a person may be said to be free only if he or she is capable of fulfilling certain specific goals and not just any goals. This gives us a concept of 'self-determination' that is defined by specific goals, and which consequently is severely limited. Only if a person realises this specific goal is he or she really free. Understanding freedom as fulfilment of a particular, specified set of goals and purposes leads, at least logically, to a situation in which some (those who formulate the set of goals) are given the authority to impose their values on others.[23] If we bear in mind the liberal idea about the state being neutral to individuals' good life, it becomes quite clear that any interpretation of liberty relying on a particular concept of the good or the right (or anything else individuals should be free to do) cannot be legitimate in any kind of liberal philosophy.

3.2.3 Positive Liberty Understood as Autonomy

To define liberty as the realisation only of a specified collective goal is, however, a quite extreme form of positive liberty. It can also be understood in a less ambitious way that is also clearly less opposed to liberal values such as moral plurality and state neutrality.[24] Freedom must not necessarily mean to be free to do or reach a predetermined goal, but can refer to socially stipulated needs, capabilities, possibilities and resources that are required for someone to realise his or her own idea about what is good.[25]

This is what we usually mean by 'autonomy'. The German philosopher Immanuel Kant (1724-1804) defined a conception of liberty, which gave support to the idea of tolerance and a limited state. Freedom meant individual self-determination, according to Kant, and was non-restrictive of options. A free individual is not ruled by others, but by himself. Kant called such an individual 'autonomous'.[26] By arguing for individual autonomy, Kant 'emancipated' his positive understanding of liberty from collective restraints. Instead a free individual is one who follows his reason, and by reason the individual will come to a moral truth: Act according to the 'categorical imperative'.

However, the concept of autonomy has changed since Kant. Instead of speaking in terms of an individual's autonomy to choose, unaffected by external or internal (mental) disturbances, the tendency today is rather to use the language of people's general ability to make choices and to formulate and fulfil their (life)plans. Viewing an autonomous individual as one who has the capacity as well as the opportunity to exercise that capacity leads the discussion onto another track.[27]

Autonomy now rather means that it is up to the individual person to decide what is good for him or her, based on his or her reflections about his or her own desires, but also the surrounding societal environment (Gray 1995:91). It also means that certain opportunities to actually make those reflections are provided. Thus, autonomy actually has two interconnected meanings: one external and one internal. Externally, it implies that individuals require some space within which they shape their lives as they choose. Without having the means to make choices and the opportunity to implement chosen plans, autonomy to choose is of little value. This, in fact, points to the internal meaning of autonomy, which is that individuals are capable of making choices and reaching conclusions and decisions which are, in a sense, 'authentically their own' (Jones 1994:125).

This particular form of autonomy is often spoken of in terms of 'well-being' (Jones 1994:129ff). In contrast to the Kantian conception, autonomy becomes an essential constituent of peoples' actual abilities to fulfil whatever plans they have. Individual autonomy no longer is a matter of living correctly or doing the right thing, but rather for someone/something to promote what is good for him or her.

To understand autonomy as presupposing 'well-being' appears to correspond well with the developmental democratic tradition. And, according to Jones, J.S. Mill can most certainly be located among the first to connect autonomy and well-being. Mill himself used the term liberty, "but much of his concern for liberty was of a sort that would be articulated nowadays in the language of autonomy" (Jones 1994:129). According to Gray (1983:80), foremost amongst what Mill called "the permanent interests of a man as a progressive being" were security and autonomy. What Mill described as 'higher pleasures' were available only to human beings who had developed a capacity for autonomous thought and action.

What would be required for individuals to enjoy sufficient autonomy to ensure their well-being? According to Alan Gewirth (1978, 1982) and many other developmental liberal theorists along with him,[28] it is possible to define certain basic needs (other than those for pure physiological survival), even if we recognise and defend the idea of moral plurality. Such needs are not related to a certain morality or a certain kind of well-being. Instead, they have to do with individual capacity for 'moral agency'. Every moral code must offer the individual some space for action. This action, whatever it may be, requires certain resources, commonly attributed as 'basic' or 'primary' goods, resources or capacities. In order to accomplish the action, it is not only required that the individual has the capacity to make crucial choices (the traditional autonomy idea); to actually act in accordance to the choices being made requires a certain degree of well-being as well.[29]

If this is a sensible interpretation of the 'modern' conception of positive liberty as 'autonomy', then positive liberty need no longer refer to a particular common good, as Hegel and others have emphasised (cf. the literature on perfectionism). Instead it is about providing the individual with the means necessary for that individual alone (in its most fundamental form) to have the space required to formulate his or her own life plan, and (in its broader form) to have the opportunity to realise the chosen life plan—whatever that plan may be. The state gives no instructions as to which conception of good is to be considered 'best'.

Figure 3.3b Developmental Liberty

Developmental (positive) liberty refers to self-determination and the
ability to do what one wishes, i.e., enabling conditions for action, but not
according to a superior goal or moral principle. Liberty is understood as
being able to acquire the socially stipulated needs, capabilities and
possibilities, as well as resources for someone to have the capacity and
opportunity to realise his or her own idea of the good life. Only if this is
fulfilled is it possible to talk about an autonomous individual. Such an
understanding of liberty presupposes a state that is active, but yet neutral
to the content of, and the major goals constituting the individual's life
plans.

In principle, negative and positive liberty seem to have many similarities.
However, this is not to say that they fit together perfectly well. In one respect
they stand in complete contrast to each other. To actually provide the benefits
of positive liberty means that there are costs that must be borne by someone.
The more that groups with scant resources are provided with enabling means,
the more this may infringe on the negative liberty of groups or individuals
already enjoying those means. But the extent depends on what means are
required and how those means or goods are to be distributed. These
implications of positive freedom lead us to the issue of equality.

3.3   Equality

"The political equality of democracy means not simply that everyone is equal
before the law, that is to say that as a subject to political authority everyone
should be treated equally. It also means that everyone should have a place in
the exercise of political authority, even if this only involves electing those who
are to constitute the government" (Weale, 1990:54)

Weale's assertion raises several important matters. Individuals ought to be
equal within a particular sphere. This is constituted by the liberal democratic
idea of freedom from coercion. Further, individuals should be treated equally
by the state. That is to say that each and everyone ought to enjoy equal absence
of coercion from the state or from others. The idea of political equality thus
implies that there should be equal opportunities to participate and to have an
equal say in political life. This idea coincides with protective liberalism. What
about developmental liberalism? There are different positions ranging from a
similar 'thin' protective understanding of equality (Dahl 1998), to more
substantial ones (Raz 1986). The reason for extending the meaning of equality
is that political equality, i.e., equal political rights to participate, is not regarded
enough for individuals to actually be equally free. In other words, political
equality alone cannot produce equal liberty (or autonomy).

Most democrats hold that equality is an intrinsic value, and that this value is best maintained within a democracy (Holden 1995). Some even argue that political equality is the actual meaning of democracy (e.g. Dahl 1956; Boström 1988). Certainly, a theory of democracy needs some degree of egalitarianism to be reasonably consistent. If the political demos comprise all above a certain age, then all these constituent individuals must have an equal right to get involved. Any other interpretation implies that one group is 'more equal' than the rest of the people. Inequality in this particular respect would give some people an exclusive position in the political sphere (Walzer 1983).

The reverse does not necessarily apply. It is not obvious that equality requires democracy. For example, neither the liberal philosopher Rawls (1972) nor Dworkin (1977) explicitly mention democracy as a prerequisite for upholding equality. Their focus is rather on the tense relationship between liberty and equality.

I argue that three different positions are conceivable (cf. Lukes 1991:48f;53). First we have the typical protective view of equality, which is no less consistent than its view of liberty. It argues that liberty is threatened by equality, either because governmental action, which is required to uphold equality, invades and diminishes individual liberty[30], or because social equality exposes social structures, which—while producing inequalities—also function as barriers against state power.[31] Second, there is the proposition that equality suffers at the hands of liberty. The more formal the liberties, the more (material) inequality we get (Holden 1995:35). Such inequalities arise from the fact that the state cannot intervene to prevent them, since state authority is limited (as a consequence of the primacy of negative liberty).[32] Finally we have the idea that liberty and equality presuppose each other.[33] As will be clear in this section, both the two latter positions are to be found among developmental theorists.

3.3.1 Protective Equality

Most protective liberal theorists argue that as long as formal political equality prevails, then economic and other inequalities are justifiable. That immediately raises questions about what kind of, and how much of, such inequalities can be legitimised. A common argument here is that people are not the same in all respects and should only be treated the same in those important regards where they actually are the same (Holden 1995:37). This is important also for us when establishing policy restrictions in Section 3.5. What are the frameworks within which people ought to be considered and treated equally?

These differences among individuals are also of significant importance for developmental equality. If people are to be treated equally and they differ in several relevant respects, then they should be 'equalised'. But what are the relevant regards in which they should, and should not be treated equally? Holding on to negative liberty, protective liberals avoid such deliberations. This issue is in fact one of the most important objections that protective liberals have to the idea of developmental/positive equality. Their objection often raised by the question "Equality of what?" (Sen 1982:476ff), where 'what' refers to all the positive means that ought to be distributed to individuals in order for them to achieve equal opportunities to act.[34]

Achieving equal negative liberty primarily requires negative resources/rights,[35] and that the liberties are distributed equally. Equal opportunities to enjoy autonomy, however, presuppose positive resources/rights,[36] which ought to be distributed in such a way that the opportunities are actually provided. While negative rights in general do not result in any significant economic costs, positive rights do.[37] Furthermore, since economic resources are limited, it might not even be possible for the state to provide all individuals with enough positive means for them to enjoy (full) autonomy. And, most importantly, any attempt to make such positive provisions inevitably threatens the provision of negative liberty.

One obvious example where negative goods/rights become threatened by demands for positive goods is when 'equality of what' refers to economic welfare. Most demands for increased welfare imply costs, which must be borne by someone. When developmental liberals speak about 'equal opportunities' as a certain equal level of welfare, they have to consider restrictions on private property. Thus, a defence of negative liberty against equality can (legitimately) end up with inequality in opportunity being legitimised by equality in the right to hold and enjoy property.[38]

The protective tradition understands equality as equal freedom from arbitrary treatment and equality before the law in the form of political and civil rights/liberties, i.e., free speech, expression, association, voting and belief, as well as the right to hold property (Held 1997:99). When those liberties are distributed equally among citizens, then there is equal political liberty. The state is separated from the rest of civil society, and is tightly restricted to allow citizens to pursue their private lives as freely as they like. From this follows that political equality in the protective sense can be expressed as an equal distribution of the liberties necessary for individuals to enjoy a space of immunity from the state and from other individuals.

The protective view of equality is thus as intelligible and straightforward as its (negative) view of liberty. Both concepts are simple and clean and they largely refer to the same thing: individual freedom from coercion. When adding equality it follows that those liberties should be distributed equally. 'What' should be equalised is solely a negative matter (that is, the goods or means necessary to enjoy negative liberty). Each and every individual has an equal right to this liberty. In the former section we asserted that the greatest difference between a negative and a positive view of liberty is that the latter advocates adding certain elements to the original set of negative liberties. These additions do not necessarily challenge the ideals of moral pluralism and state neutrality. When the same idea is applied to equality, however, the picture becomes more complicated, because when the positive features or resources are implemented, an economic resource base derived from private property is presupposed. And this, as we have seen, is an almost absolute negative liberty according to protective liberals. Thus, when it comes to practice the realisation of negative and positive liberty in an equal way, we see that there is an inherent incongruity between them, rather than a matter of moral pluralism or state neutrality.

Figure 3.4a Protective Equality

The protective liberal interpretation of equality fully corresponds to negative liberty. The state ought to make sure that individuals are equally free from coercion, and not the least that they hold an equal right to property. Since the right to hold property is so intensely defended, it follows that any definition of equality that presupposes or implies redistribution of property is unacceptable to protective liberalism.

3.3.2 Developmental Equality

Although seemingly stringent, the attempts of protective liberals to completely separate political equality from 'equality of opportunity' are confusing. We can reasonably speak in terms of opportunity also when focusing on formal political equality. With guaranteed political equality, individuals have equal opportunity to be spared coercion in a certain sphere. This opportunity is guaranteed if you enjoy negative liberties. But, political equality can also mean equal opportunity to participate in political life. Put simply, if democracy is a political system that gives people equal political rights and liberties, then democracy also provides equal opportunities to enjoy those liberties. As Dahl (1998:38) argues: "Democracy provides opportunities for 1) effective participation, 2) equality in voting, 3) gaining enlightened understanding, 4) exercising final control over the agenda, 5) inclusion of adults. If we exclude political equality from the meaning of equal opportunity, we lose the fact that developmental liberals do support the idea of a limited state as well, although not as limited as that of the protective tradition.

Therefore, in this section I argue that developmental equality comprises both the 'thinner' political equality and in various degrees also the 'thicker' equality of more substantial welfare allocation. In terms of defining policy restrictions this causes difficulties, because how does one determine the quantum of welfare required for individuals to be equally autonomous?

As with positive liberty, an extension of equality must occur within the framework or restrictions imposed by the liberal demands for moral pluralism and state neutrality. Recall that if negative liberties are not regarded as enough for an individual to be free (autonomous), e.g., there are no external obstacles coercing an individual, but he or she lacks the resources to do what he or she wants to do, then liberty must either be understood in a different way, or else the means to achieve it must be supplied in some way. Seen in this perspective, equality of autonomy refers to an equalisation of the means necessary for individuals to enjoy autonomy. This means that individuals are made equally capable of making choices and forming objectives so that they themselves are the originators of what they do (Jones 1994:125). Such an equal provision of means does not exclude freedom from restraints and coercion. Rather, such liberty is supplemented with the means necessary for action to take place. As Tawney (1931:139) emphasises:

> "In reality, of course, except in a sense which is purely formal, equality of opportunity is not simply a matter of legal equality. Its existence depends, not merely on the absence of disabilities, but on the presence of abilities. It obtains in so far as, and only in so far as, each member of a community, whatever his birth, or occupation, or social position, possesses in fact, and not merely in form, equal chances of using to the full his natural endowments of physique, of character, and of intelligence."

According to many liberal 'egalitarians', a society is less determined by formal negative rights and liberties than by practical powers. Society is not so much dependent on what its citizens may do if they are not coerced as it is on what they could do if they had the will and the powers. In trying to decide what rights individuals have, and particularly rights to liberties, Dworkin (1977:266-278) proceeds from equality instead of liberty. He asserts that government should not only treat people with concern and respect, but with equal concern and respect (ibid.273). This means that someone's liberty must not be constrained or favoured on the basis that his notion of the good life is inferior or superior to that of others. Dworkin's maxim is based on two different rights: 'equal treatment' and the 'right to be treated as an equal'.[39] He contends that it is only in very specific situations that constraint on individual liberty is allowed. First, liberty may be constrained if it is required to protect the distinct right of some individual who will be injured by the exercise of that liberty. Second, constraints may be required to reach some overall political goal. For the latter constraint to be legitimate, it must not violate the liberal principle of neutrality, i.e., the liberal notion of equality prohibiting a government from relying on the claim that certain forms of life are inherently more valuable than others (Dworkin 1977:272ff). As I shall show below, Dworkin's maxim is one of the key factors for us to understand fully the kind of equality emphasised within the developmental liberal democratic (DLD) tradition.

Equality beyond political equality is often expressed in terms of economic equality (cf. Baker 1987; Cohen 1988; Mason 1998). This extension means that one ascribes an important role to income or wealth as a means of enabling autonomy. That is, equality in wealth is required for individuals to enjoy autonomy. The extent of equality of autonomy (or rather inequality of autonomy) that people face, however, can usually not be deduced only from the extent of inequality in income. What one can do or cannot do depends also on a wide range of capabilities, physical as well as mental and social.[40]

Let us stop here for a moment and meditate what has actually been argued in these introductory pages. In Section 3.2. I claimed that the DLD version of positive liberty, i.e., autonomy, contains considerably more than just negative liberty. Autonomy refers to individuals having the resources required to choose and realise life plans that are genuinely their own. In this section it is implied that, according to the DLD tradition, these resources ought to be equally distributed. Undeniably this assertion raises a variety of questions of which I believe three are particularly important to elaborate on here. First, what resources are required for individuals to be able to enjoy autonomy and how are these resources determined? Second, can the state determine and supply these resources without compromising the principle of neutrality? Finally, can these resources be determined without leaving it to the discretion of the vast majority to decide what should be considered autonomy?

These questions are problematic and I do not aspire to produce a watertight reply. All I intend to do is to provide answers specific enough to give the DLD ideal-type as consistent and analytically satisfactory as possible, enabling me to formulate stringent compatibility criteria in the following section.

To fully understand the particular DLD position on equality and autonomy, and to be able to answer the questions above, we have to further disentangle the concept of neutrality. Raz (1986:114f) identifies three neutrality conceptions, the strict, narrow and comprehensive neutrality. The first and the third are of particular importance here. Strict neutrality largely corresponds with the protective liberal democratic (PLD) position on state action: For the state to remain neutral to the citizens' life plans, it should avoid interfering with individuals and their property.[41] Comprehensive neutrality is equivalent to DLD neutrality. Also here the state ought to remain neutral to the citizens' life plans. To meet this neutrality principle, however, the state practically has to interfere with individuals and especially with their private property.[42] The motive for this is well captured by Dworkin's maxim which says that the state ought to show all its citizens equal concern and respect (Dworkin 1977:272f). To really meet this ideal the state must not distribute resources unequally on the ground that some citizens are entitled to more just because they are worthy of more concern or because some conception of the good is superior to others. Instead the state ought to produce equal opportunities for its citizens to realise their life plans. For this to happen, the state must redistribute resources, something that, however, presupposes interference in private property. With this clarification in mind, we are ready to examine how some of the most distinguished DLD theorists have dealt with the matter of which resources ought to be distributed in order to maintain equal autonomy.

Rawls (1972, 1993) argues that autonomy presupposes certain primary goods. These goods are needed[43] by every individual to be able to form and realise his or her idea of what a morally good life is. The state can distribute these primary goods without jeopardising its neutrality because they are defined as goods that each rationally acting individual wishes more rather than less of, no matter what he or she think is morally correct. Besides basic rights and liberties, primary social goods are also included and consist of things such as income and wealth, opportunities and powers (Rawls 1972:92) and a sense of one's own worth—self-esteem (ibid:440f). As these goods neither reward nor facilitate individuals' association with a particular moral conception, Rawls' primary goods may be considered neutrally distributed by the state (cf. Rothstein 1996:62).

Dworkin uses his maxim to derive an "overall theory about equality". His idea is that for individuals to be treated with equal concern and respect, the state should provide equality of resources. This line of reasoning integrates two different rights that are included in the maxim. First there is the right to equal treatment, which requires the state to ensure an "equal distribution of goods and opportunities" (1977:27). More recently, Dworkin has expressed this as "equality in whatever resources are owned privately by individuals" (1981:283). Second, there is the right to equal concern and respect in the political decision about how these goods and opportunities are to be distributed, elsewhere expressed as "equality of political power" (1981:283). Thus, like Rawls, Dworkin includes both material and civil/political 'resources' in his theory.[44] To achieve this 'equality of resources', Dworkin advocates redistribution via income taxes (1981:312).

Both Rawls and Dworkin have been criticised for not considering the different power among individuals to convert material resources into actual capacity (Sen 1982:427).[45] Sen suggests that instead of commodities, the state should equalise basic capabilities (Sen 1982:368). According to this position, any idea about equality that is to be combined with state neutrality (whether political, social or economic equality) must take into account both citizen dissimilarities and differences in morality. State (re)distribution of resources should thus be sanctioned with the argument that they abolish or at least reduce any inability preventing individuals from living an autonomous life.

Another objection against Rawls' idea of basic goods is that such a theory may force the state to favour people with expensive tastes.

"Imagine two persons, one satisfied with a diet of milk, bread and beans, while the other is distraught without expensive wines and exotic dishes. A welfare egalitarian must, ceteris paribus, provide the epicure with a higher income than the person of modest taste, since otherwise the latter might be satisfied while the former is distraught." (Cohen 1989:913)[46]

To avoid this objection, according to Cohen, we must not be focused on primary goods to equalise the welfare of all citizens. Instead the state ought to compensate only for those welfare deficits not "traceable to the individual's choices" (Cohen 1989:914). This means that rather than concentrating on equality of welfare or resources, the state should create equality of opportunity to welfare.[47]

The Aristotelian theorist Nussbaum's analysis of welfare distribution is important not least to get an idea of the scope of resource distribution legitimate in DLD. In analogy with Sen, Nussbaum argues that each individual is different, and that different life plans require different resources. Furthermore, similar to Cohen she suggests that focus ought to be on citizens' capabilities to reach autonomy rather than on trying to specify exactly what resources the state ought to provide (1990:214)—a problem that can hardly be solved with political theory (cf. Douglas 1998; Rothstein 1996; Sen 1982 and note 44 in this section). In short she concludes that rather than suggesting a thin and fairly precise list of basic goods or resources as e.g., Rawls (1972), government should try to 'stay' within the framwork of state neutrality. Nussbaum suggests a thick and vague principle on "human functional capacities" (1990:217ff).

Nussbaum's arguments for this principle are well captured by Rothstein (1996:67). First, since the state cannot know exactly what resources are crucial to supply individuals with capabilities to realise their life plans, it is preferable that the state provides a broad set of resources.[48] Second, to remain neutral the state must not emphasise certain ways to live as more desirable than others. Therefore it is desirable that the set of resources be unspecified. This leads Nussbaum to suggest a comprehensive welfare state offering a smorgasbord of options and resources from which the individual can pick and reject as it serves him or her to enjoy welfare (or translated into DLD terms: 'a smorgasbord providing every citizen equal opportunities to choose and live an autonomous life').

Nussbaum is thelos/end oriented. Thus, her list is, reasonably, too comprehensive to be accommodated by any liberal-democratic theory. Simply put: Nussbaum's welfare state leaves practically nothing substantial for the democracy to decide since all social and economic issues are already determined.[49] Nonetheless, her principal reasoning is important since it shows that quite comprehensive resource distribution is plausible within the DLD ideal-type—provided that the aim of the distribution is not to direct the citizens towards a specific moral good, but to offer them opportunities to make themselves capable of chosing from a variety of life projects. In the DLD version, however, the determination of exactly which resources or opportunities is not a matter for political theory, but is rather for the electorate to decide.[50]

Although the objections against Rawls' and Dworkin's commodity-focus are correct when it comes to actually creating opportunities, I cannot see how the state would distribute or redistribute capacity or ability. What the state can do is to distribute goods and resources (read tools) that equalise individuals in terms of making them equally capable to make and to realise autonomous choices of life plans.[51]

In summary: even if the DLD theorists do disagree on exactly what should be equally distributed, be it goods, resources or capacities, they nevertheless have one central idea in common that is absolutely fundamental to the DLD ideal-type: The state can and even should provide its citizens with certain resources/tools that give them equal opportunities to choose among not one specific life project, but among a variety of life projects (as long as these do not harm others).

Let us continue with the crucial question whether 'autonomy resources' can be provided by the state without compromising the neutrality principle. There are two aspects to this question. First, state provision of resources implies that the state must interfere with individuals and collect these resources from those who have a surplus. This can be argued as being non-neutral. Second, for the state to decide which resources are to be provided means the state must make a moral decision, indicating that the state already knows what its citizens need in order to be able to make good choices. Also this scenario may be in opposition to neutrality. Thus, if we agree with these two conclusions, must we then not also accept that the state infringes the neutrality principle when supplying individual autonomy? My answer is no.

Just as Dworkin, Rawls, Sen, Raz, Nussbaum, Rothstein and Cohen argue, the autonomy principle demands that citizens already are in a situation where they can both make and realise autonomous choices. For this to be so, they must have access to certain goods, resources and/or capacities enabling them to make these choices. Thus, in the DLD ideal-type, the border beyond which the state becomes non-neutral is neither drawn when the state starts coercing individuals (i.e., Raz's 'strict' neutrality), nor when it starts supplying certain basic material resources/good/capacities.[52] Instead it is drawn when the state start dictating what a morally good choice is or how the provided resources ought to be used. To continue, the required resources must be collected from the surrounding society—mainly via taxes (Raz 1986:417). From a principal PLD perspective, this is never legitimate since it violates the right to private property.[53] For the DLD ideal-type, however, the right to private property is not sacred and the comprehensive neutrality principle allows for taxation—provided that the aim of (re)distribution is legitimate. If the aim of the resource provision is to show all citizens equal concern and respect by ensuring equality of resources (Dworkin), to support them with primary goods (Rawls), to provide equal capacity (Sen) or opportunities (Cohen) in order to make autonomous choices, then the aim is legitimate and the state does not violate the (comprehensive) neutrality principle when reducing the right to enjoy private property. As put by Gray: "The legitimate concern ought to be with what the state legitimately does, not with its overall magnitude" (1993:118).[54]

In fact, one can even argue that the state will act immorally if it does not endeavour to provide its citizens with equal opportunities. To quote Rothstein: "From the idea of equal concern and respect, the moral burden of proof ought to be placed upon those arguing that the state does not have obligations to provide its citizens with basic capacities to realise their autonomously chosen life projects" (Rothstein 1996:69).[55]

What then about the second conclusion that the state is forced to take a moral stand when extracting resources, and when doing so it cannot remain neutral nor maintain individuals' autonomy? The way I understand the DLD ideal, such an interpretation is based on a misconception, simply because for the state to actually be neutral it has to encourage individual autonomy. And, the other way around, to ensure autonomy the state has to remain neutral to individuals' life plans. Thus, when discussing neutrality and autonomy from a DLD point of view, we are not dealing with a state that imposes certain moral values by providing particular resources assumed to lead to 'the good life'. The whole DLD complex is instead founded on the premise that the state is obliged to provide its citizens with resources or capacities enabling them to live a life where they can make their own choices regarding what is good. Moreover, every citizen, of course, has the liberty to decline resources not contributing to his or her autonomy (cf. Rawls 1993:189).

Finally we have the argument that democratic decisions regarding what resources and opportunities should be supplied by the state inevitably end up in majoritarian utilitarianism. Throughout this chapter I have pointed out several (largely coinciding) principles which, if properly observed, would at least normatively avoid such a situation, namely:

Negative liberty: Although DLD theorists emphasise both negative and (to different degrees) positive liberty, negative liberty (i.e., civil liberties and rights) is still both fundamental and non-negotiable. It prevents the state (the majority) from dictating (1) what is morally good, and (2) which resources are required for such a 'communitarian' good to be generally realised.

The principle of equal concern and respect (ECR): Besides suggesting roughly what resources are to be provided by the state, the ECR principle also provides every citizen with a principal protection against majority discretion. To show each citizen equal respect means that the state must never circumscribe a citizen's liberty to choose and fulfil his or her life plan just because the vast majority think his or her life project is morally inferior, or that certain citizens' life projects are morally or socially superior. Thus, the ECR principle serves as a trump card in situations where a reform or a policy is in conflict with the individual's right to be treated with equal concern and respect (Rothstein 1996:40). This means that this individual right is superior to any goals formulated by the state or the collective, because the majority is never allowed to limit an individual's opportunities to enjoy autonomy merely because such a restriction would bring additional advantages to the majority.

The autonomy principle: Even if we disregard Dworkin's (1977) ECR principle, it is still reasonable to argue that the general autonomy principle serves as a protection against majority discretion. The reason is simple. Since this principle denies the state right to dictate which life plans are morally desirable or superior, all individuals consequently have a moral right to choose their own life projects. This is a principle that cannot be opposed by the majority, unless—of course—a particular life project causes harm to other individuals or constrains the legitimate realisation of the life plans of others.

The harm principle: When I introduced J.S. Mill's harm principle, I argued that it could be developed and practised also when we discuss autonomy and welfare. According to Raz's interpretation of the harm principle, a main task for the state is to create equal opportunities for people to chose any conception of the good. Now, if the state fails in fulfilling this task (e.g., because the majority disregard certain life plans), it means that the majority causes harm to those whose opportunities are not fulfilled (Raz 1986:124). Put differently: (1) The state is not allowed to use coercion that harms people. (2) The state is not allowed to harm anyone by unjustifiably diminishing his or her autonomy. (3) If the majority withholds the minority's opportunities to make autonomous choices and to enjoy chances to realise these choices, then the majority is causing illegitimate harm.

In this section we have scrutinised the DLD position on autonomy, equality and neutrality. It has been argued that as long as the aim of a state-initiated distribution is not to direct its citizens towards a specific moral good, but to offer them equal opportunities to choose among a variety of life projects, then welfare distribution is legitimate and may even be required. Furthermore, by understanding DLD in this way, none of the three entities of autonomy, equality and neutrality are in conflict with each other. We have not, however, been able to specify exactly which resources ought to be distributed in order for the citizens to enjoy equal opportunities. This 'failure' is explained by the fact that people have different qualifications and capacities to make autonomous choices and that they also have different conceptions of what constitutes the good life. Thus, exactly what resources to distribute and in what proportions cannot be derived from liberal political theory. This is not to say our examination has been useless or that we are left with no analytical framework to use when specifying criteria against which to test sustainable development policies (cf. Chapter 2.2). Even if we cannot specify exactly what the state is legitimised to distribute, we can now say quite a lot about what the state is *not* allowed to do or distribute.

Under no circumstances is the DLD state allowed to:

1) Dictate what a morally good life is —this is solely a matter for the individual to decide.

2) Distribute resources with the aim of directing individuals towards a specific conception of the good life.

3) Allow the discretion of the majority to decide which life plans are worthy of support, and which resources should be distributed—without simultaneously adhering to individuals' negative liberty, the ECR principle, the autonomy principle and the harm principle.

Figure 3.4b Developmental Equality

Equality of opportunity refers to an equal availability of the means necessary for individuals to enjoy autonomy. This refers to the goods, resources and capacities enabling an individual to choose and fulfil his or her life-plan. These means are not only political ones, like constitutional rights, but are also positive ones, like social and economic means, i.e., means that produce well-being or welfare. Extending the understanding of liberty and the reach of equality by adding positive elements makes it difficult to define the framework of state neutrality, i.e., exactly which resources can legitimately be distributed. Rather, the framework is 'negative' and specifies what the state cannot do. These frameworks lie where the active state is no longer neutral to individuals' autonomy and their concept of the good life.

3.4 Establishing Compatibility Criteria

3.4.1 Re-examination of the Relationship Between the State, Liberty and Equality

The intensity of the tensions between the state and individual liberty and equality that were stressed in the beginning of this chapter apparently depend on how we understand the three concepts and their relationship to each other. The protective liberal view of democracy sees liberty as individual freedom from coercion. Equality refers to an equal right to this freedom, and the role of the state is to make sure that neither the state nor other citizens violate this liberty. 'Absence' is the key word: a rather simple and straightforward idea.

Developmental liberalism is less straightforward in this respect. It is, however, possible to talk in terms of degrees: we either study liberty and/or equality. However, exactly how much of each cannot be determined theoretically. The main reasons for this can be traced back to J.S. Mill's ideas about 'opportunity to participate' and his 'no-harm principle'. In what spheres ought people to get the opportunity to participate, and in what respects should people not get harmed? After Mill the division into two different traditions becomes even clearer. When liberty gradually becomes 'autonomy', opportunity no longer refers solely to the opportunity to participate in political life. Liberty then becomes the right to individual self-development, which, in combination with demands for equality, profoundly challenges the protective liberal view. This becomes apparent when the question 'Equality of what?' is asked.[56]

However, even if there are great differences between the protective and the developmental liberal traditions it makes sense to place both within the framework of liberalism. None of the traditions lead to producing 'grand politics', decided in advance and in accordance with a particular definition of the good life although developmental liberal democracy certainly could. While the definition of neutrality is stretched in the developmental tradition, the state remains neutral in relation to its citizens. In contrast to the passive neutrality referred to in the protective tradition the state ought to remain actively neutral in the developmental tradition. For example, the goals of the state are certainly more numerous and socially exhaustive than in the protective tradition, which stresses a role of the state as a 'securer', rather than a 'provider'. However, ends can be means as well. This is how developmental liberal democracy is understood. The means required to fulfil individual life plans are not necessarily the same for everybody. The provision of means for the realisation of individual life plans is a goal of the state, but is not allowed to become a superior societal goal in developmental liberal theory.

3.4.2 The Compatibility Criteria

Going through the literature on compatibility between sustainable development and (liberal) democracy in Chapter 1, I criticised the analyses to date in several respects. One was that few theorists have established what they mean by liberal democracy. There is also a lack of established criteria or premises for a sustainable development policy to be compatible with liberal democracy. In this chapter, I have created two ideal-types which I argue represent the common denominators of liberal democracy. I have done this in order to establish the frameworks within which a policy can be considered 'legitimate' from a liberal democratic viewpoint. In line with what was stated in the Figures 3.2a-4a and 3.2b-4b, it is now possible to determine the policy restrictions for each ideal-type, and thus to provide the limitations encountered by sustainable development policies in such liberal democracies. That is, we can formulate criteria for judging whether or not a sustainable development policy can be considered compatible with any of the ideal-types. The criteria shown below are applied when I accomplish my type-four compatibility analysis in Chapter 8.

Figure 3.5a Compatibility Criterion Derived from the Idea of Protective Liberal Democracy

Premise 1.	The 'good life' is exclusively an individual matter.
Premise 2.	Individual liberty shall solely be understood negatively.
Premise 3.	The individual's right to hold and enjoy property is absolute.
Premise 4.	Equality only comprises legal and political standing.

Policy restriction: Thus, in order not to violate premise 1, the protective liberal-democratic state must be neutral in regard to an individual's life plans, and passive in all respects other than those presupposed in premises 2-4.

Compatibility criterion: Any sustainability policy presupposing a violation of this policy restriction is to be considered incompatible with the core values of protective liberal democracy.

Comments: The premises arise from the following figures: Premise 1 (Figure 3.2a). Premise 2 (Figure 3.3a), Premise 3 (Figures 3.2a, 3.3a and 3.4a), Premise 4 (Figure 3.3a).

**Figure 3.5b   Compatibility Criterion Derived from the Idea of
Developmental Liberal Democracy**

Premise 1.   The 'good life' is exclusively a matter for the individual to
define.

Premise 2.   Individual liberty shall be understood as autonomy
(opportunity to fulfil one's life-plans).

Premise 3.   Equality comprises opportunities to choose and fulfil life
plans.

Policy restriction: Thus, the developmental liberal-democratic state must
be neutral with regard to individual life-plans, active in the respects
presupposed by premises 2 and 3, but must never end up in a majority
violating neither a citizen's negative liberty, nor the principles of harm,
ECR and autonomy.

**Compatibility criterion: Any sustainability policy presupposing a
violation of this policy restriction is to be considered incompatible
with the core values of developmental liberal democracy.**

Comment: The premises arise from the following figures: Premise 1 (Figure 2b),
Premise 2 (Figure 3b), Premise 3 (Figure 3b and 4b).

Notes:

1 Thus, a most crucial question arises: Is it consistent to hold that democracy is the best
form of government, that the people should run this government and that the power of
this government should be limited? Those questions have no simple answer. One reason
for this is that the extent to which the state ought to be limited is not an absolute, but a
relative issue. As will be seen from what follows, the frameworks set for the 'neutral'
state are highly variable. In principal one can, however, distinguish between *passive* and
active neutrality, where passive neutrality refers to a state that is only allowed to ensure
that people enjoy their negative liberties and rights, while an active neutral state is also
allowed to provide individuals with the social and economic means required to enjoy
liberty. Raz (1986:120ff) makes a similar distinction between 'strict' and
'comprehensive' neutrality. The meaning is, however, the same.
2 Certainly, in a democracy it can always be argued that if and when people wish to
change the world, and, e.g., attain sustainable development, the world can and will be
changed in that direction. If everyone wants to change a situation (e.g., redirect society
towards sustainable development) and they possess suitable means to do this, obviously
an analysis like mine is irrelevant. But to take for granted that individuals are willing to
hand over the means necessary to make significant contributions of this kind, that there
are no institutional or normative obstacles, or to argue that if people have this
willingness, then sustainable development is not a problem, is to oversimplify the issue
significantly. Furthermore, such a position can only be examined empirically, and only
after sustainability has actually been realised. What does the philosophical debate on

compatibility between sustainable development and liberal democracy stand to gain by an ex post re-examination of whether people *were* willing to act according to sustainable development at a certain time? This is not to say that citizens are not important. Ultimately their acceptance of policies is of course essential to what the state can do (cf. Sections 8.2-8.4 and 9.1).

3 Both liberty and equality can be understood in different ways. Liberty can refer both to negative and positive liberty. The concept of equality comprises everything from formal political equality to economic equality. I discuss those views more thoroughly in Sections 3.2 and 3.3 of this chapter.

4 At least for now. I shall spend the rest of the chapter elaborating on how the relationship between liberty, equality and public authority is best understood.

5 These two are congruent with the two liberal democratic traditions ('classic' and 'social' liberal democracy) that were introduced in Chapter 1.3.

6 And several others; see Dunn (1979), Macpherson (1977), Lukes (1973), Plamenatz (1963).

7 Which is a heritage from Macpherson (1977).

8 Although such a view is questionable from a democratic point of view (reasonably freedom should mean 'having the possibility to alter the law' and that lawmakers should be accountable to the people, or the electorate, to be democratically legitimate), it probably was not such a big problem for Montesqieu, since he was not a democrat (Held 1997:87). Instead, his view was rather that the governed remained in the end accountable to the governors.

9 Such liberty is based on an idea about individual self-development, which signals a shift from a passive to an active state with the authority to provide individuals with the means necessary to enjoy such development (cf. Section 3.2 and 3.3).

10 Although he suggested a 'stationary state', this only referred to economic growth. He argued that "It is scarcely necessary to remark that a stationary condition of capital and population implies no stationary state of human improvement." (Mill 1859:169). See also Barry (1999b:72-77).

11 "It is only in the backward countries in the world that increased production is still an important objective../..in those most advanced, what is economically needed is better distribution." (Mill 1982: 168).

12 A similar kind of reasoning is common among many liberal theorists today, such as Rawls (1972), Gewirth (1982), Dworkin (1977) and Sen (1982). See my further discussion in Section 3.3.2.

13 A similar idea of self-reliance was held by earlier liberals, so I suppose Samuel meant that legislation should be extended beyond what was 'legitimate' according to previous philosophers. Perhaps one explanation is that the protective liberals stressed that it was the government that was the main hindrance for individuals to do what they would like, while the later liberals rather saw the lack of the necessary means as the main hindrance for individuals doing what they would like to do.

14 As did T.H. Green (1888). His ideas were mainly based on those of the German philosopher G.W.F. Hegel. This led Green to defend a positive concept of liberty, understood as the individual capacity for self-improvement. Such an interpretation, of course, not only allows for, but also requires, further legislation to eliminate demoralising conditions for the poor. However, I cannot fully elaborate the significance of this 'move'. Hegel very much based his thinking on the developmental republican J.J. Rousseau's thinking, whose view of individual liberty was solely 'positive'. In the next section on liberty the political implications of a Hegelian view of liberty will be discussed.

15 Thus, whether a state remains neutral, according to the developmental ideal-type, does not depend so much on the range of the measures taken, as on the aim of the measures.

16 That is, to be free is to be able to do a certain thing, and since this thing is morally valuable, the individual should be provided the means necessary to do this thing.

17 That I am not able to pick coconuts in Sweden because of the climate is not a reason for saying that I lack the freedom to pick coconuts in Sweden. That there are no coconuts to pick is a natural fact and has nothing to do with liberty.

18 As far as I understand, this conundrum can only be resolved if one out of two conditions apply. 1) Either it is wrong or analytically confusing to categorise different views of liberty as protective or developmental. The reason for this would be that only the protective tradition is fully attached to one concept of liberty (the negative), while the developmental seems to take in both negative and positive notions in its view of liberty. Since they are incompatible, according to protective liberals, developmental liberalism must emphasise positive liberty. Or 2) perhaps it is not very fruitful to speak in terms of negative and positive freedom. At least it is not straightforward to argue that they are completely incompatible. Some have tried to eliminate the difference between the two, by, for example, arguing that they actually *presuppose* each other (cf. MacCullum 1967).

19 For Hegel, liberty or freedom was a collective matter. His philosophy grasped a 'whole people's liberty, and not only that of one individual. The kind of liberty Hegel suggested led him and many of his followers to conclude that real freedom can only be achieved in a harmonious and integrated society. Both Marx and Engles were strongly influenced by Hegel (Russel 1945: 3rd book: §27).

20 I.e., a *passive* state.

21 I.e., an *active* state.

22 I say indeterminable because there are degrees of resources required, depending on how comprehensive, or far-reaching, the self-determination is.

23 In the end a rather paradoxical situation can arise. First, force may be used to guarantee someone's liberty. For example, J.J. Rousseau suggested an outspoken defence of positive liberty that makes it possible for the state to 'force someone to be free' (Rousseau quoted in Plant 1991:253). Second, one group will be given the right to not only formulate but also to implement what they hold to be the 'good life'—and this in the name of liberty.

24 Plant (1991:248ff). In the former case (the ambitious interpretation of freedom) 'to' refers to specific goals that the 'free' agent is allowed, or authorised, to strive for. That is, 'to X' indicates that X is decided on beforehand. In the latter case 'to' refers to a *variety of goals*, perhaps even up to an infinite set of goals. Thus, the government shall not ensure that its citizens become free by acting according to a particular plan, but rather it provides the means required for individuals to freely formulate their own plans. In at least one sense, this less ambitious view of positive liberty has similarities with negative liberty. In both cases, normative judgements have to be made regarding which needs, wishes and capacities are of fundamental importance, not for reaching a particular goal, but for individuals to enjoy freedom. The difference, in this respect, is that a positive view demands more social, economic and political resources to be redistributed. According to MacCullum (1967), we are not faced by a choice between negative and positive freedom, which is the case in Berlin's view. Rather, MacCullum sees freedom as a triadic relationship which he expresses as: X is (is not) free from Y to do (not do, become, not become) Z. In neither case is Z defined or decided on beforehand, which I understand is the main difficulty liberals have with positive liberty. To be free, call it positive or negative, requires means to fulfil Z, whatever Z may be. A good example is Van Paraijs (1992), who defends a neutral view of the good, but argues that for an individual to be able to do Z, certain economic resources are required. He therefore proposes a *basic income* that would provide at least the economic means required to fulfil 'basic individual goals'.

25 Such an interpretation may end up in a list of needs so extensive that little if any free choice remains (cf. Section 3.3.2). But with such an understanding, it is at least possible to build in barriers that can guarantee the individual to have some choices.

26 See Benn & Weinstein 1971:194-211.

27 The reason is well captured by Gray (1995:58) who says that: "Many modern threats to freedom—propaganda, media manipulation, and the tyranny of fashion—can be

understood, I think, only by invoking some such (open) conception of autonomy."
('open' is added by me).
28 E.g., Rawls (1972); Dworkin (1977); Arneson (1989); Cohen (1989). See my further discussion in Section 3.3.2.
29 I further discuss options to specify exactly what resources to be distributed in Section 3.3.2 below.
30 Hayek (1960) argues that liberty and equality should be regarded as two divided entities, except in one particular respect: equality before the law. Not only has liberty nothing to do with any other sort of equality; it is also bound to produce inequality in many regards.
31 To the risk of 'social uniformity' can also be added, for instance, atomisation, which J. S. Mill so intensely feared. A uniform society not only suppresses societal innovations of whatever kind, but also tends to create individuals who are vulnerable to all sorts of pressure.
32 Tawney's (1931) strict egalitarian perspective not only places equality on the same normative level as liberty, but even gives priority to the former. Equality is not solely a legal matter, but concerns capacity as well. Tawney therefore interprets equality as a positive value not unlike positive freedom. He says "its existence (equality of opportunity) depends, not merely on the absence of disabilities, but on the presence of abilities." (Tawney 1931:139). Also Dworkin uses equality as a starting point and analyses in what respects liberty can be considered to limit equality(1977:272).
33 Sen (1992:21ff) claims that there is no such thing as a 'versus' between liberty and equality. If we defend, say, liberty, then we have to decide who, how much and how equal those liberties ought to be. In fact, there is no way we can analyse liberty without either relating it to equality, or including it in the analyses. At the least, Sen stresses, equality should be seen as a supplement to liberty.
34 An interesting response to the question of 'what' should be equalised has been suggested by Sen (1992), who argues that 'what' is a matter of 'focal variables' (1992:25f). No matter what kind of liberty we defend, we will argue that some variables (negative or positive) are to be equalised, but we will have different focus. These variables are not always possible to equalise at the same time, usually because they are dependent on each other in some way. For example, if we state that everyone must have equal X in order to be autonomous, then to actually provide everyone with equal X probably demands an (un)equal redistribution of Y, leading to a conflict or inequality somewhere else. Thus, 'what' cannot reasonably refer to everything we comprehend as good, desirable or perhaps even necessary to achieve autonomy, as some full-fledged egalitarians seem to argue (Baker 1987 is a good example).
35 See further discussion in Jones (1994).
36 Usually understood as social and economic means. See my examination in section 3.3.2 below.
37 It is often claimed that 'law and order', the traditional targets for protective liberals, is relatively cheap to sustain, while general welfare is expensive and requires comprehensive taxation. That is, however, a questionable assumption. Public prisons, lawyers, courts, police and so forth certainly incur costs, and the more criminality in a country the more expensive these services become and the more restricted the right to hold property.
38 Robert Nozick (1974), for example, supports political liberties, but he also strongly defends the right to hold private property. It is the right of property holders that is the main issue, not that each and every person should actually hold property. The right to hold property effectively blocks any attempt to extend equality to something more than negative rights/goods. As far as I understand, Nozick builds his reasoning on two essential premises. The first is that no one ought to be a slave, either in whole or in part, to anyone else. This means that no one has the right to own someone else, but each and everyone is, rightfully, a self-owner. Further, since I am a sovereign self-owner, no one can lay claim to the services I produce or possess. If anyone had the right to make a claim on those services, then I would be a slave (cf. 1974: 276-292). According to Hayek (1960:139ff), it is not only the right to possess property that is central from the

perspective of freedom from coercion. To be dependent on someone who is in possession of property is a violation against liberty too. In such a view, I am free to go to Costa Rica, even if I cannot afford it. It is just not an option for me. If I get economic help from my neighbour to get there, then I have the option but I will rely upon someone else's good will, and that makes me a slave.

39 Notice that this right is not understood as an equal distribution of some good or opportunity, but as the right to equal concern and respect when it comes to a political decision about how these goods and opportunities should be distributed.

40 Others argue that economic and social inequalities threaten the coherence of society, and even tend to negate the principle of political equality. "There is, in other words no neat or clear distinction to be drawn between political equality and social and economic equality." (Arblaster 1994:76). If I am too poor and hungry I have no opportunity to participate and enjoy my political rights. Furthermore, economically and socially better off individuals, may gain an unequal impact because of this. I suppose the implication of this is that at least a certain level of basic goods is required, or should be secured for all individuals to be able to enjoy at least some kind of basic autonomy but also for society to flourish. As will be shown below, I believe such reasoning is found among most egalitarian liberals.

41 "No political action may be undertaken or justified on the ground that it promotes an ideal of the good nor on the ground that it enables individuals to pursue an ideal of the good" (Raz 1986:114).

42 "One of the main goals of governmental authority, which is lexically prior to any other, is to ensure for all persons an equal ability to pursue in their lives and promote in their societies any ideal of the good of their choosing" (Raz 1986:115). According to Raz, 'libertarian' neutrality probably ends up somewhere in between strict and narrow neutrality. "Libertarian supporters of neutral political concern gravitate towards the narrow principle" (Raz 1996:124).

43 What people *need* is hard to define. There *is* a comprehensive literature on *basic needs* and the distinction between needs and (the less vital) wants (cf. Ramsay 1992; Galtung 1990), to which I cannot fully relate in this book. To determine exactly which needs are crucial is discussed among a wide range of disciplines, such as economists (Dasgupta 1993; Sen 1981), biologists (Clark 1990), (economic) psychologists (Maslow 1943; Scitovsky 1992), ethical need theorists (Max-Neef 1991) and anthropologists (Sahlins 1968; Douglas 1986). Although a theoretical and empirical evolution is constantly taking place within this field and several attempts have been made to specify exactly which needs should be considered basic and absolutely necessary for human beings to enjoy an autonomous or even a fairly acceptable life, both theoretically (e.g Rawls 1972) and empirically—such as measurable indexes (e.g. Dasgupta 1993 and UNDP 1992) — I have found no consensus on the matter (cf. Douglas et al. 1998 for an excellent overview of the human need debate). Thus, to proceed from liberal political theory and try to identify or derive a specific list of needs that the state ought to secure, or try to identify resources that equally match these needs in order for all individuals to enjoy autonomy, is probably doomed to failure. That is *not*, however, to say the state cannot do anything without violating liberal core values (cf. my final discussion in Section 3.

44 The question of *which specific resources* should be distributed remains unanswered.

45 In much the same way the anthropologist Douglas has criticised this goods/resource approach: "Commodities do not satisfy desire; they are only the tools or instruments for satisfying it" (1998:202). Moreover, every such distribution inevitably favours those individuals whose personal characteristics are such that they, better than others, are capable of converting these resources or primary goods into *personal capacity*.

46 Against this objection Rawls argues that people with expensive tastes could have chosen otherwise, and if and when they press for compensation, others are entitled to insist that they themselves bear the cost "of their lack of foresight or self-discipline." (Rawls 1982:168-69 quoted in Cohen 1989:913)

47 Also see Arneson (1990) who argues that a principle of distributive justice in a liberal theory ought to use *individual opportunities for preference satisfaction* rather than primary goods as the basis of interpersonal comparisons.

48 Cf. Douglas et al. (1998:203) who argue that the needs of individuals are culturally conditioned leading them to claim that "without a theory of social persons we cannot start to use the distinction between basic and higher needs.

49 Cf. Nussbaum (1990:219-25) and also her comparison with welfare measurements in Scandinavian social democratic countries (ibid:240-242).

50 Cf. Sen (1992:4) who, when claiming that different theories give different answers to the question 'equality of what?' concludes that "The different answers are distinguishable *in principle* and involve different conceptual approaches. But the *practical* force of these distinctions depends on the empirical importance of the relevant human heterogeneities which make equality in one space diverge from equality in another."

51 Rothstein (1996) and Cohen (1989) call this *compensation* for inability. I think 'compensation' delimits the governmental space of action a bit too much. Certainly, the state cannot make the blind see or the stupid become intelligent, but it can compensate for such shortcomings e.g., by providing a guide dog or a remedial teacher, thus enabling (providing opportunities for) these individuals to make autonomous choices. Yet, state-initiated provisions can even be offered for other reasons (and still be considered legitimate from a DLD perspective). For example, I can hardly be compensated for lacking water—either I *have* water, or I *do not have* water. There is no substitute for water.

52 Or in Raz's words: "Since individuals are guaranteed adequate rights of political participation in the liberal state and since such a state is guided by public morality expressing concern for individual autonomy, its coercive measures do not express an insult to the autonomy of individuals" (1986:157).

53 If we scrutinise the internal logic of this line of reasoning, we immediately discover that a fully-fledged defence of private property protection forces us to conclude that not even the most minimal functions of the state, such as a police force, courts and prisons are plausible in such a system. I.e., practically every political theorist must agree that the state should provide its citizens with certain resources for them to be able to enjoy autonomy or (negative) liberty, and all such provisions incur costs and have to be paid for by the citizens (cf. Gray 1993:110-121; Raz 1986:117-124)

54 There are certainly frames though—cf. the discussion below regarding majoritarian utilitarianism.

55 We are here talking about *basic* resources/capacities that each individual should have to live an autonomous life; not just any resources. Thus, this is not about redistribution enabling every individual to eat pheasant every day and also the other way around: an individual's autonomy is not violated just because the state imposes taxes to the extent that he or she cannot afford eating pheasant every day. This is simply because eating pheasant is reasonably not a matter of autonomy (cf. Copp 1992:256-261; Edwards 1988:142-145).

56 At the same time, it appears that the protective critique of developmental reasoning is somewhat exaggerated, and positive and negative liberty are not as different from each other as has often been proposed. The right to hold property seems to be where negative liberty is most exposed to threat. Maybe Hobhouse's invitation to 'drop' the holiness of private property was the final watershed. As long as liberalism equates political rights with the right to private property, then at least no substantial economic reforms can take place without this right being violated. On the other hand, if this right were absolute, then what would be left of other negative liberties? All liberals, either protective or developmental, must accept some restrictions on property. Even the thinnest Nozickian understanding of the state is burdened by costs. Law and order is not a 'free lunch', although it is considered less expensive then economic and social welfare programmes.

Chapter 4

Sustainable Development

Having defined the two ideal-types of liberal democracy, and elaborated on the restrictions that each of them imposes on policy, the first dimension of my analytical framework is now complete. The second dimension, i.e., the specification of policies for sustainable development, requires no less than four steps. First, sustainable development must be defined. Second, a theoretical implementation of sustainable development is to be made operational and simulated through scenarios. Third, the societal changes implied by the scenarios have to be established. Finally, an assessment must be made regarding what policies are required for these societal changes to be effected. This chapter concerns the first two of these steps.

Section 4.1 presents various views of sustainable development. I conclude that sustainable development is a debatable concept and its definitions are too vague to imply any specific policies. In Section 4.2, I argue that if we go beyond the pure definition, i.e., elaborate on the conception of sustainable development (as expressed in *Our Common Future*), then the definition of sustainable development becomes more precise and allows us to derive guidelines that help us make sustainable development operational. In and of itself, the information in the Brundtland report is, however, not detailed enough to determine any policies. The report does not establish to what people could legitimately aspire, or whether there are any absolute resource limits. In Section 4.3 I continue the search for policies by specifying the case of animal food consumption, which will be my test case throughout the rest of the book. In the last Section 4.4, scenarios for a 'sustainable' global production of animals for consumption are presented.

4.1 Sustainable Development—A Contested Concept

The concept of sustainable development has been used in the environmental debate at least since 1980.[1] However, it was not until 1987 following the report

Our Common Future by the Brundtland Commission (World Commission on Environment and Development—WCED) that it became more widely accepted as a guiding principle for most environmental political policies. It has been common to approach sustainable development from quite different angles. Economists tend to relate sustainability to the productive capital stock (Munasinghe & McNeely 1995; Pearce & Turner 1990). More socially oriented scholars relate sustainability to the adaptability and preservation of diverse social and cultural systems such as institutions (Meredith 1992; Toman 1992; Freeman 1991). Natural scientists tend to relate sustainability to the resilience or integrity of biological and physical systems (Holmberg 1995; Perrings 1991). The WCED report makes clear that sustainable development can never be solely a matter of physical sustainability. It must include both global economic and social development if long-term sustainable development is ever to take place. For example, poor people will inevitably sacrifice the environment for their own survival. Thus, "Even the narrow notion of physical sustainability implies a concern for social equity between generations, a concern that must logically be extended to equity within each generation" (WCED 1987:87). Sustainable development is therefore defined as a:

"development that meets the needs of the present without compromising the ability of the future generations to meet their own needs" (WCED 1987:87).

This definition of the concept is disputed. An abundance of alternative definitions have been put forward.[2] Some definitions aim at clarifying the meaning of sustainable development by defining when the ecological or biophysical limits are met. Attempts are made to make the concept more scientifically acceptable by transforming it into something measurable (such as economic indicators) (cf. Holmberg 1995; Daly 1991; Jacobs 1991). Others assert that there is an inherent contradiction in sustainable development, since it contains the two conflicting concepts, i.e., sustainability (which implies constraints on growth) and economic growth (which implies no constraints). Economic growth requires resources to grow indefinitely even though these resources are limited. Thus, the more comprehensive the economic growth, the more resources are demanded, and the more (physical/ecological) sustainability is challenged.

Others have been disappointed with various definitions of sustainability on environmental grounds. Environmentalists and deep ecologists argue that too little attention is paid to the intrinsic value of nature. Many Greens have therefore claimed that the WCED's definition is too anthropocentric and thus invalid.[3] They argue that only an ecocentric definition, where respect for other species or for nature is included, can be considered reasonable or legitimate. Representatives of the Third World claim that while the Brundtland Commission is burdening the Third World with obligations to solve its environmental problems, it does not put (enough) emphasis on the First World's responsibilities for environmental degradation and thus those nations' primary responsibility to do something about it (Banerjee 2001; Nagpal 1995; Lelé 1991; Martinez-Alier 1987).

Admittedly, the WCED definition of sustainable development is vague and questionable. It does not provide any information on how to arrive at such a development. On the other hand, perhaps nothing else should be expected. Sustainable development, no matter what version, is a normative goal and therefore, like many other politically and normatively loaded concepts 'contested'. This means that it remains a concept that cannot be ultimately defined (Dryzek 1997:125).

Despite the alleged imperfections of the Brundtland Commission's particular understanding of the concept, I will henceforth focus on it for two major reasons. First of all, it is the most frequently quoted and politically used definition of sustainable development (Munasinghe & McNeely 1995:23). Second, a definition of sustainable development in itself does not specify (nor does it imply) how society ought to be changed in order to arrive at sustainable development. Neither does any definition indicate what political decisions are required to bring about the required societal changes.[4] To get this information Langhelle (2000c) suggests that we ought to keep apart the 'concept' of sustainable development from its 'conception'. Indisputably, as a concept WCED's definition is vague. As a *conception*, however, the WCED's discussion about sustainable development is far more precise. Langhelle refers to Rawls (1993:14) who argues that the concept is "the meaning of the term", while a particular conception also includes the principles required to apply it. In *Our Common Future*, a wide range of normative and empirical prerequisites for obtaining sustainable development are established, all of which imply what priorities must be set, and how society ought to change. At the same time Langhelle emphasises that this conception is not enough to resolve value conflicts, avoid incorrect conclusions or decide the size of the state budget. However, the conception of sustainable development as derived from the WCED report is precise enough to say something about the 'direction' of societal development (Langhelle 2000c:59).

By more closely reviewing and analysing the way sustainable development is understood in the Brundtland Commission report, we are thus able to determine its *essence*—something I will use as an *operational guide* in the work on simulating sustainability scenarios.

4.2 Sustainable Development According to the Brundtland Commission

The WCED report *Our Common Future* mediates a positive message—a belief in the future (WCED 1987:1). People *can* build a world that is more prosperous, just and secure. However, this positivism is "conditioned upon the establishment of a new era of international co-operation based on the premise that every human being—those here and those who are to come—has the *right* to life, and to a decent life." (WCED 1987:85). This right cannot be enjoyed by all of humanity unless large-scale societal changes take place. Natural resources are limited, and must be distributed and utilised differently if every member of the world's population is to live a satisfactory life. The achievement of sustainable development implies nothing less than a global revolution:

> ". . . a process of change, in which exploitation of resources, the direction of investments, the orientation of technological development, and institutional change are made consistent with future as well as present needs"(WCED 1987:9).

If people are to satisfy their basic needs and enjoy the right to a decent life, there must be global *social development*. The level of needs satisfaction, how investments are directed, and what progress we can expect in terms of technological development, depend on the level of *economic development*. That resources are limited also implies that there are *biophysical limits* to economic development, and thus to how far basic human needs can actually be met. When these biophysical limits will be reached is mostly determined by *technological* and *institutional development*. Thus, the idea of sustainable development is a demand for simultaneous social and economic development that takes place within the framework set by ecological limits, and with the important requirement to meet human needs by means of technological development and institutional change. Furthermore, the particular *lifestyles* that people adopt will affect when ecological limits are reached. Let us examine how these targets are approached in the report.

4.2.1   Social Development

The demand for social development can be divided into two levels, or targets. One concerns how to secure and fulfil *basic human needs*. The second target is the fulfilment of human *aspirations* for a good or decent life. It is difficult to keep those targets apart completely. According to the Brundtland Commission, the most urgent goal for the world is to combat poverty. This fight is independent of any requirement for sustainable development, because poverty is an "evil in itself" (WCED 1987:8). Thus, solutions to the poverty problems must be dealt with, regardless of any prospective environmental concern. *Yet*, there is an important connection between poverty and ecological degradation that must not be forgotten: "A world in which poverty is endemic will always be prone to ecological and other catastrophes" (WCED 1987:8). Simply put, poor people are forced to impoverish the environment to avoid poverty, or even to survive. But social development is not only about human survival and the fulfilment of basic needs. It is also about goods and services needed for a good life:

> ". . . sustainable development requires meeting the basic needs of all and extending to all the opportunity to fulfil their aspirations for a better life." (WCED 1987:8)

". . . beyond their basic needs these people have legitimate aspirations for an improved quality of life."(WCED 1987:87)

What aspirations are legitimate beyond basic needs are not specified in the report. However, "quality of ", "decent " and "better" imply considerably more than just the bare necessities of life. This is very important because the more goods and services we include in 'legitimate aspirations' on a global scale, the more resources will principally be demanded. Food can serve as an example. Food is clearly a basic need, and something to which all people can aspire legitimately. However, there are different diets, ranging from low to high resource consumption. There is a great difference between the diet required for an individual to survive (staple food), and the 'standard' diet required to avoid undernourishment (a diet including protein). In terms of resource use, the standard diet is still moderate compared to the average diet in the industrialised world.

Yet:

". . . sustainable development *requires* that societies meet human needs both by increasing productive potential and by *ensuring equitable opportunities for all*." (WCED 1987:88 my italics).

This is a strong requirement that gives rise to difficult issues. For example, what would happen if the overall global population was guaranteed the opportunity to fulfil its aspirations for a daily food intake equivalent to that of the industrialised world?[5] Since it is not specified to what human beings can aspire legitimately, we can hardly conclude that even if the opportunities existed, it is unlikely that (most) people would be content with a lesser resource demanding diet or lifestyle than they know exists elsewhere.

4.2.2 Economic Development

Today it is difficult to imagine a world where each and everyone has their aspirations fulfilled (not even the most fundamental ones). Hundreds of millions of people are starving, and additional billions of people are suffering from poverty. The Brundtland report contends that to change this situation, continued economic growth is needed—thus not limited economic growth as many ecologists have recommended:

"If large parts of the developing world are to avert economic, social, and environmental catastrophes, it is essential that global economic growth be revitalised. In practical terms, this means more *rapid economic growth in both industrial and developing countries*, freer market access for products of developing countries, lower interest rates, greater technology transfer, and significantly larger capital flows, both concessional and commercial" (WCED 1987:133 my italics).

However, the Brundtland Commission does not refer to the kind of growth we have experienced during the 20th century. First, it points to a rate of economic growth that inevitably includes the developing countries: Meeting essential needs depends in part on achieving full economic growth potential, and sustainable development clearly requires economic growth in places where such needs are not being met. Only if the poor countries enjoy significant economic development can they avoid poverty and create the opportunities to meet the aspirations of their people.

Second, the Brundtland Commission foresees (re)distributed economic growth. By themselves, developing countries are not capable of reaching the social and economic levels needed to ensure equal opportunities for all. Therefore redistribution of resources is required to attack poverty. "Resource flows from rich to poor—flows improved both qualitatively and quantitatively—are a precondition for the eradication of poverty" (p.113) . 'Quantitatively' here refers to the amount of aid and other support required for the developing world to meet its needs. The Brundtland Commission establishes that today's economic and technological flows are far from sufficient and must increase considerably.

Third, future growth must be ecologically sustainable, because 'qualitatively' refers to how growth is developed. Sustainable economic growth, in both developing and developed countries, must take place within ecological limits. It must be made " less material- and energy-intensive, and more equitable in its impact." (WCED 1987:96). This is a challenge to the traditional green view which holds that the higher the economic growth, the more natural resources are demanded and destroyed.

Finally, the commission demands 'just' growth. It must be more "equitable in its impact", meaning that all human beings ought to have "equitable opportunities" today and in the future (WCED 1987:88). It is an "assurance that those who are poor get their fair share of the resources required to sustain that growth." (WCED 1987:8). I interpret this requirement as more substantial than just a reference to preconditions such as the lack of legal or institutional hindrances. A globally improved quality of life is an absolute requirement and an equal right for all[6]. Thus, global and equitable economic development is required to ensure global social development. However, economic growth must not go beyond ecological sustainability, i.e., biophysical limits.

4.2.3 Staying Within Biophysical Limits

The Brundtland commission has received much international attention because of its simultaneous demand for social, economic and ecological concern. Economic growth is a prerequisite for social development, but it must never jeopardise the fundamental physical conditions for life. It is difficult, however, to extract a consistent position on biophysical limits in the Brundtland report. On the one hand the Brundtland Commission argues that economic growth does not have any set limits as long as no ecological disasters are impending (WCED 1987:89). On the other hand it contends that:

"The concept of sustainable development does imply limits—*not absolute limits* but limitations imposed by the present state of technology and social organisation of environmental resources and by the ability of the biosphere to absorb the effects of human activities" (WCED 1987:8 my italics).

This implies a society that is capable of avoiding scarcity, and of making sure that biophysical limits are not exceeded. However, the report *also* argues that " *Ultimate limits there are*, and sustainable development presupposes that long before these are reached, the world must ensure *equitable access* to constrained resources, and reorient technological efforts to relieve the pressure" (WCED 1987:8; my italics). What makes it even more difficult to find a guiding principle for establishing biophysical limits is that the commission does not think that economic growth—which apparently is necessary to ensure equitable opportunities and to promote an ecologically sound lifestyle—can take place without interference with the biophysical system: " Every ecosystem everywhere cannot be preserved intact" (WCED 1987:89).

The reason for this ambivalence seems to stem from techno-optimism: "The commission found no absolute limits to growth. Limits are indeed imposed by the impact of present technologies and social organisation on the biosphere, but we have the ingenuity to change" (Gro Harlem Brundtland quoted in Hardin 1993: 205). The report is clearly aware that the present use of resources is unsustainable, and that if the whole of humanity is to improve its life situation with *today's methods*, then the availability of many resources is limited.

Still, by improving the organisation of resource use and by further improving technology, significantly more goods and services can be produced in the world, without jeopardising the life-support system: "Technology and social organisation can be both managed and improved to make way for a new era of economic growth" (WCED 1987:8). Thus, thanks to technological development there is a great potential to "produce more with less" (WCED 1987:15).

4.2.4 *Technological Development*

Social and economic development as well as the requirement to stay within biophysical limits are usually seen as the three main elements of sustainable development. Technological development should be viewed as an important means to achieve sustainable development: "Human progress has always depended on our technical ingenuity" (WCED 1987:81). The Brundtland Commission puts great confidence in technology; many discussions about solutions[7] in *Our Common Future* circle around issues regarding what technological improvements can be expected in different areas. One example concerns the technological potential for global food security:

"Blends of traditional and modern technologies offer possibilities for improving nutrition and increasing rural employment on a sustainable basis. Biotechnology, including tissue culture techniques, technology for preparing value-added products from biomass, micro-electronics, computer science, satellite imagery, and communication technology are all aspects of frontier technologies that can improve agriculture productivity and resource management." (WCED 1987:182)

The Brundtland Commission's strong emphasis on technological development may well offer some hope for the future. Yet, it also implies great social and cultural changes—quite different from the traditional green small-scale ideals. "Many essential human needs can be met only through goods and services produced by industry, and the shift to sustainable development must be powered by a continuing flow of wealth from industry." (WCED 1987:16).

There are also important distributional aspects involved here. More efficient technology is not globally accessible and obtainable by all.[8] It is therefore not enough that new technology is to be innovated. Like economic development, technology must be *spread* to where it is needed—not only where it has a market value and presumably generates greater profit (WCED 1987:104). Unless developing countries get access to new and better technology they will continue to be dependent on the good will of the industrialised world. "A continuation of economic growth and diversification, along with the development of technological and managerial skills, will help developing countries mitigate the strains on the rural environment, raise productivity and consumption standards, and allow nations to move beyond dependence" (WCED 1987:133). There is a case for matching technology to the cultural and educational environment into which it is introduced. This is relevant for any strategy that moves towards global equality.

4.2.5   Other Means for Sustainable Development

Technological development is an often-recommended means for reaching sustainable development. However, the Brundtland Commission also recognised institutional changes and changes in lifestyle as important principle means. Both of these can alleviate the need for and/or supplement swift technological development. For example, if institutions regulating land ownership were changed to spread ownership in many developing countries, more people could have their basic needs fulfilled by cultivating the land. Institutional land reform would thus be favourable from a sustainability perspective. Technological development may not even make any difference unless institutions are reformed to be more equitable.

Furthermore, sustainable development requires international co-operation. Today, however, there is no international body that can claim responsibility for, much less initiate, redistributive action. Thus there is a requirement also for institutional change at the international level. Furthermore, changes in lifestyle will be necessary. The present energy consumption in the industrialised world is not maintainable if the developing countries are to be given the opportunity to develop their well-being through rapid industrialisation.

To what extent and in what combination technological development, institutional development and changes in lifestyle ought to be used to bring about sustainable development is not particularly clear from the Brundtland report. There is no thorough investigation of any specific problem. This makes it practically impossible to tell what effect these means would have for instance on losses of arable land, and it is certainly difficult to tell how extensive the changes would have to be in order to achieve any sustainable development.

4.2.6 Summary

The chart below represents what I interpret as being the essence of *Our Common Future*. This understanding will serve as an operational guide when the scenarios are modelled in the last Section of this chapter.

Figure 4.1 Operational Guide for Calculating Scenarios

---

(1)   Each and everyone, within and across generations, should be
      ensured of the opportunity to:

(a)   *Be spared from poverty by having basic needs fulfilled*
(b)   *Have aspirations for a decent/good life ensured and fulfilled.*

(2)   Equitably distributed economic development is a prerequisite for
      combating poverty, for ensuring human beings the opportunity to
      fulfil their aspirations, and for financing the development and global
      distribution of new, efficient and appropriate technology.

(3)   Economic development must stay within biophysical limits, now
      and in the future.

(4)   Biophysical limits are variable, and when their limits are reached depends on

(a)   *Quality of technology*
(a)   *Access to technology*
(c)   *Institutional design*
(d)   *Lifestyle patterns*

As the Brundtland report does not specify to what levels human beings have the 'legitimate right to aspire', it provides no guidance as to the natural resources needed or how comprehensive economic development needs to be, nor how extensive the redistribution of economic resources must be to fulfil aspirations. Thus, it leaves undetermined the range of social, economic, technological and natural inputs needed to fulfil social development.

For my own purposes this poses a problem since it leaves us with no clue as to (1) whether any biophysical limits will be reached, and thus (2) how extensive technological development and other measures must be to avoid going beyond those limits. If we wish to establish more firmly what policies are required to obtain sustainable development, the range of inputs must be determined, and the effects of applying the measures be estimated as fully as possible. We need information going beyond that in the Brundtland Commission report to be able to assess properly the Commission's argument that "painful choices have to be made" (WCED 1987:9).

What these painful choices (or challenges) are must be clarified and specified in terms of policies. That is, the scope of the whole 'revolution' must be assessed in order to provide the information needed to say something substantial about social transitions and decisions. For this purpose, I will apply the operational guide to a more specific case, which I present in the next Section.

4.3 Global Animal Consumption

In his famous *Essay on the Principle of Population* (1798), the economist Thomas Robert Malthus, argued that the world population would come to reach a level beyond which no further maintenance capacity was possible. Why? First, the population growth cannot be prevented since the passion between the sexes is too fundamental. Second, population growth is exponential, i.e., 1,2,4,8, while the production of food can only increase arithmetically, i.e., 1,2,3,4 (Harrison 1993:11). This eventually leads to a situation where food demand exceeds food supply.

Yet, 200 hundred years later humanity still earns the capacity (in principle anyway) to feed itself with the resources available on earth. New land has been exploited, new plant species established and more efficient agricultural methods developed. At least statistically, enough food is produced for everyone to have their basic food needs satisfied (Alexandratos 1995:40; Tims 1995; Smil 1994:258-260). In spite of this, more than 800 million people suffer from severe starvation, and an additional 2 billion are undernourished, according to the FAO/WHO criteria (FAO 1998; Jones & Hollies 1997:137).

Even if Malthus' grim forecasts have not come true in absolute numbers, he raised a question that is still burning: How many more human beings can be born and fed? Some scholars still maintain the Malthusian paradigm. They assume that together with poverty the size of the population is the main cause of starvation (Ehrlich 1968; Meadows et al. 1972). Others maintain that the content of the global diet decides whether people starve or not. If people ate less resource demanding foods, then today's total world food production would be more than sufficient to nourish the world's population (Smil 1994; Boongarts 1994; Bender 1994). There is no unambiguous answer to the question of how many people the Earth can feed. According to the most pessimistic estimates, the number is limited to around 7-7.5 billion people

(Boongarts 1994). More optimistic studies come up with numbers of 12-15 billion people (Smil 1994; Brown 1954).

Regardless of whether we project the future global population to be 7 or 15 billion people, an increase in food production will be required. Since the world population is increasing by approximately 80 million annually, food production must also increase constantly (Leach 1995).[9] As the current food production, which maintains the present world population (6 billion), already causes great damage to the environment, this does not bode well for sustainability.

4.3.1 The Struggle for Food

Non-renewable resources have been the subject of most attention in sustainability discussions (Ohlsson 1999:15-18). Several studies of global food production and future agriculture point out that the more rarely noticed scarcity of *renewable* resources tends to increase too (Jervas 1997:10). Water is a pronounced example. Continued population growth and expansion of global agriculture may come to have exceedingly negative consequences for the water resources in the world—something that is especially worrying seen from the perspective of future generations.[10] How extensive the demand on water reserves will be largely depends on what kind of food we choose to produce and consume in the future, as well as where we produce it.

Figure 4.2   Biomass Requirement Per Food Unit for Different Kinds of Animal Food

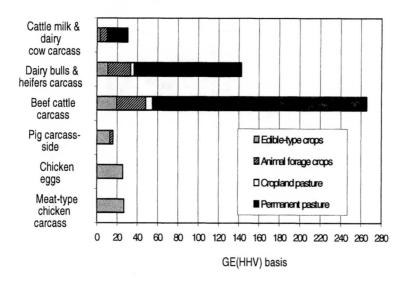

Explanation: Figures are global averages. Figure 4.2 shows on the one hand how much biomass is required to produce one unit of animal food (from milk, cattle, beef, pork,

eggs and chicken), and on the other hand how the biomass is constituted for each kind of animal food (the content of the bars). All figures are global averages.
Source: Wirsenius (2000: 157).

What kind of food we consume also determines future access to *land*. Production of animals is far more demanding on land areas than production of vegetables and serial crops (Karlsson & Pettersson 1998:44; Kumm 1998:26f). Globally, the most commonly produced animals are ruminants (cattle, buffalo, sheep and goat), pork and chicken. Also products like eggs and milk are included with animals. As indicated in Figure 4.2, cattle are the most resource demanding animals in terms of biomass and land. In this context, pork and chicken are thus relatively resource efficient. In Figure 4.3, the biomass efficiency for different kind of food is specified.

Figure 4.3   Biomass efficiency for different food categories. Refers to energy content in food intake divided by energy content equired in biomass production (on land). Global averages for the years 1992-1994

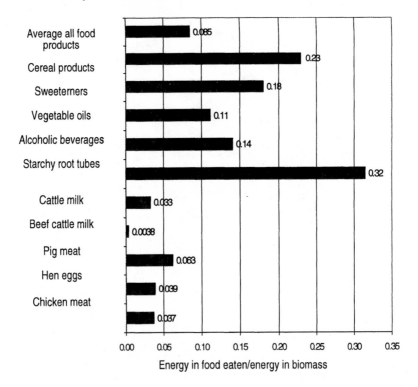

Explanation: Figure 4.3 should be read in the following way: Of all energy contained in a unit of biomass from arable or pasture land (1.0), the length of the bar expresses how much energy is left when the final product is eaten.
Source: Wirsenius (2000: 122, Fig 3.19)

As shown in Figure 4.3, considerably more biomass is required to produce one unit of animal food, compared to any vegetarian food. Cattle are more energy demanding than pork and chicken. Animal meat does not come close to the resource efficiency of any of the vegetables. Now, if for example cattle production is so resource demanding, why is it produced? First, cattle production is subsidised in most industrialised countries, which makes such production relatively profitable for the individual farmer.[11] Second, cattle (and other ruminants) can be produced where other livestock like pigs and poultry are not able to utilise the biomass energy (Alexandratos 1995:382). Globally, there are, for example, large areas of pastureland, and the energy stored in such vegetation can be utilised by ruminant animals but not by pigs and poultry (SEPA 1996:29).[12] This is an important explanation as to why African and Latin American countries mostly produce cattle and other ruminants. Third, closely connected to ruminant production is also the fact that animal pasture is a low-capital business. Few investments are required to start up a production. Fourth, in many developing countries, grazing animals also serve other important functions or purposes, e.g., as draught animals and as food reservoirs.[13] Finally, a most important explanation is that animal food is popular.

4.3.2 Human Consumption of Animal Food

On average, people consume a lot of animal food. Yet, according to Figure 4.4, the consumption varies quite considerably among regions. The global average is about 13 per cent. In the industrialised world, 30 per cent of the total food intake is constituted by animal food. In Africa and South Asia, however, only 6 per cent of the total food intake comes from animal food. Recall that the numbers in Figure 4.4 are averages for the regions. Had we been able to study the *individual* diet, it would certainly look different. We would then find that in some regions, most people's diets hardly contain any animal food at all. Differences in income is usually regarded the most important explanation for this variation.

About 40 per cent of all cereals produced today are used for producing animal food (cf. Figure 4.5). Furthermore, a large amount of forage plants (for animal production) are produced on arable land. These numbers help us explain why about 2/3 of all biomass produced in the food sector (i.e., on both arable and pasture land) is used for animal production (see Figure 4.5). At the same time, only 13 per cent of the total diets contain animal food. Thus, animal food is relatively resource demanding (cf. Figure 4.2). These numbers certainly give support to voices claiming that practically no matter what the size of any future world population's, it can *easily* be supported with food provided that each person entirely converts to a vegetarian diet (cf. Waggoner 1994; Borgström 1970).

Figure 4.4   **Food intake per capita and how animal food and vegetable food production are distributed world-wide by region**

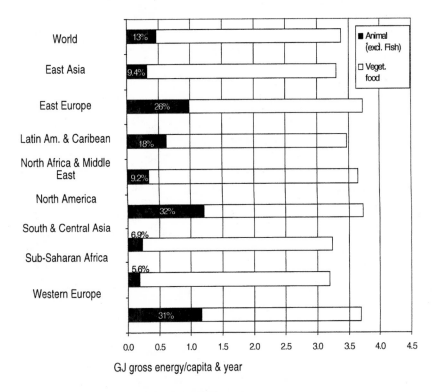

GJ gross energy/capita & year

Explanation: The bars in Figure 4.4 show how the share of animal food consumption (the darker part of the bar) and the share of vegetable food consumption (the lighter part of the bar) are distributed in different regions of the world.

Source: Compiled from Wirsenius (2000).

Such a conversion would, however, be quite an arduous task and appear so unlikely as not to merit consideration. There is in fact a strong demand for high-quality food. Thus, even if we assume only moderate income increases globally, we should expect to see some of this increase spent on a richer food intake.[14] When we examine Figures 4.6 and 4.7, these expectations gain further support.

Figure 4.5 Current agricultural input and output. Distribution of biomass between production of animal food and vegetable food and the total output from each sector

EJ Gross/energy/y

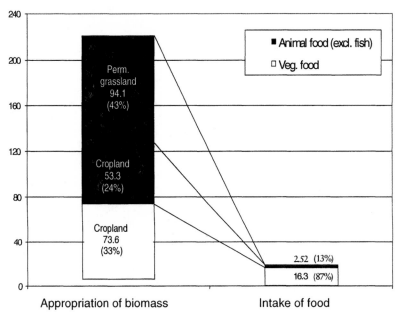

Explanation: Figure 4.5 shows the biomass required to produce animal food and vegetable-based food. Of all the biomass produced on land, approximately 67% is used for the production of animal food corresponding with 13% of the total human diet (the share constituted by animal food).

Source: Wirsenius (2000: 117, Fig. 3.12).

Figure 4.6 shows the relationship between a country's gross domestic product (GDP) per capita and the average share of animal food in the diet. The share of animal food increases with GDP. For obvious reasons the consumption curve for animal food is eventually levels off, since hardly anyone consumes meat exclusively. This connection has been demonstrated several times (Popkin 1993; Bender 1994; Smil 1994), and the tendency is claimed to be indisputable: the higher the income people have, the more animal food they consume.[15] Thus, increases in economic and material welfare in a country or a region leads most probably to a simultaneous increase in animal food consumption.[16] This is exactly what has happened during the 20th century; as the global average per capita income has increased, animal food consumption has increased too. The scope of this increase is illustrated in Figure 4.7.

Figure 4.6   The correlation between animal food consumption and GDP per capita

Share animal food in diet

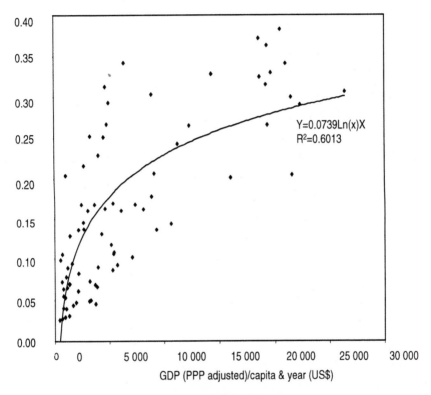

GDP (PPP adjusted)/capita & year (US$)

$Y=0.0739Ln(x)X$
$R^2=0.6013$

Explanation: Figure 4.6 shows the correlation between a country's gross domestic product (GDP) per capita (PPP adjusted) and the average share of animal food in the diet. The share of animal food increases when GDP increases. Eventually, the increase levels off (which has occurred in the Western world where animal food consumption has plateaued at around 30% of the total diet).
Source: Wirsenius (2002).

Figure 4.7 shows the increase in animal food consumption per capita for the 1961-1994 period. Animal food consumption increased during the whole period. On average, every individual today consumes about 25 per cent more animal food than thirty years ago. According to FAO (1998), the most important reason for this development is the contemporaneous economic growth.[17]

To provide the amount of food from animal food necessary to meet the expected demand if consumption to date and economic trends continue, the production of biomass must increase considerably. To bring this about, three paths are conceivable: (1) to cultivate more land area, (2) to make the production in the food sector more efficient, (Lu & Kelly 1995:268) or, as implied in *Our Common Future,* (3) to change the pattern of food intake. The first alternative is severely circumscribed. *Land* is the prime resource being exposed if we think in terms of increased animal food production, and the potential for expansion is limited. Thus, it is the two other measures that are of major interest. It will be shown in the following chapters that neither of these alternatives is without problems (especially if we have global application in mind) and both postulate great demands on society.

Figur 4.7   The increase in animal food consumption (in kg per capita and by year) 1961-1994

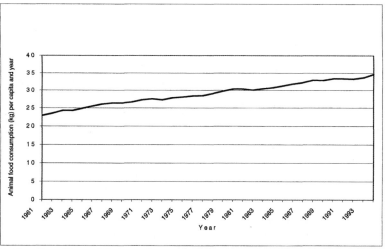

Explanation: Figure 4.7 shows how animal food consumption has increased per capita and over the years during the period 1961-1994. Each person consumed an average of approximately 27 kilograms per year in 1961. In 1994, the average amounted to 34 kilograms.
Source: Compiled from FAO Statistics (1995).

4.4   Calculating Scenarios for a 'Sustainable' Animal Production—A Thought Experiment[18]

We have now established that animal food production is resource demanding. Biomass is needed to produce animal food, and producing biomass presupposes limited resources like land. There is also an efficiency problem, e.g., production of animal food demands considerably more biomass than production of vegetables. This indicates that the character of food intake decides much of the pressure on food related resources. At the same time, there seems to be a strong demand for animal food (cf. Figures 4.4 and 4.6). This has important implications for the objectives expressed in *Our Common Future*.

Seen from a sustainable development perspective, increased global animal food consumption is not a problem *per se;* rather to the contrary. The Brundtland Commission states that a richer diet is a prerequisite for a great number of people (who are starving or undernourished) to be ensured an equal opportunity to have their basic needs fulfilled and especially to enjoy a decent life. Yet, how much animal food this requires is not established. If we embrace continuing, or even increasing economic and social development, including in the developing world, we are reasonably safe in assuming an overall increased animal food consumption. Furthermore, our figures imply that this increase will occur quite rapidly. Even relatively moderate income increases will generate noticeable increases in animal food consumption. Thus, there are two main reasons for studying the case of global animal consumption and production more closely. First, the Brundtland Commission practically expresses a common right to consume animal food. Second, it seems that if we assume increased global social and economic development, one effect will be an increased demand for animal food.

If we relate the case of global animal production and consumption to the matter of sustainable development, the previously raised question (cf. Section 4.2) becomes unavoidable: What would happen, in terms of resource demands, if we assumed an equitably and globally distributed increase in economic growth, which resulted in global increases of animal food consumption, i.e., a fulfilment of the two first guidelines suggested by the Brundtland Commission?[19]

The answer is obvious. Animal food consumption would increase enormously, and the accompanying resource extraction would probably burst every conceivable biophysical limit connected to the global food system— practically the *antithesis* of the Brundtland Commissions directives. At first sight, the social and economic objectives (as well as their effects) are thus in conflict with the objective of staying within ecological limits, i.e., the third target in *Our Common Future*. But to stop there would not be a fair reading of the report. As was argued earlier, although social, economic and ecological sustainable development are the three core objectives in the report, these goals are conditioned by the three measures of technological and organisational development and changes in lifestyle patterns. In line with our operational guide, we must therefore also ask: Is it possible to meet the increase in demand for animal food by increasing production efficiency through any of the measures suggested in the Brundtland report?

4.4.1 Applying the Operational Guide

For these questions to be answered,[20] the earlier derived operational guide (cf. Figure 4.1) has been applied to the issue of animal food production through the modelling of *scenarios*. These scenarios are calculated for a global population of 9.4 billion people. Our model of sustainable development is out of necessity simplified. It focuses only on one specific issue: animal food production. Such an approach is unavoidable if we wish to get a more specific idea of what social challenges an, albeit theoretical, implementation of sustainable development implies, and consequently, what kinds of policies are required for such an implementation to be realised.[21]

Besides scenarios for sustainable animal production (SD-scenarios), two other states have been calculated. First, we have estimated the total production of biomass for animal production at the present time. Second, we have calculated a 'business as usual' (BAU) scenario illustrating (roughly) how much biomass would be required if present trends in population growth, economic growth, increases in animal food consumption and level of productivity[22] continue until the year 2050.

When modelling the sustainability scenarios, the 'Operational Guide' specified earlier (cf. Section 4.2) was interpreted and applied in the following way:

1. Each and everyone, within and across generations, will be ensured the opportunity to:

(a) Be spared from poverty by having basic needs fulfilled.
(b) Have aspirations for a decent/good life ensured and fulfilled.

When these criteria are applied to the case of animal food consumption, we do not *primarily* deal with basic needs, because people can reasonably be spared from poverty and starvation without eating animal food. Our focus is instead on aspirations: people obviously want animal food. Furthermore, the Brundtland Commission emphasises the importance of a richer diet for the vast majority of the world population (WCED 1987:98-99; 162-188). In our scenarios we have seized upon this by assuming ensured animal food consumption for all. Today, the global average is 13% of the diet. We have increased this to 30%, i.e., the level of Western Europe. We have furthermore assumed that all 9.4 billion people will consume this much (mainly because the scenarios are based on a global economic standard far above today's averages).

2. Equitably distributed economic development is a prerequisite for combating poverty, for ensuring humankind to have the opportunity to fulfil its aspirations, and for financing the development and global distribution of new and efficient technology.

We have interpreted 'equitable' to denote an economic baseline that is ensured and shared by all the 9.4 billion people. In the scenarios, this is expressed as a global minimum economic level corresponding with Western Europe today. The Brundtland Commission's version of sustainable development indisputably implies a global welfare state. Thus, although a Western European economic standard may be seen as an 'over-kill', at least a significantly improved economic welfare environment is projected in *Our Common Future*. Furthermore, to be able to assume a major increase in productivity (through technological development), substantial economic and institutional upgrading is required.[23]

3. Economic development must stay within biophysical limits, today and in the future.

In animal food production, the prime resource being exposed is *land*. Any economic development assumed in the scenarios must therefore stay within the physical limits of land. Because of local and regional differences, as well as uncertainties regarding how much additional land is actually available (largely an issue open to debate), it is practically impossible to fully estimate the land area needed to produce the amount of animal food indicated in the scenarios. We can, however, get a hint by specifying (1) how much biomass is required to produce the current amount of animal food, and (2) how this biomass is produced. In the scenarios, the primary unit of analysis is therefore *the total annual demand for biomass*. 'Biomass' refers to both production on cultivated land (arable land) and permanent pasture land (land solely used for pasture).[24]

(a)   Quality of technology

To lower the total land demand implied in the scenarios, we have assumed significant technological development. In the case of animal food production, 'technological development' refers to two different but related measures. First, technological development means increasing productivity/efficiency in animal production, i.e., we get more (animal food) with less (land).[25] Second, changing methods to produce biomass can decrease the strains on land.[26] To be consistent with all other assumptions in the scenarios, we assume an average technological standard similar to today's Western Europe (in the sustainability scenarios SD1—SD4).[27] Despite these extensive assumptions put into the scenario-model, we arrive at biomass numbers far above the ones produced today. Also, a large share of this biomass is produced on pastureland, which is considerably more land-consuming than cultivated biomass. In spite of an originally high technological level, we thus arrive at resource demands probably exceeding the limits for additional land exploitation.[28]

(b)   Access to technology

As with the case of economic standard and animal food consumption, we have assumed an *equitably* distributed minimum standard of technology, which is equivalent to Western Europe's as it is today. When, in the latter SD-scenarios, we increase the technological level even further, the increases are assumed to be *spread globally.*

(c)   Institutional design

How the food sector is organised is an important issue. Improved institutions are certainly a crucial measure for any sustainable development to be realised. However, this measure is not included in our scenario model, since we cannot quantify how much more efficient the land-use would be by organising it differently. Thus, when *modelling* the scenarios, no particular attention is paid to this measure.[29]

(d) Lifestyle patterns

In the context of land-use as well as animal production and consumption respectively, changes in lifestyle patterns refer to two different measures. Pressure on land can be lowered if we assume a lesser consumption of animal food. This variant is left out from the analysis.[30] The second measure is to change the dietary composition. This is motivated by the fact that some animal foods are more resource demanding than others. We have dealt with this by assuming a decreased consumption of cattle, and simultaneously an increased consumption of chicken and pork. Thus, the average diet still contains 30% animal food but the composition of the food sources has changed.

4.4.2   The Scenarios

The first bar in Figure 4.8 illustrates how much biomass is used for animal production today (refers to the years 1992-94). In total, about 15 000 Tg (or 15 billion metric tons) of biomass is required annually. The largest amount of biomass is produced from areas characterised as pastureland. Edible crops, e.g., grain, oil plants and sugar crops, constitute the second largest share. The rest of the bar is constituted by fodder plants and pasture from cropland.

The second bar (BAU) is a traditional trend extrapolation and shows how much biomass will have to be produced if the present rate of increase in animal food consumption continues for the next 50 years, i.e., a 'business as usual' scenario. The objective of this scenario is to serve as a *reference* for the succeeding sustainability scenarios (SD1-SD4). In the BAU-scenario, upward adjustments have been made for a human population of 9.4 billion people and for an increased animal food consumption per capita (as a result of assumed general economic growth in all regions). Furthermore, we have assumed an increased productivity in animal food production, approximately in line with the trend since the 1960s. This forecast is proportional to GNP estimates for the year 2050. The consumption numbers are based on consumption figures found in Figure 4.6. When examining the BAU-scenario we find that it indicates a radical increase of both pasture and forage plant production compared to the present. The same is true for production of edible crops. Also notice that besides permanent pasture all biomass is produced on cultivable land. There are three main reasons why this scenario is making use of considerably more biomass than any other scenario. First, it is because Sub-Saharan Africa and South Asia (India among others) are assumed to have a continued low degree of efficiency in their production. Second, because of continuous economic growth, these regions are assumed to increase their animal food consumption. Finally, population growth is assumed to be high and more than threefold, according to UN predictions for the 1990-2050 period (FAO 1998). The BAU-scenario therefore implies a large-scale exploitation of additional land area.

The (i.e., 'less unsustainable') sustainable development scenarios (SD1-SD4) are different. In principle we have proceeded from the same basic parameters as in the previous BAU-scenario, i.e., *population* and *economic* growth. We have, however, also established a general minimum consumption level and operated with the two variables *technological development* (degree of efficiency) and *lifestyle pattern* (composition of diet). In these scenarios we have interpreted '*ensuring* equitable opportunities for all' to mean an attempt to *provide* all people with the amount of animal food to which they may reasonably aspire. To say the least about the difficulties here, it has been far from obvious what consumption level to choose.

As pointed out earlier in principle, people do not need animal food to survive. Vegans (who have been that for a long time—and are still alive) are living proof of that. Nonetheless, people do demand animal food, and this is what we have taken into account. We have tried to be consistent with the results in Figure 4.6 and 4.7. That is, if we assume a global radical increase in welfare, we should also expect animal food consumption to increase quite dramatically. Today the average animal food consumption is about 13%. Whether we assume a 100% or a 200 % increase is of less importance for our purposes. The point is that if we take the Brundtland Commission report seriously and actually assume the kind of economic growth advocated there, then we have reason to suspect that animal food consumption will increase in the world (unless dramatic changes in dietary preferences take place) and from this also follows an increased land and biomass demand.

In scenario SD-1, we derive the biomass numbers required for a global population of 9.4 billion assumed to have a food consumption, productivity and efficiency corresponding to that of present Western Europe. Compared with the BAU-scenario, less biomass is demanded. This is mainly explained by the fact that we assume a higher productivity in the SD-scenarios. Compared with present conditions, however, the global demand will more or less double. There is hardly enough land to produce these amounts of biomass. The significant differences between scenario SD1 and present conditions (92-94) therefore call for endeavours to further decrease the total demand. According to our operational guide, such decreases can take place through further improvements in technology or changes in consumption patterns.

Figure 4.8   Specification of scenarios for the year 2050 with respect to biomass production for food consumption assuming a world population of 9.4 billion people

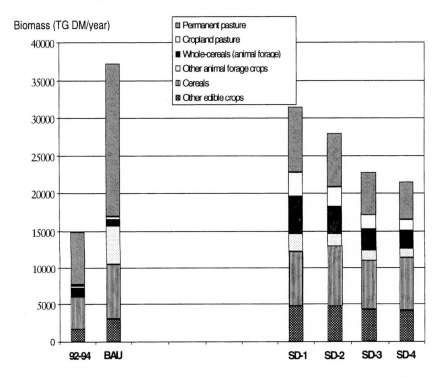

Explanation: Figure 4.8 shows different scenarios of the future biomass production required to meet different global levels of food consumption. The bars specify 6 different forms of biomass production. The 92-94 bar specifies the total biomass production required to meet the food consumption. The BAU (Business As Usual) bar specifies the amount of biomass required to meet the food consumption that will occur if current global trends continue until the year 2050. The bars SD1-SD4 specify the biomass production required to satisfy assumptions of global food consumption, and with an animal food consumption averaging 30% (SD1), increased efficiency (SD-2), a dietary change (SD-3) and a combination of SD-2 and SD-3 (SD-4).

In scenario SD2, average productivity in animal and vegetable food production has increased by yet another 17%, which is above the present Western European level. Even assuming such increases probably means that we will still reach the biological limits beyond which no further increases in productivity can be assumed.[31] At the very least it is a maximum level given present knowledge. The additional increases in productivity result in a decreased demand for biomass needed to satisfy the goals established earlier. Although the introduction of further productivity lowers the total demand for biomass, scenario SD-2 still presupposes considerably more biomass than that required today.

In scenario SD-3, we move to the option of *changes in lifestyle patterns* discussed in the Brundtland Commission report.[32] We cut down the amount of cattle food by 25 per cent and replace that decrease with an equal share of pork and chicken food. In all other respects, the assumptions are the same as in scenario SD-1. Obviously, reducing the demand for cattle will have significant effects on the total biomass demand. Furthermore, when we replace cattle with pork and chicken, less grazing land is required. Thus, this can be assumed to have a redoubling affect on land use.

Finally, in scenario SD-4 we have *combined* changes in dietary composition and productivity. When the two measures are combined, far less biomass is demanded compared with the BAU-scenario. Furthermore, when these two measures are taken simultaneously, a global animal consumption equivalent with Western Europe's only requires some 30% increase in biomass production over what is currently produced.

Although a comprehensive global economic growth and a corresponding animal food consumption were assumed in the SD-scenarios, only relatively modest increases in biomass production are required to maintain this consumption. This holds only if the dietary composition takes the shape we have assumed and if some of the future economic growth is used for investments in, and global distribution of, technological development. The character of the biomass production also changes: from today being produced mainly on pastureland, more and more biomass becomes cultivated. Thus, the final 'ideal scenario', SD-4, may actually illustrate a scenario that requires less land than is required today. *At the same time,* we must not forget that these scenarios are great simplifications of the global food system.[33] Furthermore, the assumed economic and technological developments, as well as the changes in lifestyle patterns, presuppose a wide range of factors. In fact, if these assumptions and measures are ever to be realised, a large number of challenges linked to demands for biophysical, technological and socio-economic inputs must be dealt with successfully. In the two following chapters I identify and discuss some of these challenges.

Notes:

1 The World Conservation Strategy is usually seen as one of the first to combine the two concepts 'sustainable' and 'development'. However, Langhelle (2000b:9) has traced the concept back to 1976, and then to a report made by a working group within the World Council of Churches.

2 I am not going to discuss the comprehensive debate on how to define sustainable development thoroughly, since this issue is a book on its own, but I will indicate here that there is no common definition that satisfies all political and scientific parties, as well as other interest groups that are involved in the debate. As early as 1994, Torgerson counted over 40 different definitions (1994:303).

3 A popular way to characterise different definitions of sustainable development is to maintain a division between 'weak' and 'strong' sustainable development. Viewing

sustainable development in this way, the Brundtland commission's report is usually seen as a fairly weak version of sustainable development, while the definitions made by, e.g., deep ecologists and other more environmentally committed groups are considered stronger. The more that concern for the value of nature for its own sake is included, the closer   the definition is to strong sustainability (cf. Dobson, 1998; Baker et al 1997:16ff).

4 Both points are of vital importance for my final compatibility analysis.

5 According to Our Common Future, many desires are culturally determined and therefore, for example, we should perhaps not expect too many people to adopt a western world lifestyle. Such expectations are, however, not much of a safety net, something that will become clearer after the next Section of this chapter.

6 cf. the first general principle in 'Summery of proposed legal principles for environmental protection and sustainable development' adopted by the WCED experts group on environmental law, in Our Common Future, Annexe 1, p.392 which says: "All human beings have the fundamental *right* to an environment adequate for their health and well-being."

7 This point is not absolutely fair. A large proportion of the solutions suggested refer to institutional and legal changes. However, these suggestions do not differ much from the solutions suggested in the earlier debate on development.

8 The commission does not claim that technological development is an *exclusive* good. For example "while this technology offers the potential for slowing the dangerously rapid consumption of finite resources, it also entails high risks" (WCED 1987:4-5 see also 104-106). The debate about biotechnology is an illustrative example. While such technology is said to be a promising weapon against poverty, at the same time it risks impoverishing many resources needed for food production. The Commission also emphasised regional differences far more than I have done. There are some regions which may need more advanced technology, while others perhaps need a technology which allows low-intensive sustainable production but where the problems are institutional and consist of organisational hindrances that ought to be changed, e.g., an *inequitable* distribution of land or water.

9 Although 80 million people every year is a very high number, it could have been worse. If the average birth rate of 5 children per woman (which was the case in the early 1960s), continued the annual increase would be approximately 160 million. As a result of active family planning (among other things) the average today is 3,3 children per woman, which gives an increase of over 80 million people per year (Engelman & LeRoy 1993:5)

10 "Today with 5.5 billion people and well-drilling technologies capable of reaching water buried in the earth, human populations for the first time are capable of depleting and polluting fresh water supplies on a massive scale." (Engelman & LeRoy 1993:33)

11 Not least the case in the EU, where beef is heavily subsidised on many levels (SOU 1997:26).

12 This approach is far from a matter of course, however. The food sector is motivated by demand, and if something other than pasture was demanded, many of those areas could be cultivated, or used for other purposes—for example for producing biofuel or as nature reserves.

13 See further examples in Wagner & Hammond (1997) and Sausoney (1995)

14 "Urbanisation, together with income increases, will change the eating habits from root crops, leguminous plants and low-qualitative grains to high-qualitative grains such as rice, wheat, meat and vegetables:" (Ohlsson 1997:262)

15 This can also be expressed in the following terms: the income effect on animal consumption is great.

16 A very important question is, of course, why this connection exists? Within the scope of this book, I do not have the means to fully establish the specific causes. But, such an investigation is certainly most valuable if anyone wish to break this connection.

17 The composition of animal food differs between regions. In some areas, certain animals are excluded. E.g., the cow is sacred in Hinduism, and the consumption of beef is therefore relatively low in countries like India. Yet, although few eat beef, a range of

milk based products is still consumed (e.g., 'ghee'). Another regional affect relates to the Muslim population, which does not eat pork. From the point of view of resource efficiency, this is unfortunate since large amounts of mutton and lamb are consumed instead, which are about as biomass demanding as cattle (Wirsenius 2000).

18 In Chapter 2, I examined critically how the scenarios have been created, what assumptions are behind them, and how we have been reasoning. Thus, here I limit the background discussion to the most basic facts needed to understand the scenarios and the forthcoming analyses of them.

19 By only studying the Brundtland Report we cannot determine the level of animal consumption beyond which the physical land limit is reached. In fact, it is not even certain that it will be reached. First of all, some additional resource exploitation may be allowed, according to the Brundtland report. It is not realistic to demand that from tomorrow, no further resource exploitation be permitted. To produce more animal food with the same amount of (or less) land, implies a huge transition, and an increased efficiency that cannot be obtained overnight. Second, the quantum of resources needed to meet future sustainable animal food consumption is dependent on the quality of technology, and how it is distributed, and furthermore on how global animal production is organised, and what lifestyle people adopt. Thus, the estimate of whether any resource limits are met largely depends on these three variables.

20 To say "answer" is somewhat presumptuous. Of course no absolute answers can be offered to these kinds of questions. To get an 'idea' is perhaps a better expression.

21 *First*, it gives us an idea of the quantum of resources required to fulfil the kind of social revolution implied by WCED. That is, how extensive the resource *requirements* actually are when we speak of sustainable animal food production, given that 'sustainable' also takes into account the social and economic goals expressed in the Brundtland report. *Second*, by applying the measures suggested in the report, our scenarios give us an indication of (some of) the *social transitions* and challenges set in motion when discussing implementation of sustainable development in the grander global scheme. Rather than a well-captured image of what sustainable development would looks like, we ought to see such a scenario analysis as a *qualified thought experiment*, where the WCED guidelines are applied as far as possible.

22 Recall that *productivity* (P) and *efficiency* (E) are not the same thing and may not even coincide. It is fully possible to increase the productivity in, e.g., crop production on a unit of land, without actually increasing the efficiency in this production. For example, by adding additional fertilisers, water and technology we might increase the total output of crops. However, since we then also increase the use of, e.g., energy, we have to weigh the additional output against the increase in energy use before we can judge whether the shift has resulted in energy improvements. To establish efficiency 'more with less' is the guiding principle.

23 This economic standard may not take place in all countries by their own volition (at least not to start with), but will most likely requires a global economic as well as institutional (cf. DeSoto 2000) redistribution (something the Brundtland commission is not against, as we have learned)

24 Even if the unit of analysis is biomass, far more information is included in the unit. To produce biomass, several things are required. Besides land, also sunlight, water and carbon-dioxide is required. To further increase the production of biomass might also require plant-nutriment (fertilisers). Therefore, if we assume an increase in the production of biomass, the use of these underlying factors will increase. When we thus see a change in the scenarios (the demand for biomass is increasing, or decreasing), then we actually see a change in demand for these factors—although this demand cannot be expressed precisely.

25 Increasing the efficiency in animal production can take place in two different ways. Either (a) through relatively conventional methods, such as breeding in farmhouses instead of grazing, using concentrated fodder, keeping animals healthier by using, e.g., antibiotics, or (b) using more unconventional methods, i.e., biotechnology in particular.

26 Here there are conventional and unconventional methods. Starting with conventional methods, biomass can be produced either in the wild or by cultivation. The latter is far

less demanding of land. The less conventional methods usually require large-scale investment. Examples are use of fertilisers, pesticides, advanced irrigation systems and also biotechnology. The more efficient animal and biomass production is assumed, the more use of new technology is also intimated. In the final scenario, less conventional methods must be assumed to be used.

27 It can be questioned whether Western European agriculture ought to be regarded "sustainable". It probably should not (see Frankenhuis 1994:46f). But following the Brundtland Commission's instructions, and the additional assumptions we make, this kind of agriculture at least comes near the goals expressed by WCED.

28 These requirements should be put against the land requirements arising if current trends continue for another 50 years (cf. the BAU-scenario). A continued unlimited increase in land for animal food consumption biomass results in increases much greater than any of the SD-scenarios.

29 This is not to say that I disregard it throughout my analysis, rather to the contrary. When I analyse how to achieve, e.g., the assumed technological improvements, and make sure they are distributed to where they are needed, then I carry out far-reaching discussions about the institutional challenges involved in such development.

30 It should be quite clear that a lower demand for animal food results in a lower demands for land—provided that all other assumptions remain unchanged. Certainly, we could have calculated a scenario where the global average consumption was assumed to be e.g., 20%. If every other assumption remained the same, then such a decrease would have significant affects on the total annual biomass production. The problem is to find realistic motives (other than normative) for assuming these lower levels.

31 Thus, even if the Brundtland commission has a strong belief in, and refers to further production through technological development in agriculture, e.g., "Biotechnology, including tissue culture techniques, technology for preparing value-added products from biomass, micro-electronics, computer science, satellite imagery, and communication technology are all aspects of frontier technologies that can improve agriculture productivity and resource management." (WCED 1987:182), all such development has limitations. For example, no matter how much we manipulate a plant, add nutrition, and improve the growing conditions, only a certain portion of the planet can be utilised.

32 One option is to assume that people will choose or be forced to eat *less meat* in general. That would, however, jeopardise people's opportunity to aspire to what they wish. Thus, before any such assumptions are made, we need to investigate if changes in the dietary composition will have any effects on the total demand for biomass.

33 For example the use of fish is excluded.

Chapter 5

Challenges Connected to Physical Resources and Technological Supply Requirements

The scenarios presented in the previous chapter are based on expected *demand*, i.e., they illustrate how much biomass will be demanded depending on our initial assumptions. Thus, they say nothing explicit or substantial about all the conceivable inputs needed for the scenarios to be realised. Neither can we identify the social consequences should the scenarios be realised, nor what happens if critical inputs are missing or inadequate.

In our scenario model there are mainly two aspects that generate challenges. The scenario requires inputs and also gives rise to conflicting interests. In principal, three inputs are needed for scenario SD-4 to be realised:

(1) *Physical resources*
(2) *Technological resources*
(3) *Economic and social resources*

Each of these three categories is derived from the specifications of sustainable development in our Operational Guide in Chapter 4. Physical Resources must be supplied to produce the amount of biomass implied in the scenarios. The development of new technology is an important means for producing the biomass within resource limits. Social and economic resources are required both for people to afford new technology and for securing welfare. However, besides input challenges I argue that scenario SD-4 may generate:

(4) *conflicts of interest*

I do this for two reasons. First, for scenario SD-4 to be realised, we assumed dietary changes. Unless these changes take place voluntarily, they will give rise to disapproval among certain interest groups—not least consumers. Second, the scenario requires significant changes in agricultural practises, implying comprehensive social changes. Consequently I argue that scenario SD-4 produces both winners and losers.

The objective of this chapter is to discuss the challenges connected to the first two categories, i.e., the supply of physical resources and technological development. In order to supply enough resources without jeopardising the needs of present and future generation, cautious and optimal use of these resources is required. The demand for technological development generates two kinds of challenges. First, the appropriate technology must be developed per se. Apart from the fact that this is difficult in itself, the demand for technological development also generates political challenges since it implies an active support for, e.g., the provision of healthy business environments and adequate funding and rewards for research. Second, technology must also be accessible to those who need it or ought to use it according to scenario SD-4 (cf. Chapter 4.2).

In Section 5.1 I argue that the use of these resources must be globally co-ordinated and controlled if scenario SD-4 is to be realised without requiring extractions beyond resource limits. I substantiate my argument by analysing three inputs: access to land (5.1.1), water (5.1.2) and nutrients where I have focused on phosphorus (5.1.3) in relation to the demands implied in the scenarios.

In Section 5.2, I claim that the technology required by scenario SD-4 presupposes not only challenges connected to technological development, but also more 'distributional' challenges. I do not argue that all the hypothetical problems that I discuss here *will* and *must* occur if attempts are made to implement scenario SD-4. If anything, my discussion in both of the two following chapters should be seen as an attempt to lay out the worst case scenario, i.e., to outline as many as possible of the principal challenges that the political sphere *may have to cope with and form policies for* if scenario SD-4 is to be realised. To investigate if such policies can be regarded legitimate from a liberal-democratic viewpoint, I consider it more useful to overstate the challenges rather than to avoid or neglect even those that are less likely.

5.1 Global Co-ordination and Control of Resources

5.1.1 The Case for Land Use

Only about 25% to 30% of all the world's land area (approx. 13 billion hectares) can be cultivated (Alexandratos 1995:58ff; cf. Leach 1995:28f; WRI 1986). The rest is too dry, cold, steep or in other ways inappropriate. This gives us reason to investigate whether our scenarios' demand for more land is attainable. The lower estimate (25%) implies that about 3 billion hectares can be cultivated. Less than half of that area (about 1.4 billion hectares) was cultivated by the beginning of the 1990s (Alexandratos 1995:18; Fageria 1992:1). At least theoretically, this leaves space for expansion.

However, the potentially available areas are not waiting to be cultivated. Either they host forests, or they are characterised as grassland or pastureland (Alexandratos 1995:155ff). Furthermore, expanding cities and infrastructure compete for those areas (Goklany 1999:270f). This implies that even if the potential land is not cultivated today, it is not necessarily *unused*. "Some potentially arable land exists in areas of unreliable rainfall. But in most regions today, new cropland can be gained only at the expense of forests, pasture land or wetland, all of which supply other valuable resources or ecosystem services to the human enterprise" (Ehrlich 1994:23). Any exploitation of these areas would thus affect a range of other societal and ecological functions and interests; the expansion *potential* is actually a function of all alternative land-use.

The limited supply of additional land caused us to calculate several scenarios that illustrate different levels of biomass demand, and to assume a more efficient production on areas already cultivated. This is very important since the food sector gradually may have to compete with other land-users, e.g., the energy sector (Azar & Berndes 1999).

The range of the demand for biomass is wide across our scenarios. The BAU-scenario implies more than a redoubling of today's demand. In the SD-1 scenario we have assumed a high level of efficiency. Despite this, its realisation requires almost twice the amount of biomass produced today. The increase is explained by the comprehensive animal food consumption assumed. Since much of the biomass in these two scenarios (especially the BAU-scenario) is produced on relatively low-productive pastureland, these scenarios imply *extensive land exploitation*. Only when we increase agricultural efficiency even more, and assume dietary changes, do we arrive at levels of biomass consumption resembling the present figures, i.e., scenario SD-4.

There is no unanimity among scholars regarding how much more land *can* be exploited. The most pessimistic ones argue that the land area already cultivated is a relatively good indicator of how much land is actually available.[1] However, this is not an indicator of how much biomass *can* be produced. The amount of cultivated land has only increased 10% during the last 45 years, while food production has more than doubled. This increase in food production is mostly a result of a constantly increasing productivity per hectare (Postel 1998:629; Ehrlich 1994:23). At the same time, we note that less than half (1.4 billion hectares) of all available land (3 billion hectares) is used today.

Land scarcity does exist, but is largely a *regional phenomenon*. While the potential for expansion in, e.g., Southern Asia and Europe is limited, or sometimes non-existent (de Vries et al. 1997:918), there are large land reserves potentially available in both Africa and South America (Leach 1995).[2] Under present conditions these land reserves are running the risk of either being used in a detrimental way, or if used, having detrimental effects on other things.

There are several reasons for this. One frequently expressed reason is that land in Africa and South America is *unevenly distributed*. The vast majority of people are forced to support themselves on small allotments that allow for neither crop rotation nor fallow periods (the most common ways to keep land productive in the long-term). Because of this, much land is more exposed than it needs to be and much is ruined or degraded yearly.

Therefore many scholars call for a more rational land-use policy or 'good governance' (Hjort af Ornäs & Strömqvist 1997:247ff; cf. Ehrlich 1994; Kates & Haarmann 1992). The aim of such a policy should be to extend the size of allotments, and thus allow for better long-term use of land. While this might be ecologically sound, it generates issues of how the land should be (re)distributed. What comes first? If sustainable land-use policy means ensuring larger plots, then it also places great demands on societal order and structuring as larger plots (in the longer run anyway) generally result in many people having to *leave* their small allotments, i.e., the same development as we have experienced in Western Europe. Since scenario SD-4 is a global goal, we can expect that such a development must be matched also with global societal order, change and restructuring.

Another reason to suspect that the land-use implied in scenario SD-4 requires global co-ordination and control is that a large share of all available land is located in regions with an uneven and unreliable distribution of rain. The only way to guarantee an optimal global harvest would be to control and regulate what ought to be cultivated on these land areas. Finally, exploiting new land may cause severe damage to other important values. For example, the greater part of any prospective land expansion must take place at the expense of forests, pastureland or wetlands—all of which host other resources and ecosystems regarded as valuable by many (Ehrlich 1994:23; WRI 1992). I contend that solving this dilemma also implies co-ordination and planning. Let me give an example using rain forests and biological diversity.

A major part (approx. 45%) of all land reserves accommodates tropical and sub-tropical *rain forests*, considerable parts of which are forests with high biological diversity (Alexandratos 1995:225). Certainly, many of these forests can be cut down and replaced by, e.g., cultivation of biomass for feeding animals or for grain for human beings. This would increase food production, implying that scenario SD-4 may be realisable (at least as seen from an 'area perspective'). However, such land management would be controversial—to say the least.

Even if scenario SD-4 only requires an additional 30% of biomass, and thus not much more land than today, these figures are built on the assumption that the average soil quality is rather high. If it is not, our assumed biomass production will require considerably more land area than today. Where is such high-quality soil to be found? Large parts of the remaining land-reserves (not covered with rain forest) are more difficult to develop in the shorter run than the ones hosting rain forests. However, developing the rain forest areas both exposes the fragile soil (with the risk for causing erosion, cf. Goudie 2000:185-

194) and makes the rain forests vulnerable and exposed to continued encroachment (Ehrlich 1994:23). The risk is magnified no matter whether we expect the global per capita consumption of animal food to increase at the same rate as during the 20th century (approx. the BAU-scenario), or if the rate of increase takes place as assumed in scenario SD-4.

If the demand for biomass continues to increase as indicated in scenario SD-4, the *economic incentives* to convert forests to cultivatable land with, e.g., fodder plants, in order to earn 'quick money' increase. For scenario SD-4 to be realised without jeopardising remaining rain forests, some kind of *supervision* is necessary. There should be an *international body* with the authority to both control and regulate the use of valuable forests. This would be a great challenge for the world community, not the least since such a body would have to consider overruling national sovereignty to hold up laws safeguarding the *national* private property right. Obviously rain forests contain enormous short-range economic values, and so does the land on which they grow. Thus, to convince the landowners to *keep* the forests for the sake of ecological, ethical or perhaps even long-term economical reasons, the counter-incentives must be strong and have global backing whether we have a 'stick' or a 'carrot' in mind.

Biological diversity is closely tied to the use of rain forests. An overwhelming majority of all animal and plant species existing on earth are located in those forests. If they are cut down, biological diversity will diminish substantially. Besides being politically and ethically problematic (not least because of internationally agreed conventions), it jeopardises the ability of future generations to fulfil their needs. The increased animal food consumption intimated in scenario SD-4 will threaten biological diversity. The enormous increase in efficiency assumed in this scenario should, however, offer a degree of protection. A great future challenge is to establish a sustainable *balance* between a level of animal consumption that fulfils human demand on the one hand, and maintains biological diversity on the other. The responsibility for future generations therefore forces today's society to *plan* and *balance* its continued expansion in such a way that the least possible harm is made on accumulated resources, *including* bio-diversity. Only then can the Brundtland Commission's recommendations be realised, and thus, an implementation of scenario SD-4 be considered fulfilled.

Summary: To expand the production of animal food without causing comprehensive damage to remaining land places great demands on societal order, structuring and planning. Here I have pointed mainly to the uneven distribution of land, the irregular distribution of rain, the need for an optimal use of land, the preservation of rain forests and biological diversity as reasons for why scenario SD-4 presupposes global co-ordination and control of land resources. The list could, however, be made longer.

5.1.2   The Case of Water Use

In the SD-scenarios we assumed that both productivity and animal food consumption corresponded with those of Western Europe. According to scenario SD-1, such animal food consumption levels would more or less double the total biomass demand compared to the present. These assumptions have consequences also for the global demand for water. The Western world agriculture requires large amounts of water every year. Even if water supplies in the US and Western Europe have not been *acutely* insufficient so far, several US regions, like California and the Colorado River, are approaching water scarcity (Falkenmark 1997:207; Engelman & Leroy 1993:27). This occurs in spite of a relatively good access to water compared to many other regions in the world. If we assume global biomass productivity similar to that of Western Europe, we thus assume an increased demand for water.[3] Consequently in the first SD-scenario, at least, we can expect the global water demand to increase quite significantly.

The SD-2 scenario assumes increased productivity (17%) but we only found a marginal decrease in total biomass demand. Even so, we have good reason to expect that the demand for water has decreased quite significantly, because when increasing productivity, we simultaneously have to include a more efficient use of water.[4] The kind of irrigation we are assuming is much more sophisticated, and manages to adapt the amount of water uniquely for every individual square metre of a cultivated field.[5]

In the following scenario, SD-3, we instead assumed a dietary change. This change causes two other changes with repercussions on the demand for water. First, noticeable decreases occur in total biomass demand with consequent reductions in water demand. Second, the production of cattle decreases. Since production of cattle requires large amounts of water, notably for growing feed for cattle and for milk production (Rifkin 1992:218ff), a reduced cattle production would have additionally positive effects on total water demand (Smil 1994:265).

In the final scenario, SD-4, we combined dietary change with further improvements in agricultural efficiency. This had perceptible effects on total biomass demand. Even if the scenario illustrates a situation where 9.4 billion people are consuming animal food at the present Western European rate, only an additional 30-40% of biomass was required to reach this position. Although less biomass usually implies less demand for water, this is not the case here. Recall that production has changed from mainly pasture to fodder production. This shift affects the global water-use because when shifting from pasture to fodder, we may also have to assume a change in water *provision* from mainly rainwater to irrigation, thus implying a totally new agricultural infrastructure but also *global co-ordination and control* of water assets. This is mainly for two reasons. First, unless controlled, sub-soil water may be pumped up as a (non-sustainable) substitute for the scarce water that occurs naturally.[6] This would mean a complete violation to the core premises of scenario SD-4.

Second, irrigation water is used for other purposes such as for households and industry, implying potential competition.

How much water do the scenarios require?[7] The American hydrologist Sandra Postel (1998) has estimated the amount of water needed to produce enough biomass to support the global population by the year 2025. These calculations are also useful for our aims.[8] Of the roughly 40,700 km³ that run into the sea each year in rivers and aquifers, only about 12,500 km³ are actually accessible for human use (e.g., irrigation) (Postel et al. 1996). This amount is what we have to 'play with', besides annual rainfall. Recall that the figures in Table 5.1 are estimates of how much water the *crops* need to grow appropriately, and not of the total amount of water needed for *producing* the biomass. These figures depend on factors such as water productivity, i.e., how much water is *wasted* between source and target use (the plant).

Table 5.1 shows that water demand varies significantly among the scenarios. Our BAU-scenario indicates a water demand (20,000 km³) 2.5 times that of today (8,100 km³). Scenario SD-3 and SD-4 only exceed today's figures by about 30-45%. The most important difference is that *the ratio of pasture to total land is decreasing* in all the SD-scenarios. This might be desirable from a pure productivity point of view. However, pasture and enclosed pasture are mostly low-capital methods. Many of the other land uses specified in the scenarios may require *refinements* such as water supply and fertilisers. Thus, if we assume that some of the land that is presently used for pasture is to be devoted to crop or fodder production, then new demands are made on these areas. Even if some current pasture areas have a sufficient water supply thanks to rich rainfall, this is not valid for all areas—rather on the contrary. A significant deal of steppe and savannah that can be used for pasture would require *irrigation* to produce any reasonable crop yields.

Even if the total biomass demand and thus the total demand for water goes down as we move from the BAU-scenario to any of the scenarios SD-1 to SD-4, we have to remember that the demand for *irrigation water* remains approximately the same. This demand may even increase, since an increasingly larger share of the total biomass demanded is produced on cultivated land. To this fact should be added that access to water is unevenly distributed (Fernie & Pitkethly 1985:120) and access to cultivatable land often does not coincide with access to water.

When we view this from a global management perspective, we understand that for any of the SD-scenarios to be realised, a minimum demand is that all available areas are mapped and co-ordinated in order to obtain the largest possible return from the least amount of land area, and with a minimum use of water.

Table 5.1   Current total water demand in the BAU scenario and in the different SD-scenarios

Scenario	Biomass Demand	Water demand	Water demand
	(TgDM)	Total area (km³/year)	Cultivated area (km³/year)
1992-94	16212	8100	4000
BAU	40 215 (150%)	20000	8000 (40%)
SD-1	31500 (94%)	15800	10000 (63%)
SD-2	28143 (73%)	14100	9000 (64%)
SD-3	23582 (45%)	11800	8000 (68%)
SD-4	21446 (32%)	10800	7500 (69%)

Explanation: Table 5.1 shows how water demand increases when crop productivity increases. Within parentheses in the *biomass column* we find the percentage of *additional* biomass required for the scenario to be realised, and within parentheses in the column for *water demand in cultivated areas*, we find the share of irrigated water of the total water demand (based on the somewhat exaggerated assumption that all cultivated areas require irrigation). As we see, the share of irrigated water increases as the scenarios become less biomass demanding, i.e., the share of irrigated water increases when we move towards scenario SD-4.

Comment: Water demand for each scenario is based on the following calculation. An expression for total water demand is given by the equation [0.5l /g DM x X x 10^{15}], where X represents total biomass demand. Water demand for cultivated land is also given by the equation [0.5l /g DM x W x 10^{15}], but here X represents biomass demand on *cultivated area*. The expression [0.5l/gDS) says that in general 0.5 litre of water is required to produce 1 gram of biomass (water excluded, i.e., *dry matter*, DM). The assumption that 0.5 litre of water is required to produce 1 gram of biomass is a general approximation, and varies depending on the crop used (some crops require more and others less water). According to Postel, however, this is the best available approximation when calculating total water demand with regard to global biomass production.

Source: Postel (personal communication)

This line of reasoning is supported by Jones & Hollier (1997:169f;267f) who argue that any such global co-ordination necessitates efficient international agricultural politics, something far removed from today's international political scene. Since water is used for many purposes other than agriculture, a more comprehensive international *water policy* is essential. Since access to water for irrigation is limited, and the water demand implied in each of the SD-scenarios is so high (although not necessarily exceeding *available* water supply), the global use of water must be monitored and co-ordinated for the total water reserves to be *optimally used*, i.e., where it is most needed and productive.[9]

However, there are other reasons for expecting some kind of control and regulation of the global use of water. One is the responsibility for future generations that is built into the scenario. Today some countries not only harvest their water assets, but they also make use of their water *reserves* (Cunningham & Saigo 2001:431ff). This means that they not only use the 'interest' of annual water provision, but also draw on *accumulated* capital, i.e., the fossil water reserves. It goes without saying that such consumption is precarious, especially in the long run. Such use may supply the demand for water for one or even several generations, but will gradually impoverish the reserves, which will eventually affect future generations. Thus, unless these countries change their current behaviour, either of their own accord or through help from outside (with any of the previously discussed methods), one of the most crucial objectives of sustainable development (regardless of which version) will be violated, i.e., to *save for future generations*. Water is not easily substituted, which means there is no simple 'solution' to the intergenerational dilemma (Jones & Hollier 1997:268). [10]

Implementation of scenario SD-4 risks *aggravating* the water situation for future generations. The total water demand in scenario SD-4 is estimated to be about 40% more than today's figures,[11] and most of this additional water is supposed to be used in areas *already short in naturally produced water*. Thus, when adding the needs of future generations to the list of people to whom the world community has obligations and responsibilities, the need for efficient technology and support for *cautious water use* becomes even more pronounced. Unless the global community manages to keep down the use of water, a great debt to future generations will be created; one that jeopardises their ability to maintain life, and reduces the prospects for 'realising' scenario SD-4.

Summary: Although I cannot conclude that scenario SD-4 implies water demand that cannot be globally maintained, our comparison still points to a need for co-ordinating and controlling global water supplies. This is mainly for two reasons. Competition among users: When realising scenario SD-4, we increase the use of irrigation substantially. This means that competition for water increases. For this water to be enough for all purposes, global assets have to be controlled and co-ordinated. Responsibility for future generations: To ensure the needs of future generations, hardly any fossil water reserves can be used regularly for irrigation. Food production thus has to be supported by renewable water. To actually ensure this will be a difficult political challenge. It would probably require a control system where water extraction is regulated and limited by stipulated annual amounts of available water.

5.1.3   The Case of Phosphorus

A common way to increase agricultural productivity is to fertilise the soil through livestock manuring or synthetic manuring. One of the most important fertilising elements is phosphorus. Whether we speak of plants or animals, this element is necessary for all life. These phosphorus fertilisers are extracted from minerals, i.e., phosphate rock, and therefore finite, or reproduced only over geological cycles.[12] As with other non-renewable resources, it is thus reasonable to inquire how long these minerals will last with present and expected extraction.[13] Phosphorus is relatively abundant (SEPA 1997b:7). However, this gives us no certainty about how long the mineral will last. That, of course, depends on the scope of extraction and availability. It is notable that large amounts of the estimated reserves are not economically viable to extract mainly because the minerals occur too sporadically in the earth's crust. Based on current usage "extractable supply is estimated to last for another 350 years (pessimists) or perhaps for another 1200 years (optimists) " (SEPA 1997b:5).

Increased or decreased use can thus affect the time interval quite significantly. About 90% of all extracted phosphorus is used in agriculture, especially in farming in the Western world. Some phosphorus used is wasted, mostly because of agricultural leakage, which in the longer term causes severe environmental damage through contamination of lakes and oceans (Smil 2000). Thus, continued and excessive use of phosphorus is problematic for mainly two reasons: (1) The availability of phosphorus mineral is limited, which generates questions about potential resource scarcity. As we will see, this risk is not imminent. However, (2) the use of phosphorus is also causing environmental disturbance, such as eutrophication, and furthermore, it may be toxic. Largely these arguments lead me to conclude that the global phosphorus reserves ought to be globally co-ordinated and controlled to prevent environmental and health damages, which would prevent the realisation of scenario SD-4. Significant efficiency improvements have marked effects on the scenarios. For example, the changeover from grazing land to cultivated land (i.e., to replace present pasturage with feed crop production) would improve the production of fodder per unit of land. Such a transition, however, would also change agricultural conditions significantly, because feed crop production requires both a relatively stable contribution of water and fertile soils. This is usually obtained by soil improvements such as draining, lime-washing or by adding fertilisers.[14] Increased efficiency in animal food production includes an increased use of phosphorus. It seems realistic to assume that for any of the SD-scenarios to be realised, a significantly increased use of phosphorus-based fertilisers would be required. This is particularly the case in scenario SD-4 where we assumed the largest proportions of feed crop production, the least land-use and the highest productivity. I.e., improvements would only be possible with an average soil of high quality.[15]

Table 5.2 is based on approximations made by *The Fertilizer Society* (TFS) and shows how the occurrence of phosphorus mineral is distributed in the world.[16] More than half of all phosphorus reserves are found in Morocco. The US, Russia and the rest of Africa (South Africa especially) also have large reserves. Potential resources and geological reserves are included in the table. At current extraction rates, according to TFS, the reserves are assumed to last for another 180 years. In addition to those reserves (i.e., the numbers of resources considered economically and technologically possible to extract *today*), additional resources (resources that may become economically and technologically possible to extract in the long run) are estimated to last for another 450 years.[17]

Table 5.2   Annual   production   and   estimated   phosphorus   mineral reserves in the world (billion tons)

Land/area	Prod. 1992	Reserves	Pot. Reserves	Geol. Reserves
Europe				
(excl. ex - CIS)	0.1	6	6	30
ex - CIS	3	110	654	1396
US	6	161	581	3504
Latin America	1	92	166	490
Morocco	3	1589	5141	6877
Africa	5	1961	5644	7706
The Middle East	1	145	517	1786
China	2	884	884	1257
Asia				
(excl. the Middle East)	3	906	957	1475
Availability				
(number of years)				
at *present* extraction		**179**	**452**	**671**

Comment: These estimates are made by 'The Fertilizer Society' (TFS). The calculations of the period over which phosphorus can be economically and technologically extracted are based on several assumptions, in most cases more pessimistic than the ones made by TFS.
Source: SEPA 1997b:8

Access to phosphorus must not be considered a problem within the medium term. This is, however, a rather 'relative' conclusion, because the scenarios do not tell us how much the use of phosphorus will increase in the future (provided that any of the SD-scenarios are realised). What can be said is that the more extensive our crop-productivity assumptions are, the more the demand for phosphorus increases. This demand is also dependent on soil quality. The more we use less fertile soil, the more phosphorus is required for high productivity (Sanchez & Leakey 1997:16). Most likely we will face a substantially increased use of phosphorus in the future, regardless of which SD-scenario is chosen.

Whether this use will cause any acute scarcity, I cannot tell. However, such an increased use of phosphorus may cause *severe* environmental problems.

Thanks to the poor management of phosphorus, today's usage causes much of the *eutrophication* of lakes and oceans. According to the Swedish Environmental Protection Agency, agricultural leakage is the single largest environmental problem associated with phosphorus (SEPA 1997b:28; 1997c:24). Some of the phosphorus added to farming is washed away on the land surface and leached via soil, and is thus never taken up and utilised by soil or plants.

A waste-product following the use of this phosphate mineral is cadmium. This is a toxic heavy metal that is taken up by plants and transmitted to animals and humans, causing, e.g., damage to human kidneys (Järup & Berglund 1998). As the availability of cadmium-poor phosphorus resources decreases, cadmium poisoning may increase appreciably. Even if Sweden almost *exclusively* trades with cadmium-poor phosphorus (extracted from eruptive phosphate rock), the average per capita intake is already today close to recommended limits.

Unless a well functioning recycling system is established, the continuing and increasing global use of phosphorus may lead to considerably larger eutrophication problems than we see today. If scenario SD-4, with its appreciable increase in phosphorus use, is to be realised, one must be aware of the risks of eutrophication that are connected to this scenario. There is no simple 'technological fix' for recycling phosphorus, or to prevent eutrophication. Furthermore, since the global access to cadmium poor phosphorus is constantly diminishing, the risk of increasing discharges of cadmium is running parallel with the assumed increase in phosphorus use. This is important information for the wider understanding of our scenarios.

Summary: Phosphorus use is perhaps not in urgent need of being restrained per se. However, there is still every reason to be cautious about the way it is used. Each of the SD-scenarios does imply an increased use of phosphorus and from that follows a range of challenges. While there are large amounts of phosphate rock in the earth's crust, low-cadmium phosphate mineral is relatively rare, and unevenly distributed. In addition, phosphorus is difficult to separate from the cadmium that often goes along with cheap phosphorus. For (mainly) poor countries (to start with anyway) not to be compelled to use this cheaper and perilous fertiliser when increasing their agricultural production as implied in scenario SD-4, this scenario reasonably presupposes both a control system to prevent spreading of toxic fertilisers, and a distribution of pure phosphorus according to where it generates the largest harvests (i.e., according to efficiency) rather than according to where it fetches the best price. Also the use of phosphorus is problematic. Leakage from agriculture is one of the most important factors behind the increasing eutrophication of lakes and coastal zones, with negative affects on marine plant life and fishery. Moreover, leakage of phosphorus is an international phenomenon affecting even neighbouring countries. Both of these factors provide reasons for (1) being cautious with the use of phosphorus and (2) finding ways to use it globally without risking any damage to human beings and other life forms, thus implying a use that is globally or internationally controlled and co-ordinated.

5.2 Development and (re)Distribution of Technology

Improved efficiency is mainly a matter of technological development (including education and training). However, agriculture in most of the less developed countries is highly underdeveloped when compared to, e.g., Sweden or any other developed country. To assume a Western European standard in those countries therefore implies a multifold increase in productivity. Such an increase would be technologically and economically strenuous. Europe's advanced farming developed over a long period of time. The process was costly, and purged many small-scale farmers. Present Western European agriculture is largely constituted by technologically intensive large-scale farmers with high earning capacity and requirements (Tims 1995:115). I argue that to introduce a similar system in the developing world, within the short time-span we have assumed in the scenarios, would be socially and politically demanding on a massive scale. First, it presupposes that partly new technology is invented and developed, implying a favourable research climate and business environment. Furthermore, this technology must be developed even if there might not be any clear demand for such technology in the countries where the development is expected to take place.[18] Second, the technology must be distributed to where it is needed and required for scenario SD-4 to be realised, and not necessarily to where it gets the highes price. Third, but not least important (but less relevant when we have Western liberal democracies in focus), it must gain the willing acceptance of those expected to use it.

To state the reasons for my argument, I discuss technology aimed at improving the use of water (and thus also of land) and of phosphorus.[19] This discussion also includes bio-technology.[20]

5.2.1 The Case of Irrigation Technology

"The full potential of agronomic crops is seldom reached because of limitations, on physiological and morphological processes imposed by environmental stresses. The single most important factor limiting productivity of crop yields on a worldwide basis is drought." (Fageria 1992:215)

The annual *increase* (growth) of irrigated areas diminished from about 2% per year during the 1970s to 1.3% between 1982 and 1994 (Postel 1998:633). The single most important reason was *cost increases* associated with the design and construction of new irrigation projects. The reduced number of places and areas where ecologically and socially sustainable dams and river diversions can be built largely explains why the costs are accelerating. The more unsuitable and inaccessible these areas are, the steeper the cost increases (cf. Bongaart 1994:20).

This has caused several international donation funds and governments to cut their investments in such projects (Postel 1998:633). The four largest and most influential investors, The World Bank, the Asian Development Bank, the US Agency for International Development and the Japanese Overseas Economic Cooperation Fund have nearly halved their investments in new and ongoing irrigation projects during the last fifteen years (Rosegrant 1997). A large number of governments have made comprehensive cuts in their appropriations to irrigation projects (e.g., China, The Philippines, Bangladesh, India, Indonesia and Thailand). These cuts have been made in the face of the highest expected population growth during the next fifty years—a development that will multiply the need for water and food. Also globally, irrigation has increased at a lower pace than population growth. The highest rate of irrigated area per capita occurred in 1978, but has since decreased by about 7% (Gardner 1997 quoted in Postel 1998:633). This implies that more and more people have to live with water scarcity.[21]

In a world of constantly increasing water shortage, land with abundant rainfall becomes all the more important for the global food supply. This implies a need to manage such land with particular caution. An area with soil erosion (e.g. because of bad management) is not helped by high precipitation. National and international achievements are important to lessen the demands on such land and to increase water productivity (Engelman & Leroy 1993). What is required to cope with such long-term development? First, improved irrigation technology is needed to increase productivity and thus produce more food per hectare with the same or a lower input of water. Second, technology is required to economise and optimally utilise, recycle and store water (Alexandratos 1995:277f; Bongaart 1994:20). Let us start with the first one.

Because of the level of high productivity that was assumed initially in the SD-scenarios, global access to efficient irrigation technology will be a prerequisite for any of the scenarios to be realised. Advanced irrigation technology is expensive and places great demands on economic development in those countries assumed to require such technology. If the economic means are missing, and we still assume the scenarios to be realised, it is up to the rest of the world to make sure that such technology becomes obtainable and is actually used.

In addition, each of the SD-scenarios, and especially scenario SD-4, implies a significant increase of feed crop production, i.e., cultivated land. We thus have additional reasons to expect a comprehensive world-wide use of irrigation. This must, however, be a highly efficient form of irrigation with few if any losses, according to the figures in Table 5.1.[22] Thus, when saying 'irrigation', we are referring to the most advanced and efficient methods existing today, i.e., systems where few water losses occur between source and utilising plant. This brings me to the second option of utilising and storing water.

Water scarcity is becoming more and more common around the world, not only in regions suffering from drought, but also in regions with abundant rainfall. This is mainly explained by a systematically inefficient use of water, and aconstantly increasing water consumption per capita (Bongaart 1994). According to some scholars, this development is possible largely because water is inadequately priced (Postel 1997:165ff). Because of its relatively low economic value, few if any measures are taken to lower the consumption, and large amounts of water are lost annually. This, however, only explains some of the losses. Even with the most modern systems, up to 20% of all water is wasted.

Furthermore, in many cases, hygienically pure water is needlessly used (Postel 1997:126ff). Much of all water used by households need not be perfectly pure, and much of it can be recycled and used for other household purposes, or for gardening. In fact, between 60% to 80% of all household water could be recycled at a minimum cost. Since water is still relatively cheap, domestic recycling systems are seldom economically justifiable. Along with the decreasing availability of water, this development will probably be met by increased prices, which will encourage the use of water recycling in individual households (Jones & Hollier 1997:256-263).

Water is also inappropriately used within industry and the energy sector. Pure and hygienic water is often used for cooling, dust suppression, dilution of pollutants from chemical and petrochemical works, and for transporting waste products and effluents away from factories. It would be possible to introduce recycling processes that contribute to a sounder water management policy. As with households, a decreasing supply of water is expected to advance the price and thus make recycling more viable in the future.

Yet, to primarily invest resources in these sectors would only have moderate effects on global water assets. Neither industry, nor the domestic sector is the greatest user of water. Agricultural consumption of fresh water accounts for the vast majority of total water use, with irrigation accounting for up to more than 60%. Table 5.3 shows an aggregated picture of how water is distributed among the three sectors in the world's main regions.

In the most pronounced agricultural regions, e.g., Africa and Asia, agriculture accounts for the largest part of total water consumption, while in Europe industry holds that position. To recycle industrially used water would thus have significant effects, at least in those regions with a large consumption of water for industrial purposes. The overall picture is yet overwhelming: about 70% of all fresh water is used for agricultural purposes, making the global food sector the prime consumer. Unfortunately, this sector requires the most water during the driest months of the year when water is least available. That is when livestock needs additional supplies of drinking water, and crops need extra provision through irrigation. Thus, the drier the climate the greater the demand for water for agricultural purposes (Allison 1992). In countries facing the greatest imbalances between water supply and demand, it would probably even be necessary for farmers to install water tanks or underground storage in the water table for a scenario like SD-4 to be realised (Jones & Hollier 1997:260).

Table 5.3   **Global water use, specified for regions and sectors (for the year 1990)**

Region	Household	Industry	Agriculture
Africa	7	5	88
North and Central America	9	42	49
South America	18	23	59
Asia	6	8	86
Europe	13	54	33
Former USSR	6	29	65
Pacific Ocean	8	23	69
The entire world	8	23	69

Source: Jones&Hollier (1997:260) with data from WRI 1994

Other ways to facilitate a more steady supply of water, but also to improve efficiency in agricultural operations, would be to *combine* storing and recycling systems with advanced irrigation; that is, to replace spray irrigation with small-bore trickle-feed pipes, i.e., delivering water more directly to the roots of the crop (Postel 1997:101). There are even more advanced systems. Common among Western world farmers today are computer-controlled irrigation and fertilising systems, providing every individual square meter with the optimal amount of water (U.S. Congress 1992:6ff). Compared with traditional irrigation (flood irrigation, ditches and spray), such precise systems are *far more* efficient. However, the global distribution of these systems is slow, because of the high costs associated with such technology (Postel 1997:115f). Distributing it globally would be quite a task:

> "Most of these changes are expensive to implement and farmers will need to be coerced by government policy and assisted by financial subsidy to make changes in the way they use water" (Hollier & Jones 1997:260).

The challenges associated with irrigation and the recycling of water are similar. Most of the technology that has been discussed exists today, which of course improves the prospects for producing the amount of biomass indicated in scenario SD-4 without having to reach the global limits for water, i.e., one must not be forced to make use of subsoil water. Although they can most certainly be further improved, the great challenge here does not seem to be only the actual development of the technology[23] but also its distribution. Since access to water is irregularly distributed, both seasonally and geographically, measures must be taken to overcome these problems. Thus, it is not sufficient to conclude that there is water enough to produce the biomass figures indicated in the scenario. Water must be optimally used. Besides being irrigated efficiently, it has to be extracted where accessibility is most favourable, and (partly) stored until it is most needed. The more efficient these methods are the more expensive they are initially as well. For scenario SD-4 to be realised we are probably dealing with the most efficient systems available, and therefore also the most expensive ones. Thus, it will be costly to actually provide the amount of water needed for scenario SD-4 to be realised globally, without having to pump up sub-soil water. As indicated before, some of the regions where such technology would be most required are among the poorest in the world.

Summary: To arrive at scenario SD-4, it is required that irrigation and water storing/recycling technology is distributed to where it is needed, and not to where it fetches the best price. For this to take place may require a redistribution of either technology and/or finance from the rich to the poor world.

5.2.2   *The Case of Recycling and Purifying Phosphorus*

The most common way to increase efficiency in the use of phosphorus is to recycle it through manure. But only some is reused, namely that which is taken up by plants. Thus, a great deal of the phosphorus used leaches out of the ground and finds its way into watercourses, or becomes difficult to reuse in other ways. If scenario SD-4 would be realised, the amount of phosphorus rich manuring would increase significantly. One suggested and, not the least in Sweden, often applied method to avoid eutrophication from manuring is to spread it over larger areas (SEPA 1997c:8). Such methods are applicable in Sweden where access to additional land is relatively easy. When applied on a global scale, however, the same methods are less applicable. Neither now, nor in 50 years' time will it be possible to 'pick and reject' among the land areas suitable for cultivation and/or available for pasture. Nor do any studies suggest that it might be possible to reject land because it has an inferior capacity to absorb and utilise phosphorus.

This reasoning is valid for all the SD-scenarios. A decentralisation of the global animal food production by increasing animal food production through pasturage is not a realistic option in any of our scenarios. On the contrary, the scenarios (particularly SD-4) point to a radical decrease of freely grazing animals. Our figures imply that most of the animals in the scenarios will be kept in stables or the like, whether we speak of cattle, pork or chicken. When worrying about future eutrophication of phosphorus it thus appears that we are forced to pin our faith on not yet invented or developed technology and methods to mitigate leaching and eutrophication, rather than on additional grazing areas.[24]

What about purification? It seems as if there is no global panacea to the problem of increasing the use of phosphorus without bringing increasing contents of *cadmium* into agriculture. Hitherto, farmers in mainly rich countries have managed to keep down the levels of cadmium since the market has been able to supply them with affordable phosphorus fertilisers low in cadmium. However, in the future access to such fertiliser can be expected to decrease perceptibly. By then technology to purify the mineral from toxic substances will be essential (Elinder & Järup 1996). There might be reasons for a certain optimism. Several purification methods are conceivable, and successful tests have been accomplished in laboratories. Admittedly, available methods are expensive but studies have shown that the costs are strongly related to the size of the sewage-treatment plant.[25] The larger the size of the plant, the lower the expected price. Compared with today's price for pure phosphorus, the purification procedures are assumed to be relatively cheap in the long run, indicating good prospects for such technology to become more generally accessible in the future.

If this is correct, then there are prospects for scenario SD-4 to be realised without forcing us to expect large parts of the global population to become victims of cadmium poisoning. At the same time, much support for technological development and diffusion of such technology is required for our global scenario SD-4 to be carried out at full scale. Although challenging, such support and diffusion (redistribution) is necessary because the core premises behind scenario SD-4 do not allow for any farmers (whether rich or poor) to be denied access to purifying technology and/or pure products since this would constitute an obvious violation of the social aspects of sustainable development.

Summary: To realise scenario SD-4 with the help of phosphorus, two things appear to be required. (1) Support for developing both recycling methods and purifying technology, e.g. healthy business environments and substantial investment in research. The most challenging is that the aim of the purifying technology (to start with anyway) largely is to make it possible for poor farmers to use clean phosphorus in their agriculture, while the technology is assumed to be developed in the rich world. (2) Distribution of technology. Since the rich world can still afford to buy naturally pure phosphorus, and purifying plants are expensive to develop, it appears as if the affording world (whether it is in urgent need of the technology or not) has to bear the initial costs in order to lower the costs to a level that is attainable for the poor. Or, it has to give sufficient economic support for the technology to be diffused.

5.1.4 The Case of Biotechnology[26]

In the original sustainability scenario, SD-1, we established that the demand for biomass was too extensive to be realised with today's knowledge. Quite comprehensive assumptions about dietary changes and further improved productivity were necessary for the total demand to approach today's biomass figures. In light of what has been said regarding access to land, water and phosphorus resources, enormous achievements are needed for global agriculture to enjoy such a production system. The scenarios postulate a global food system where neither water nor phosphorus is overexploited and where land is thriftily used—all this so as not to cause needless devastation of e.g., rainforests, or exploitation of land not suited for cultivation, thus avoiding jeopardising the fulfilment of the needs of present and future generations.

The sooner such a vision is to be realised, the faster the distribution of technology must be, and the more concentrated the initial costs will be. Biotechnology is one increasingly discussed methodology to speed up the reductions in water and phosphorus use, while keeping down the costs. Since the 1970s, the advancements within genetic research have been unprecedented. Today several of the larger food producers deal with genetically modified products. Since the demands for such products are still rather low, and vigorously opposed in some quarters, no comprehensive diffusion of technology has yet taken place.[27] However, genetically modified plants and animals may become increasingly common. Elements of genetically modified food will accordingly be more common in our food stores. There are arguments both for and against biotechnology.

On the one hand, such technology may mean that the human race is encroaching on the innermost spirit of nature (Thompson 1997:148). First of all, it can be held unethical to place humanity above nature by interfering with nature in such a way. Second, such methods can be viewed as unethical acts against the animals being manipulated. Third, although the two former arguments perhaps can be refuted, many people still worry that knowledge received by manipulating plants and animals can be used also in experiments on humans.[28]

On the other hand, biotechnology may offer unimaginable possibilities to improve agricultural efficiency and food. Thus, it may become one of the most important means to solve future food supply problems and mitigate resource demands (Morris & Bate 1999; Wagner & Hammon 1997:89; Lindgren 1996). It is already possible to develop animals with significantly improved capacities to utilise energy in fodder, making them grow faster while at the same time demanding less food. But not only animals can be manipulated. So far, agrarian biotechnology has mostly been oriented towards plants. The purpose has been the same as in more traditional plant breeding, namely to develop more 'appropriate' species. When making such a comparison, the principal difference between traditional and modern plant breeding seems to be the alteration rate.

Traditional plant improvement is based on a generation-wise trial and error procedure, where new plants are gradually taking on more advantageous properties. With biotechnology, however, crossbreeding can take place in single experiments, thus speeding up the results and shortening the lead-time to actual use. In some cases, crossing is not even necessary; changing a particular quality in an existing gene composition is enough. By doing so, one can relatively quickly develop plants that provide a larger yield per unit. It is also possible to develop species that can grow in environments where they would not otherwise survive, e.g., in cold, humid, dry and warm or other extreme conditions.

Do we have reasons to believe that scenario SD-4 requires biotechnology to be realised? Most likely that is the case. However, there is no unanimity among scientists on the potential of biotechnology as a method to facilitate the future food sector. I argue that at least for scenario SD-4 to be realised, a quite comprehensive use of biotechnology will be required.

Smil (1994) contends that biotechnology certainly has qualities to improve productivity within global agriculture. At the same time he claims that such technology need not be developed for society to manage its future global food maintenance. While this may be encouraging if we see to the maintenance of scenario SD-4, we should remember that Smil presupposes considerable dietary changes in the Western world, and that the developing world under no circumstances can imitate the present consumption patterns in the developed world. In the long run he thus assumes a much lower share of animal food in the average diet than in any of our scenarios.

On the other hand one can assert that biotechnology is not enough to support present needs within agriculture. The heydays of the 'Green Revolution' are forever gone. Only massive changes of lifestyle patterns and dietary habits/wants can provide long-term sustainable solutions:

"No technological encore that could match the multiplication of average yields of major crops produced by the green revolution over a few decades is waiting in the wings. Biotechnology, for all the hypes, may make a series of useful contributions to agriculture in the next decade or two, but these will contribute more to security of production than to dramatically larger harvests." (Ehrlich 1994:26 cf. Gasser & Fraley 1989)

Following the line of reasoning of these scholars we should perhaps not pin our faith on biotechnology as the solution to the realisation of SD-4, but rather on additional dietary and social changes.

Other scholars maintain that biotechnology is absolutely necessary for future agriculture to provide all people with sustainably produced food (Lu & Kelly 1997; Frisvold & Condon 1998; Smith & Okoye 1994; Wagner & Hammond 1997). Lu & Kelly declare that a sustainable agriculture will look radically different from today's production. If we forecast future global agriculture by proceeding from how both demand and supply have historically increased, we not only get a good illustration of how much biomass must be produced, but also a terrifying image of an agricultural production that uses masses of pesticides and detrimental fertilisers to produce enough food (1997:269). The forecast that Lu & Kelly are referring to, has similarities with the BAU-scenario presented in Chapter 4, they provide additional arguments for society to strive for faster improvements in global agriculture than is implied in that scenario.[29]

According to Lu and Kelly, too large-scale use of fertilisers and pesticides cannot realistically be included in a sustainable agriculture because such methods would not only impoverish the soil, but also give rise to additional resource extraction and threats to biodiversity (1997:263-270).[30] Some other scholars even argue that such damage reduces the prospect of maintaining all life on Earth (cf. Brown 1994; Benbrook 1991). Thus, instead of using too many detrimental substances, *resistant crops* must be made available to agriculture.[31] Furthermore, agriculture ought to develop crops that, in an optimal way, can utilise nutritious substances in the soil.[32] In most cases, traditional plant breeding can be used to develop such crops. However, Lu & Kelly argue that such methods are not efficient enough. With a constantly increasing human population, the development of 'optimal' crops and animals must take place much faster than can be achieved using traditional methods, i.e., through biotechnology. Only then can society simultaneously supply tomorrow's demands for food and sustainability (1997:275f).

If Lu and Kelly's conclusions are correct, then biotechnology is probably one way to avoid, or at least reduce, the pressure on our specific key resources. By developing less sensitive and more productive crops, the need for irrigation goes down. Also the demand for phosphorus may decrease thanks to biotechnological advances. If animals can be developed that grow more quickly and produce more milk on less fodder, the global biomass demand can probably decrease quite significantly. These are most important implications for our scenarios. The larger the productivity assumptions that we make in the scenarios, the more likely we have also built in, or assumed, the use of biotechnology to arrive at these figures. Even if that is not specified in any of our calculations, at least our 'ideal' scenario SD-4 can probably be realised only with massive use of biotechnology. I suppose no productivity figures such as ours can be attained globally unless both crops and animals are modified to become optimally productive in the various conditions characterising our world. By this specification I also think many of our comprehensive and sometimes utopian productivity assumptions, on which our SD-scenarios are based, become more intelligible. At the same time it also provides us with a clearer view of the challenges required to reach scenario SD-4, because:

"Biotechnology for the better utilization of animal genetic resources to achieve necessary production and productivity gains require *sound policies, capital, trained people,* well equipped *research laboratories* and *infrastructures* for the *diffusion* of improved animals, prerequisites which in many countries are not available and unfortunately in many instances will not be so in the medium term." (Wagner & Hammond 1997:89 my italics)

Several of these major and necessary conditions for a global introduction and massive use of biotechnology in agriculture are not only expensive for the average farmer. A controlled and co-ordinated use of biotechnology also requires knowledge and infrastructure that is presently, and increasingly, in the hands of giant corporations in the wealthiest and most educated countries in the world. To the list of challenges I would like to add a public that at present is very sceptical and suspicious of the development of biotechnology (cf. Chapter 6.2). To change this pattern in order to supply the global demand for food, or scenario SD-4, is a political challenge of a magnitude that the global community may find overwhelming (Lindgren 1996).

First, the technology has to be developed, implying the same kind of support for research as was indicated for purifying phosphorus. This can prove to be extremely challenging for several reasons, e.g., much of all biotechnology applied to food is controlled by transnational corporations which may have opinions about the development of such technology becoming regulated. Furthermore, a majority of the Western world's public is sceptical about biotechnology in general and suspicious of it particularly when applied to the food sector (cf. Section 6.2). Second, it is not only a matter of developing the technology and its applications. The initial costs may have to be borne by those who can afford them (which largely coincides with where the technology is developed). Furthermore, it also has to be distributed to where it is required for scenario SD-4 to be realised, something that again may be in conflict with the objectives of the great corporations. In addition, if some 'needy' groups lack economic means to buy the technology at hand or to acquire the proper knowledge, then distribution of it ought to be according to scenario SD-4 rather than to purchasing power, implying redistribution of both technology, economic resources and, not least, education and training.

Summary: I conclude that when studying the case of biotechnology we have reason to believe that a realisation of scenario SD-4 would give rise also to comprehensive political challenges, mainly in the form of (1) Giving support to technological development and (2) (re)distributional help via (i) bearing the initial costs, providing (ii) technology per se, (iii) economic resources and (iv) educational resources.

Table 5.4   Challenges derived in Chapter 5

- Global co-ordination and resource logistics in order to attain the animal food production assumed in scenario SD-4 with the least possible demand on resources such as land, water and phosphorus.

- Production of technological development as well as adaptation of available technology to local conditions, aimed at achieving the production requirements indicated in scenario SD-4.

- Transferrence and (re)distribution of technology in order to attain the demands for a global efficient resource use.

Notes:

1 As was indicated earlier, these figures can be questioned. However, even if there are additional areas to win, much of this land is less productive than that currently cultivated. As Bongaart (1994:23) asserts: "There can be no doubt that the land now used for growing food crops is generally of better quality than unused, potentially cultivable land."

2 I say 'sometimes', because there are great differences within those regions regarding capacity to ensure food production and capability to produce it. Compare, for example, China, which already today imports large amounts of grain and other food because it is lacking cultivable land, with India which has problems largely because it is short of water (Brown & Kane 1994).

3 This largely depends on how the biomass production is taking place. I return to that issue in Section 5.2.

4 Without doing so, any such assumptions are implausible.

5 Also see my discussion in Section 5.2.

6 Cf. Section 5.2 on irrigation technology.

7 It is probably not possible to calculate this other than very approximately. One of the main reasons is that the volume of water that a given crop uses will vary by crop type, climate, season and other factors. Nonetheless, the basic linear relationship between dry matter production and transpiration used in our calculations (i.e., Postel's [1998]) holds for all crops and growing environments (largely supported by Kramer & Boyer 1995).

8 Before applying her calculation on our scenarios, however, a few remarks are appropriate. Postel does not assume that total animal food consumption will increase by as much as we do. Accordingly, the estimated demand for biomass is less in her scenarios than in ours. Furthermore, her study only covers the year 2025 (i.e., she does not calculate for the same population growth that we do). Also, she assumes a lower agricultural efficiency than we assume, resulting in a more comprehensive water demand compared to our case. All these factors bring about results that cannot be directly compared to ours. Important, however, is the fact that Postel makes the same assumptions that we do, namely that water demand decreases when agricultural efficiency increases. Postel concludes that total water demand will double until the year

2025. When we apply Postel's calculations, we (not surprisingly) arrive at different results depending on the particular starting scenario. In Table 5.1, the results are specified.

9 In the name of common sense, any such global prospects of course have to be matched with national and local water management as well (as is also claimed in *Our Common Future*), not least by encouraging and urging agriculture to safeguard and utilise as much rainwater as possible (Bongaart 1994:20; Brown 1995). For example: "terracing, mulching, contour bundling (placing) stones or vegetation along contours and other methods of capturing rain-water to enhance soil moisture have proven effective in increasing yields of rain-fed crops." (Postel 1998:632)

10 Recall that inefficient use of water not only implies *less* water in the future, but also, and not the least important, inefficient use of water today increases the *price* for water in the future. As argued by Daily et al: "if individual farmers, when drawing water from an aquifer, ignore the fact that their extraction will increase other's future extraction *costs* because of a lowering of the water table, the social costs of agricultural production would exceed the farmers' costs" (Daily et al. 1998:1291).

11 See Chapter 6.1.3

12 In the literature that has been available to me, the terminology on phosphorus is a bit confusing. In the SEPA reports (1997b and 1997c), 'phosphorus' is mainly used, while in much of the international literature, 'phosphate rock' is more commonly used. Phosphate rock only contains a certain amount of phosphorus (approx. 15% [SEPA 1997b:27]). To extract the phosphorus, large amounts of sulphuric acid are added. In fact, over 60% of the world sulphuric acid production is used in the fertiliser industry (Demandt 1999) (which, by the way, is an interesting resource aspect of phosphorus use as well).

13 Regarding phosphorus as a finite resource, a deceptive measure of usage is commonplace in the literature. Phosphorus is not an element that is gradually running short. However, because of, e.g., leakage caused by farming, its availability is decreasing over time. Thus, from a purely physical perspective, phosphorus continues to exist, although increasingly in a form which makes its extraction for farming purposes prohibitive.

14 Including nitrogen-based fertilisers.

15 There are conceivable techniques to keep down the need for phosphorus. Biotechnology is one (cf. the next Section 5.4).

16 It is uncertain whether the phosphorus mineral referred to in the table actually refers to phosphate rock, or phosphorus. For our purposes, this is, however, of less importance because what we are after is not the absolute amount of phosphorus available, but for how long it will last (which is reasonably the same whether we calculate for phosphate rock or phosphorus).

17 However, there is an additional difficulty here. Much of the "phosphorus" mined is more or less rich in cadmium (which is a highly toxic heavy metal causing great damage to the environment and to human beings). If we only assume a use of phosphorus poor in cadmium, the reserves are considerably more limited than indicated in the table. With current use, the pure phosphorus would most likely run out within only a few generations.

18 See especially the discussion on biotechnology in Section 5.2.5.

19 I do not enter any deeper into discussions regarding particular products or inventions, but stick to principal matters. For example, I only mention different methods to improve irrigation efficiency, but do not present in detail how these methods work. Such a discussion would add nothing to my overall purposes in this book. Consequently we

have not specified or calculated what specific methods might constitute the technological improvements assumed in the scenarios.

20 Besides the ones I refer to, there is a wide range of supply-related factors and resources that I do not discuss, but which are required. A few examples are worth mentioning. In case any of the SD-scenarios are realised, large parts of global pasture will be replaced with modern breeding technology. Such a shift requires large investments, not least in cowsheds equipped with feeding- and hygiene plant etc. It also assumes that crop management is made more efficient. Sowing and harvesting technology must thus be developed, as must technology for distributing fertilisers as efficiently and optimally as possible. Furthermore, modern farming presupposes the use of large amounts of fossil fuel (SEPA 1997e:13-24). Seen from a wider sustainable development perspective, today's machines and vehicles must be replaced with technology demanding less fossil fuel per unit of useful work. All these things are assumed, but are not discussed any further in the analysis.

21 We mainly find this scarcity in agriculture, not in households.

22 Cf. the discussion we had in the former Section on water availability. We then established that there seems to be enough water to supply the amount of water that the crops require, but how much water must be extracted to provide all crops with that much water is a figure that depends largely on how much water is wasted/lost in the system.

23 E.g., in the form of governmental subsidies "Firms investing in the discovery of new technologies may only capture a small part of the net income gains resulting from it. This reduces their incentives to invest in research, with the consequence that 'too little' research may be produced by relying on the private sector only" (Alexandratos 1995:277; cf. several contributions in Timmer 1991).

24 One way could be to improve a plant's capacity to utilise fertilisers (cf., the next paragraph on biotechnology).

25 At least this is the case for the kind of technology suggested in the SEPA report (1997b).

26 Biotechnology is not a very substantial heading. It is a concept gathering research and production within a wide range of areas. If anything, the concept has a particular emphasis on industrial and technological development. When I speak of biotechnology in this chapter, I refer to agrarian research aimed at changing the gene structure of a plant or of an animal with the intention to develop and improve a particular attribute, e.g., resistance to a particular disease, or improving productivity under certain conditions such as drought or cold weather.

27 With certain exceptions, however. For example, genetic modifications of soya beans have been going on for a long time, and their distribution has been extensive. Some scholars and NGOs expect it soon to be practically impossible to guarantee that a soya based product does not contain genetically modified protein (cf. several contributions in Kungl. Skogs- och lantbruksakademien/Royal Swedish Academy of Agriculture and Forestry [RSAAF] 1997)

28 I discuss the moral and ethical objections to biotechnology more thoroughly in Chapter 6.

29 Reading Lu & Kelly (1997) also enriches our picture of what an (uncontrolled) improved agricultural efficiency *may lead to*. Using plant and insect pesticides can certainly improve productivity. At the same time, however, such methods can have detrimental effects on both soil and on the surrounding eco-systems (e.g., Carson 1962)

30 According to some scholars, biotechnology will be especially important in developing countries' agriculture. There, food production is especially challenged by factors such as climate-related strains, diseases, energy-poor crops and the diminishing

biological diversity of wild animals—all of which can be mitigated by extensive use of biotechnology. At the same time these countries usually suffer from limited or insufficient market structures, under-developed policies, limited research capacity and economic boundaries thus reducing the potential to introduce new technology into agriculture. Many of the products and techniques so far being developed in the industrialised world are not designed to satisfy specific problems in developing countries. An elucidation of what is required is thus necessary, but such an elucidation presupposes well-developed market structures, policies and knowledge about biotechnology's mode of operation (Wagner & Hammond 1997:83)

31 Examples of improvements that may be attained by using biotechnology instead of, e.g., pesticides are: resistance and toleration of hereditary diseases and bacteria, toleration of water shortage and marginal fertility, toleration against extreme climatic conditions and adaptation to prejudiced cultivation (Wagner & Hammond 1997:83).

32 With biotechnology it is also possible to lower the agricultural discharges of phosphorus (cf. earlier in this chapter). This is done by adding the enzyme called *Phytas* to pork and chicken fodder. This enzyme is developed by genetically modifying certain micro-organisms. When the phosphorus is released in the fodder, growth is stimulated and the animal is able to further utilise mineral substances. This means that the total amount of phosphorus in manure decreases, which in addition decreases agricultural leakage and leaching into watercourses.

Chapter 6

Socio-economic Challenges

I began the previous chapter by arguing that an implementation of scenario SD-4 would be challenging mainly for two reasons. First, the scenario requires certain inputs. I contended that the major inputs in our model are physical resources, technology and social and economic resources. Second, I said that an implementation of scenario SD-4 may give rise to conflicting interests. In the former chapter 5 I focused on the first two input categories. I argued that input of physical resources presupposes both control and co-ordination across national borders. I further claimed that the implied demand for technological development in scenario SD-4 generates both supporting and distributional challenges.

In this chapter I continue by discussing challenges connected to the third supply category, i.e., demand for social and economic inputs. Furthermore, I discuss how an implementation of scenario SD-4 may give rise to conflicting interests.

6.1 Implied Redistribution of Food, Physical Resources, Money and Other Socio-Economic Goods

"Calling for the financial resources required to achieve *sustainable food security* is not to suggest simply reprogramming funds within today's inadequate *foreign aid* budgets. What is needed is not benign neglect or band-aid approaches but measures that enable *subsistence farmers* around the world to *feed themselves*, their communities and their nations while *preserving the resource base*. Representatives of the world's governments agreed in Cairo that sound population and agricultural development policies work together to *improve social well-being*. Among the steps needed are the *elimination of trade barriers* against developing world exports and reduction of developing-world dept." (Engelman & Leroy 1995:35 my italics)

This quotation captures several important socio-economic aspects applicable to scenario SD-4 and its basic assumptions. What kind of aid does such a scenario imply? What kind of agriculture is intimated? What is required of farmers in the developing world to produce food as efficiently as assumed in the scenario? How is self-sufficiency attained, and what happens if not all areas, regions and countries attain it? Besides the challenges that I postulated in Chapter 5, I claim that a significant redistribution of resources will be required to maintain scenario SD-4. However, this does not concern only aid in the form of financial support (even if that is one option). I contend that redistribution of a range of goods is implied by scenario SD-4, such as physical resources, food, education and perhaps even support of institutions and actions to bolster political stability. This is at least required if we have reason to believe that not all countries in the world will be able to reach a generally high economic and social standard without external help. I emphasise a generally high standard, because if some countries lag behind significantly, then there is a risk that scenario SD-4 will actually produce more starvation, poverty and political instability than is the case in the world today.

6.1.1 Competition for Land vs. Redistribution of Food and Economic Means; The Case of Energy Demand

Discussing the physical potential for cultivation in Chapter 5, we found some scholars estimating the remaining (unused) land-areas to be considerable (e.g., Fageria 1992). If we temporarily accept these figures, the competition for land may not be acute, except locally or regionally and especially in areas that are exceptionally fertile and/or attractive for living.[1] However, these 'available' land areas also produce a range of other goods and services, and furthermore, there might be competition for biomass as well. This implies price increases of basic goods like food, thus hitting people with inadequate purchasing power. Therefore I contend that unless matched by food aid or some kind of economic support, the massive demand for biomass in scenario SD-4 may price some people out of the food market.

One could argue that any increases in animal food production ought to be focused on cattle and other ruminants, rather than pork and chicken as suggested here. Such animals can utilise the energy in plants growing in areas that are not cultivable (Kumm 1998:26; SEPA 1997a:51f; see also Ely 1994 and Webster 1994) or are otherwise 'useless' for agriculture. That would invalidate the argument to reduce cattle consumption as is done in scenario SD-4. By increasing the use of such uncultivable pasture land for cattle production (grazing), animal food production can increase without necessarily threatening bio-diversity or forcing out competing claims for land since society then makes sensible use of areas that can merely be used for pasture. But does not our scenario introduce methods that actually reduce the total share of pasture?[2] From a purely agricultural 'utility-perspective', it would be wasteful to let land areas remain unused instead of producing something for which there is a strong demand, in this case cattle. Yet, this reasoning only covers traditional agricultural business i.e., crop and animal production. As the number of alternative land-uses increases, competition for land is intensified.[3] Admittedly, our scenario analysis focuses solely on animal food consumption, thus actually leaving out many challenges generated by scenario SD-4. The competition from the energy sector is one important example:

"If all energy for human use was provided by well-managed energy crops, every individual would need 0.2-2 ha. The land required for green energy would be an order of magnitude larger than that for food. If all the land in Europe that may become available in the next decades is planted with energy crops (19 Mha) then its contribution to Europe's energy consumption will still be only 8%." (de Vries et al. 1997:926)

Conscious attempts to reduce the global carbon dioxide emissions may increase the demand for bio-energy significantly. The reason is that growing energy crops is a relatively cheap method of compensating for the drop in energy when the use of fossil fuel is eventually reduced.[4] Most scenario analyses on energy-crops assume that the total area available for energy-crop production is all the cultivable land left after a satisfactory global food supply has been 'secured' (Azar & Berndes 1999:157). Such scenarios, however, tend to disregard the principal factor determining land-use, namely demand. If the global community strives for reducing the total carbon dioxide emissions, e.g., by introducing carbon taxes, the energy price will increase. If the price increases are high enough, it will become more and more profitable to produce energy crops. Above a certain level, it may even become more profitable to produce energy crops than grain or other food. Thus, for the farmer not to change over to energy crop-production, the price for grain may eventually have to increase (de Vries et al. 1997:926).

If the demand for animal food increases in the developed countries, then farmers will have incentives to start growing fodder plants instead of grains and other plants directly usable for human consumption. As in the case of energy crops, such development may force food prices to increase. This in turn hits back at poor people who do not own any cultivable land. The scenario assumptions about a global increase in the economic standard of living are perhaps not realistic, but may very well be required to prevent future starvation.[5] As the competition for land and biomass increases, so will food prices. Furthermore, the Brundtland Commission argues that starvation can be eradicated only if everyone enjoys a certain degree of economic development. This places great demands on the rich world both now and in the future, especially if the connection between economic standard of living and animal food consumption is as strong as indicated in Chapter 4 (cf. Goklany 1999:260ff). Of course, the stronger the average economy becomes, the higher the prices that can be paid for food. However, if some people do not enjoy any economic improvement or are not ensured a sufficient economic and social standard in some other way, then the objectives of scenario SD-4 can hardly be fulfilled.

> *Summary*: Unless matched by either some kind of economic support and/or food aid, the massive demand for biomass in scenario SD-4 may price some people out of the food market.

6.1.2   *Redistribution of social and economic goods; The case for self-sufficiency*

In order to underline the importance that the economic and social standard in the world increases significantly, to a fairly equal level and simultaneously, I discuss what may happen if economic development will not occur in all parts of the world.[6]

> "Many countries such as Bangladesh, cannot afford to buy food from abroad and thereby compensate for insufficient natural resources. These countries will probably rely more on food aid in the future." (Bongaart 1994:24)

Both the price of land and of crops follows a rather direct mechanism; increases in demand and/or decreases in supply are immediately reflected in price increases. This has, however, not been the case with water (at least not for agriculture). Even if water is a scarce resource, locally and regionally, and also of vital importance for all humankind, the price has remained fairly low. The most common explanation is that there is no working market. Water, like air, is regarded a 'common good' that can hardly be subjected to mining claims and is nothing to make money from (Cunningham & Saigo 2001:442f; Jones & Hollier 1997:25).[7] Thus, even if we make the assumption that the price for water remains stable, even when it is scarce, the price for much of what water is used for can still increase, e.g., food or biomass. If a country suffers from water shortage, it may lose its self-sufficiency.[8] Even if this does not indicate that a country loses its capacity to maintain itself, it becomes more exposed to market fluctuations. This has important implications for the understanding of our scenario, since it is based on increases in both population and animal food consumption.

Such continued increases reasonably increase the demand for, and consequently raise the prices of, e.g., land and fertilisers. This also affects the price of crops and biomass and thus of food. Most of the countries currently suffering from water shortage, or that are expected to do so within the next 25 years, are among the poorest in the world (Postel 1998:635). They are also expected to contribute the most to global population growth during the period in question. For these reasons, such countries are particularly vulnerable to water shortage (or to any other shortage forcing them to import their food).

This line of reasoning can be developed further. A country not self-sufficient in food is dependent on imports. This means it must have capital and financial resources to maintain the food supply.[9] If the demand for biomass increases, as in scenario SD-4, the price of biomass probably increases. This eventually gives rise to competition between what cultivable land ought to be used for, and what kind of biomass is to be produced; in this case, competition between grain and animal fodder (cf. Leach 1995:37). Price (along with agriculture policies, presumably) will decide what cultivable land areas are used for. Since rich countries can afford to continue demanding animal food products, even if the price for biomass increases, this economic capacity may also contribute to an increase in the price of grain.[10] Even if such competition does not affect the rich world appreciably in spite of the increased price of animal food and other food, it will strike hard against poor countries, and especially those countries which are not even self-sufficient in most elementary staple crops. This is because poor peoples' demand for food is much more sensitive to changes in price and income (Timmer et al. 1984; Alderman 1986). For those who are self-sufficient among the poor countries, raised demand and prices will be less noticeable, and under certain circumstances even advantageous.[11] For those who are both non-self-sufficient in food and too poor to provide sufficient social and economic development/standards, such a development may be completely devastating.

To keep scenario SD-4 from contributing to such a development[12] a generally high economic standard is required to match price rises when demand for biomass increases as indicated in scenario SD-4. So far it is not lack of food that mainly explains starvation in the world, but rather lack of purchasing power (Bongaart 1994:24; Sen 1993a, 1981). A generally high agricultural productivity, including efficient use of water, is also required.[13] If we assume that not enough of the food needed can be produced within the country and/or that the population cannot afford to buy it from the international food market, then ensured provision of food (cf. Chapter 4.2) requires one or several of the following conditions: (1) A redistribution of food from where there are surpluses to where there are needs; (2) A redistribution of resources required to domestically produce enough food; (3) Economic support comprehensive enough to fulfil e.g. the food requirements to maintain the standards outlined in scenario SD-4.

> *Summary*: Unless a generally high economic standard is ensured, either by domestic efforts or through aid, in parallel with the extensive biomass and animal production assumed in scenario SD-4, the scenario may make life even worse for those who are left in poverty.

6.1.3 Call for Redistribution of Physical Resources; The Case of Water

Water is a basic good and a necessary resource for all living beings. It is, however unevenly and irregularly distributed around the globe (Jones & Hollier 1997:242), which calls for redistribution if scenario SD-4 is to be realised.

Socio-economic challenges

Because of its character, this is easier said than done, and implies *great social and economic costs* practically no matter what method we have in mind.

Table 6.1   **Grain import in African, Asian and Middle Eastern countries whose water per capita assets fall below 1700m³ per year**

Country	Water access m³/cap & year Year 1995	Net import of grain Share of consumption (%)
United Arab Emirate	158	100
Singapore	200	100
Kuwait	0	100
Djibouti	500	100
Oman	909	100
Lebanon	1297	95
Jordanian	249	91
Israel	309	85
South Korea	1473	77
Algeria	489	70
Yemen	189	66
Armenia	1673	60
Mauritania	174	58
Cap Verde	750	55
Tunisia	393	55
South Arabia	119	50
Uzbekistan	418	42
Egypt	29	40
Azerbadjan	1066	34
Turkmenistan	251	26
Morocco	1027	26
Somalia	645	26
Rwanda	808	20
Iraq	1650	19
Kenya	714	15
Sudan	1246	4
Burkina Faso	1683	2
Burundi	563	2
Zimbabwe	1248	2
Nigeria	380	1
South Africa	1030	-3
Syria	517	-4

Comment: Water access does not include river water inflows from other countries. This is to avoid 'double counting'. Only Armenia, Azerbadjan, Djibouti, Iraq, Mauretania, Sudan, Turkmenistan and Uzbekistan would have more than 1700m³ / capita and year if such additional inflows were included.

Source: WRI 1994, FAO 1995, USDA 1997, specified and summarised in Postel 1998.

Constantly increasing imbalances between population size and water supply result in more and more countries no longer being self-sufficient in food. When annual runoff levels per capita fall short of the general figure of 1700m^3 per year, it is considered difficult for a country to maintain complete self-sufficiency (Postel 1998:634).[14] Below this level, there is not enough water to meet all the demands from industry, cities, households, agriculture and different ecological functions. In principle, such countries then have to import water, for the most part in the form of grain. In Table 6.1, import dependency on grain is specified for countries in Africa, Asia and the Middle East that are short of water.

This table is an oversimplification,[15] but still brings the message across. Only two of the countries (South Africa and Syria) are not net importers of grain. Half of the countries are forced to import 50 per cent or more of their total consumption. As the world population continues to grow,[16] the number of countries falling below the 1700m^3 limit of self-sufficiency will also increase. Needless to say, the situation will be even more difficult for the countries already listed in the table.[17]

By the year 2025, about 40% of the world population will not be self-sufficient in water, according to Postel (1998:635). Thus, dependency on water imports will become an even larger problem in the future. This is important for our analysis of the scenario. If the import dependency is expected to increase, even with a quite moderate increase in global animal food consumption (around today's per capita consumption, i.e., 13% of the total diet), our scenario SD-4 implies an even larger share of redistribution.[18]

As we learned in Chapter 5, limited water resources do not mean that availability must be an acute global problem (even if regional and local shortage obviously is common). However, to redistribute or transport water from rich to poor areas is not an easy task. Besides great losses along the way, such systems are costly. Yet, they are most needed.

A strict interpretation of the Brundtland Commission's demands for social justice compels us to assume fully ensured access to water. This should also be claimed for the water demand implied in scenario SD-4. New questions arise immediately, for example about how to make global water assets available for all,[19] meaning how to distribute it to where it is needed.[20] At least three starting points are possible. Water can be distributed either by (1) moving it, (2) redistributing it via grain, or (3) moving people who need water. While all three methods are possible, they also involve costs.

Moving water. To satisfy the demands for water in scenario SD-4 by physically moving it to where it is needed is theoretically possible. To maintain areas short of water by transporting it is quite common (Cunningham & Saigo 2001:436). Northern California supports its southern parts, making those areas considerably more productive than would otherwise be the case. However, such transportation can vary in efficiency and is expensive. In scenario SD-4, we assume the most advanced and efficient methods available. This assumption should here be understood as transportation by pipelines. However, such costly methods are mostly found in richer countries. The most common alternatives, i.e., canals and ditches, are cheaper, but also less efficient. Our reasoning thus ends up with the question: Who is to pay for such transportation systems? If we assume a global economic standard equivalent to Western Europe, then perhaps all countries could afford such transportation. But what if the economic development demanded by the Brundtland Commission turns out to cover only the bare necessities of life, thus making the costs for transporting the water implied in scenario SD-4 to those who need it prohibitive? Morally and politically it must be up to the remaining 'affording' world to make sure that those needs are satisfied, at least if scenario SD-4 is to be realised.

Transportation in itself is hardly a panacea for global water provision. By *redistributing water via grains/food*, i.e., 'virtual water' (Wichelns 2001), much of the needed water and the water-related services can be provided without incurring many infrastructure changes and costs and needless waste of water. However, again we must ask who is paying? Redistribution of grains aims at lowering the demand for water in countries with a water shortage. In rich countries, the population may afford a satisfactory water supply for itself without help from elsewhere. Poor countries require economic assistance. Thus, even if their water supply is increased by grain imports, we cannot exclude an active involvement by the rich world for scenario SD-4 to be realised. My point is that redistributing water by grain production may be efficient but does not eliminate the need for redistribution of economic means.[21]

Solving water shortage by *moving the shortage-suffering people* is yet another option. Whether this solution is 'organised' or not, there is a risk that large groups of people will be forced to move, in order to survive, especially if scenario SD-4 becomes realised without sufficient control. Such migration already occurs in e.g., Africa. With a more than tripled population within the next 50 years in Africa, the likelihood for more comprehensive migration increases. Consequently, the pressure on surrounding countries also increases (Ehrlich 1994:31ff), in turn implying a need to ensure political and social stability (cf. Section 6.1.3)

> *Summary:* Quite clearly, active participation from the affording world appears to be required for scenario SD-4 to be realised, no matter what alternative we assume. To ensure that people get the water to which they are entitled, but may not be able to afford, implies support probably in each of the forms suggested above.

6.1.4   Redistribution of Social and Political Stability; The Case of Water Scarcity

While discussing water I will now take the opportunity to point out still another 'good' that may have to be redistributed or provided if scenario SD-4 is to be realised, i.e., provision of social and political stability. Water scarcity is considered a major factor behind national and international conflicts (cf.

Ohlsson 1999, Homer-Dixon 1995 and Harrison 1993). When water scarcity reaches a certain critical level, then the propensity for conflict increases. The strained relations between Egypt and other countries along the Nile can be explained mainly by the fact that Egyptian agriculture is vulnerable to water extraction done upstream (Hollier & Jones 1997:241). In fact, periodically hardly any water reaches the estuary. Similar phenomena are found in the US. The Colorado River is more or less 'finished' before it reaches the Pacific Ocean (Goudie 2000:206).

This conflict hypothesis supplies us with additional reasons to reflect on our scenario. What would the international political consequences be if a realisation of scenario SD-4 actually increases water scarcity in the world? Unless efforts are made to maintain supply to the already most exposed countries and regions, they will suffer even more from water scarcity within the next 25 years (cf. Postel 1998:635). These regions largely coincide with the regions where the greatest population growth is expected. They also coincide with areas where agricultural expansion is assumed to be most tangible in scenario SD-4. Thus, unless endeavours are made to support and maintain these most exposed regions, this scenario might not only cause even worse water shortages, but also internal and international struggles.[22]

To prevent such a development, achievements that ensure peaceful and efficient solutions are needed. This implies both economic and political support. Global water use can be significantly more productive, e.g., by applying highly efficient irrigation technology. This would diminish the risk of disputes. At the same time such technology is costly, and the greatest risks of conflicts are in countries with unstable economic and political systems.

> *Summary:* If the countries with a propensity for conflict cannot afford to pay for the needed technology, while at the same time the Brundtland Commission's requests for social and economic sustainability are to be realised, then help must be provided from somewhere else, not only in the form of financial resources and technology, but most likely in the form of institutions necessary for political and social stability.[23]

6.1.5 *Redistribution via Duty and Subvention Cuts; The Case of a Deregulated Food Market*

It is not within my competence to evaluate the actual effects and consequences of a deregulated global food market. However, my ambition to describe a worst case scenario entices me to at least reflect upon this option. It is commonly held that such deregulation would have (1) positive consequences for the developing world (Bhagwati 1993), and (2) negative consequences for the rich world (SOU 1997:26). However, I argue that it is reasonable to claim that in a world where some key resources are scarce, poor people may be worse off in a deregulated food market.

An often-suggested method for improving the lives of Third World farmers, and to avoid extensive aid, is to deregulate the global food market (cf. the introductory quotation in Section 6.1). The basic idea is that by doing so, farmers in poor regions could sell their products and thus yield capital to use for social, economic and technological development. Deregulation would thus function as an alternative to the kind of economic support that has been discussed in this chapter. This may be correct in the short run. The average farmer in developing countries would sell more at higher prices than before, and therefore be free of import duties, consequently earning more money.[24]

In the longer run, the picture may be somewhat different. Unless this 'new competition' really propels more efficient technology in the developing countries, as assumed in our scenario, several of the resource scarcities discussed earlier may arise,[25] in turn raising food prices further. For farmers continuing to produce food at competitive prices, such a development would be most advantageous (cf. Luc & Jeffrey 1997:315f), but it would hardly improve the lives of the poorest sections of the population. That is, an increasing resource scarcity increases resource prices. If this assumption is correct, then a deregulation of the food market may push us back to a situation similar to the one discussed in Section 6.1.2, where we concluded that the poorest populations, unless they have enough purchasing power, may be less well off following a scenario realisation. This reasoning can be developed further. Food prices vary considerably by season, by world demand, and locally depending on regional differences in harvest yields. Thus, in a completely free market some farmers may go broke because they are unable to sustain a number of bad seasons.

> *Summary:* If scenario SD-4 is to be realised (partly) by deregulating the food market, then there is a risk that this scenario make life *even worse* for those who are left in poverty. Thus, deregulation of the food market may have to be matched with regulations such as additional economic or food support at least to ensure the welfare of those lacking purchasing power and to provide assistance to producers to withstand severe seasonal variations over time.

6.2 Giving Priority to and Ranking Interests

Even if the dietary change assumed in scenario SD-4 was shown to have favourable effects on the total demand for biomass, such an assumption can prove problematic and challenging when it comes to actual implementation. Such a change would affect ranges of groups, perhaps negatively sometimes, and we can therefore not take for granted that they would be willing to participate in such transitions voluntarily. Just to mention a few groups who may come to be affected by such a change, let me refer to consumers who are used to eating plenty of beef, producers who are used to grazing, anyone who appreciates the aesthetics of a grazed landscape, those who rely upon tourism, and religious and cultural groups who do not eat pork or chicken. I mainly discuss consumers and producers here, but the principal problem is the same for all the groups: if they have good reason to oppose the implied changes, they must be convinced of the greater good or forced to accept the changes.

6.2.1 Give Priority to Future Generations; The Case for Dietary Changes

With only a few regional exceptions, most people who can afford it eat food produced from animals. The largest consumption is found in Western Europe, USA and South America. People there are used to eating meat, and especially meat from cattle (Rifkin 1992:9-66). It is not self-evident that such habits can be changed solely by free will.[26] When critically examining scenario SD-4, it is important to reflect on the prospects for such changes, i.e., how would Western world consumers respond to such a dietary change? To my knowledge, no study of people's willingness to change their animal food consumption has been done (at least not looking at the benefit to the global environment). However, other studies can shed some light on the public opinion about the relationship between diet and the environment.

In a survey study done by the Swedish national food administration (Livsmedelsverket 1996), respondents were asked to judge the 'importance' of 16 different food attributes. The feature "produced in a way that does not harm the environment" ranked number ten among those characteristics. The quality considered least important was "ecologically produced". Thus, judging from the study carried out by Livsmedelsverket, the environment is not a quality that people mainly consider when choosing their diet; the individual's well-being has priority. This is perhaps not too surprising; people's own well-being is probably a reasonably strong driving force while their support for the environment is not powerful enough to override personal preferences.

Some support for such a 'hypothesis' is provided by the study carried out by the Swedish aid organisation SIDA (1998). The environment is not given any prominent concern, but Swedes at least appear to have a certain willingness to support environmentally related projects in other countries. Without hesitation, however, most support is given to projects in the 'social sectors', such as health care and education. High priority is also given to human-rights related projects. Furthermore, the interest for environmental aid is mostly directed towards projects in neighbouring regions and countries. The further we move away from Europe, the lesser the propensity for giving aid seems to be.

A similar conclusion is drawn in Carlsson & Kumlin's (1998) study, which is based on a nationwide Swedish survey.[27] Two conclusions are of particular interest here. First, the willingness to economically support environment-related projects is generally low. Compared with most other sectors, especially the economy and employment, the environment is a low-priority issue (cf. Bennulf 1997, 1999). Second, the willingness to pay for measures improving the environment decreases with the distance from the own home municipality to the target of the contribution. Thus, support for international environmental improvements in, e.g., Africa, can be expected to be pretty low.

The empirical evidence is not strong enough to draw any far-reaching conclusions. However, the results at least indicate one thing. A government conducting an open and conscious environmental and consumption policy with the global aim of letting animal food consumption increase further, while at the same time keeping down the strains on resources such as land, water and phosphorus, will probably be met with public opposition.

This also has implications for our assumptions about dietary changes. To increase the social and economic development and also the animal food consumption as done in scenario SD-4 with little harm to the environment thanks to efficient production, it is important to make the citizens aware of the environmental harm that their animal food (cattle especially) consumption may cause unless it is produced under optimal conditions. The lesser the value people ascribe to environmental and global social development, the stronger the politics and the more powerful the political system must be.[28] No matter how politically challenging this may be, these challenges have to be met if scenario SD-4 to be realised, while still fulfilling the demands of the Brundtland Commission. Otherwise the comprehensive consumption in scenario SD-4 may develop towards our BAU-scenario, something that could lead to irreversible damage to both the poor population of the world, as well as to future generations.

Taking my objective of discussing a worst case scenario seriously, I wish to underline further the demand and scope for dietary changes in, e.g., the Western world. The scope of the dietary changes assumed in scenario SD-4 may be affected by cultural and religious factors. Recall the scenario SD-4 assumption that chicken and pork would replace some of the global beef consumption (including sheep and goat), since such animals are less resource demanding. At the same time, however, e.g., pork is a culturally controversial meat, i.e., consumption of it is often afflicted with religious and other restrictions. For example, a future transition to a more 'pork-oriented' consumption may prove difficult in many Muslim countries even if the population growth is expected to be very extensive there.[29]

Unless dietary content becomes valued differently within, e.g., religiously oriented countries, the animal food proportions assumed in scenario SD-4 can only be reached provided that other less culturally and religiously affected parts of the world change their diet even more than the 25% already assumed. This does not change the principal challenge of convincing or forcing people to change their diet. However, it certainly increases the scope of the change, and perhaps also the range of measures needed to have the dietary changes implemented.

Summary: Unless Western world consumers voluntarily change their diet, largely for the benefit of the poor and for unborn generations (and perhaps even for other groups, e.g., to enable them to exercise their culture) such changes must be forced using political power for scenario SD-4 to be realised. According to my (limited) data, there is scant evidence in favour of voluntary change.

6.2.2   *Give Priority to the World's Poor; The Case of Biotechnology*

It is not only assumptions about dietary changes that give us reason to expect that other groups must be given precedence over western world (liberal democratic) citizens if scenario SD-4 is to be realised. Another example I wish to discuss is the assumed use of biotechnology. Most of all such technology is developed in the Western world, and in Chapter 5 I indicated that such development ought to be governmentally promoted and supported if scenario SD-4 is to be achieved. How likely is such support if the public is against biotechnology? Here I argue that with the present attitudes to biotechnology in mind, it is not enough to inform people about its advantages and that it may not cause any personal harm. The negative attitude is largely explained by moral and ethical objections, and these objections presuppose political force no matter how we try to overcome them.

Today, biotechnology is mainly (although not exclusively) used for medical purposes (Andersson & Wahlberg 1996: 21ff). Most research is done on hereditary diseases and in the development of medicines. Biotechnology is also used in food production. So far, most food research has been done on crops. It will probably take quite some time before food from genetically modified animals is introduced on the market. According to the Swedish Gene Technology Advisory Board (Gentekniknämnden/GN), consumer demand and attitudes largely decide whether the market is ready for biotechnology and genetically modified food (GN 1997:5). One way to estimate the opinion about biotechnology and how important it is considered to be is to measure awareness and knowledge among citizens (Hoban 1997:232). General public awareness of biotechnology has remained stable over time. In 1997, American citizens were only a little more aware of it than in 1992, despite the fact that several products were introduced during this period (Hoban 1997:232f). Outside the US, attitudes and knowledge vary significantly. In Europe, for example, countries can be roughly divided into two different groups.[30] Knowledge about biotechnology is largest in the northern countries, where more than 70% of the citizens have some knowledge, while the figures in the southern countries vary between 35 and 50% (GN 1997:15f).

The EU citizens have become clearly more sceptical about modern biotechnology over time (Fjaestad & Ohlsson 1997:13). This should be contrasted with the American people who have been, and still are, more positive than the Europeans. However, even if the Americans are more positive with regard to all fields of application, there are differences (Zechendorf 1994:870ff). The public is at its most positive with regard to medical research, e.g., pharmaceutical production and diagnoses of hereditary diseases.[31] Also, genetic modification of micro-organisms earns relatively strong support, while genetic modifications of crops are weakly supported. The American people are most negative to biotechnology applied to animals.[32] Genetic engineering of food does gain certain support, provided that the aim is to make disease-resistant crops, but the support is much weaker if the aim is to, e.g., increase the rate of protein in the food, extend the length of shelf life or improve the taste (Fjaestad & Ohlsson 1997).

Should we then conclude that "acceptance for biotechnology increases with both knowledge and understanding" (Zechendorf 1994:875; cf. Frewer 1997:139)? According to the Swedish Gene Technology Advisory Board, it is not possible to assert a general connection between knowledge and attitude when it comes to biotechnology.[33] This becomes evident when studying several countries with either a generally high or low knowledge of biotechnology. If anything, people are either highly knowledgeable or have no knowledge, but are still positive towards such technology. However, with the "increased number of correct answers on the knowledge-related questions, both the share of positive and negative expectations is increasing." (GN 1997:26).

Thus, to explain attitudes to biotechnology we have to supplement the picture with additional factors. Risk and health factors are generally ascribed as significant determinants in opinion formation. If people consider an activity as risky or unhealthy, they tend to have a more negative attitude towards it. This has been the understanding of authorities, corporations and researchers informing the public, but it has also been the basis for legislation and other rules aimed at counteracting risk (GN 1998:29ff). Yet, neither the risk nor the health argument seems to explain much of people's positive and negative attitudes to biotechnology:

> "Surprisingly enough, there is no connection, whatsoever, between how risky the respondents estimate an application to be, and how willing they are to encourage further development and use of it!" (Fjaestad & Ohlsson 1997:14, *my translation*)

What does seem to be a powerful motivator is people's moral and ethical conception of biotechnology. According to Gaull (1997:38-42), it is the national ethos that explains why it has been relatively easy to implement biotechnology research and products in the USA compared to Europe. Fjaestad & Ohlsson draw a similar conclusion; it is first and foremost moral and ethical deliberations that determine attitudes to biotechnology, and not utility or risks (1997:14; cf. Zechendorf 1994:874). According to Bruhn (1992:80), conceptions connected to social justice also seem important when people form an opinion on these matters. For example, compared with only benefiting a few large companies, citizens are more positive to biotechnology if they think its application will benefit humanity as a whole. To get an idea of the political challenges connected to implementing a comprehensive use of biotechnology—

as implied in scenario SD-4—we thus ought to enter somewhat deeper into the moral objections that have been put forward against biotechnology.

I know of no empirical attempts to specify which moral motives are behind attitudes to biotechnology, and which of these are most important. We should also keep in mind that there are ethical arguments in favour of biotechnology. For example, such technology may be a means to avoid starvation (Lu & Kelly1997:256).[34] I have no intention to advocate any particular stand in this matter. My sole aim is to outline certain commonly recognised moral objections that may come to form hindrances for any global application of such technology, and thus for scenario SD-4 to be realised. In this context, it is important to find acceptable arguments against the following objections, or methods to avoid what they are referring to, if the general public is ever to become reconciled with the idea of mass-producing and consuming genetically modified food.[35] If not, only political force can bring about the promotion of the biotechnology required for scenario SD-4 to be realised on a global scale. The potential moral objections include the following:

• *Animal well-being.* Different applications of biotechnology may cause animals to suffer. Another objection is that animal 'interests' are harmed when they are genetically modified for the sake of satisfying human needs. Simply put, what is the 'status' of animals if human beings consider themselves to have the right to manipulate animals for the purpose of improving the well-being of humanity (Shiva 1998:25-30)?

• *Mankind's right to play God.* It is morally questionable to change the *nature* of animals or the nature of any other biological organism (Thompson 1997:148).[36]

• *Religious objections.* Several religions demand *full control* over the diet, which is lost when food is genetically manipulated.[37] Many critics also argue that biotechnology is connected to a range of ecological as well as religious risks; not least the risk that modified genes may spread to wild species (GN 1998:14f). Such an uncontrolled distribution of modified genes would obstruct the exercise of religions demanding full control of dietary composition.[38]

• *Individual liberty.* Present demands for labelling genetically modified food differ among countries. If the labelling system becomes comprehensive, then the consumers can *freely* choose what products they wish to buy. There is, however, a fear that the labelling system about to be developed will not be taken seriously; food producers may mix genetically and non-genetically modified products. Such a development is seen as a violation of individual liberty (Thompson 1997:148).[39]

• *Genetic erosion.* The view that each and every species on Earth has an intrinsic value[40] and therefore ought to be protected was probably one reason why the convention on biological diversity was constituted. The fear of devastating natural resources with future potential for humanity was certainly another. An uncontrolled distribution of genetically modified plants and animals could risk ousting not only many existing plants and animals, but also possibly useful species that are supposed to develop in the future (Frisvold & Condor 1998:553ff; Greenpeace 1996:7f).[41]

- *Property legislation, in opposition to biological diversity?* The prospect of property legislation on genetic material and engineering is unclear. The primary supplies of biological diversity, crops and the principal sources for genetic raw material are found in developing countries. At the same time, Western world corporations wish to appropriate the right to patent genes that they find in those plants, claiming to have 'invented' these genes. A double standard arises in the interpretation of the convention on biological diversity. Mainly Western world biotechnology is regarded as intellectual property, providing it legal protection, while developing countries' raw material is to be preserved, but also available for all. Thus an identified gene can be patented, while legal protection for the possession of the gene-carrier is missing (Oksanen 2001).[42]

- *Unfair patenting—'biopiracy'.* The patent legislation has developed massively over the last hundred years. Today it comprises not only mechanical inventions, but also intellectual property and rights (Frisvold & Condor 1998:553). As just stated, naturally occurring plants or animals are still considered a public good (not possible to patent). When it comes to an isolated (and perhaps slightly adjusted) gene, however, it is a private good. This asymmetrical definition of property rights is criticised by many as 'biopiracy', since it produces negative and unfair consequences for poor countries and farmers (Shiva 1998:7-11; Rifkin 1998:48-56).[43]

We have implied that the future for biotechnology within the food sector is dependent on consumer demand and attitudes. Furthermore, we have established that ethical concerns and lack of fairness (social justice) are factors that determine consumer attitudes. These attitudes also determine the prospects for promoting the development of such technology. If we consider the foregoing moral objections to biotechnology, we find that they are not only directed at animal well-being or risks to humankind, but they are also largely directed towards those who are developing this technology at present. I therefore contend that to be able to promote biotechnology in order to realise scenario SD-4, some kind of political regulation or other force is probably required.

On the one hand, this political force can be directed towards citizens, meaning that the public (moral) attitude must either be changed or disregarded, i.e biotechnological development is promoted regardless of public opinion. However, if the government instead chooses to conciliate the public, political force will still be required, not against the citizens but against the biotechnological corporations. This is because moral and ethical objections are largely the base for public opinion. If positive public opinion is required for biotechnology to be developed and globally distributed without political force, the development and use of it must be so comprehensively regulated that as few as possible of these publicly perceived ethical constraints are violated. Thus, in the latter case the political force is directed towards the corporations developing the technology.

> *Summary:* To promote development of biotechnology, political steering and control appears unavoidable. Either political force is required to overrule public opinion, and/or political force is required to regulate the biotechnological industry. In both cases, a liberal democracy faces great challenges. In the first case, it has to prioritise scenario SD-4 (largely the starving world and perhaps also future generations) rather than its own voting citizens. In the latter case, it has to prioritise the well-being of, e.g., third world farmers ahead of enormously powerful corporations.

6.2.3 Give Priority to the World's Poor and Future Generations; The Case of Western World Producers

In this section I contend that crop and animal producers constitute another interest that may be negatively affected and partly disregarded if scenario SD-4 is realised. This is politically challenging, not the least since Western world producers are well organised and very powerful (Rifkin 1992). Thus, unless those interests agree voluntarily to the transitions required to implement scenario SD-4, we can expect them to put up strong political resistance. This implies a need for political steering and value priorities. To run my argument I discuss the following: (1) government withdrawal from the food market, (2) parallel regulation in the form of food redistribution, (3) dietary changes, (4) conflicting values and (5) political steering of what ought to be produced.

(1) Government withdrawal. As was discussed in Section 6.1.4, an often-suggested method for improving the lives of farmers in developing countries and to avoid extensive aid, is to deregulate the global food market (SOU 1997:10). Such a change would probably be advantageous at least for some farmers, but not necessarily for all. According to several commentators, deregulation of the food market would have negative effects on agriculture in, e.g., the EU, the US and Australia (SOU 1997:115-131). Demands for high yields are extensive in those countries. To remain competitive against the rest of the world, often far less capital intensive (but also less efficient) methods in terms of land-use, high import duties and producer subventions are used (Waggoner 1994:7ff). If these restrictions were reduced or abolished, then the prices for, e.g., European-produced food would increase considerably, and the EU farmers would no longer be competitive (SOU 1997:124ff).[44] Other regions would certainly gain from this, as would perhaps also EU citizens generally. If deregulation of the food market is required to realise (or at least to facilitate) an implementation of scenario SD-4, a great political challenge looms for Western

world governments because disregarding the interests of their own producers
for the benefit of farmers and people in less developed countries would
probably be perceived as, if not bordering on political suicide so at least
politically strenuous.[45]

(2) Additional regulation. If scenario SD-4 is implemented, global food
production will probably take quite a favourable turn for many farmers. After
all, the scenario implies a huge market, and an enormous demand for food.[46]
Thus, those who manage to meet the productivity demands assumed in the
scenario can look forward to a future characterised by a stable demand. In the
short run, at least people in the poor world will gain from deregulation. The
average farmer in developing countries will sell more at higher prices than
before. Farm producers will be freed from import duties and consequently earn
more money. However, in the longer run, the picture may be somewhat
different. Unless this 'new competition' really propels more efficient
technology in the developing countries, several of the resource scarcities
discussed earlier may arise (cf. Chapter 5.1-5.3).[47] This in turn raises food
prices (cf. Section 6.1.2). For farmers continuing to produce food at
competitive prices, such a development will be advantageous (cf. Luc & Jeffrey
1997) but will hardly improve the lives of the poorest population whose basic
needs are among the key targets in the Brundtland Commission report. So, for
scenario SD-4 to be realised, access to food and animal food must be
distributed more equitably than today.

Unless deregulation fully meets the demands in scenario SD-4, continued
regulation and steering of the market will also be needed. However, the aim of
any such regulation would not be to support inefficient or over-capitalised
farmers, but to ensure that people have access to the diet to which they are
entitled to aspire. Thus, a 'worst case scenario' for Western world farmers
would be one where they (a) lose their subsidies, (b) become exposed on the
international food market because of withdrawn import duties, and where they
(c) would suffer some of their products being redistributed, instead of being
disposed at market prices.[48]

(3) Dietary change. Unless consumers change their diet voluntarily, we
concluded that government regulation is required to realise scenario SD-4. This
dietary change not only affects the consumers, of course, but also the
producers. Thus, the implied political force, aimed at changing the consumer's
diet, also affects the farmers. Within the EU, the US and South America,
agricultural interests traditionally enjoy a solid political position. There is
strong support for animal food in general, and beef production in particular
(SOU 1997:71-77; Rifkin 1992:42f, 49ff, 163f). To advocate a decrease in beef
production under such circumstances may be self-defeating and politically
highly challenging—especially since the need for reduction in beef production
is far from being a universally accepted concept.

(4) Conflicting values. It is true that our scenario SD-4 is based on the
assumption that increased animal food consumption ought to be matched by
decreased beef consumption, mainly because the latter is very demanding of

biomass and of land. However, this is not an obvious starting point. There are strong voices claiming that ecological sustainable agriculture ought to build on more pasture and cattle production than today.[49] This is asserted in two 'futurological' scenarios made by the Swedish Environmental Protection Agency (SEPA),[50] called the 'road-winner' and the 'path-finder' scenarios respectively.

In terms of production, the 'road-winner scenario' shows some resemblance to scenario SD-4. Sustainability is sought by using fertilisers, pesticides and concentrated fodder (distributed with great precision), and high-yielding animals dominate the animal production. The 'path-finder scenario' is instead characterised by diversity with close links between crop rotation and animal food production. To a larger extent, animal food production is based on pasture. When comparing the two scenarios, SEPA concludes that both scenarios can obtain a fairly high degree of sustainability, but that they also have shortcomings. The road-winner scenario tends to diminish the areas of naturally enclosed pasture. The path-finding scenario hardly fulfils any of the demands of energy-crop production, reduction of carbon dioxide emissions and discharges of poisonous substances because most of all available land will be used for food production. Despite this, SEPA maintains that cattle production ought to take place mainly on pasture. For Sweden, with plenty of available land, this is perhaps a reasonable conclusion. Seen from a global perspective, however, the conclusion is less convincing. Still, nearly the same conclusions are also drawn in SEPA's global futures study, "Omvärlden år 2021" (SEPA 1997:4726). In that report, a global concentration of cattle production and a reduced production of chicken and pork are recommended.[51]

It is disputable whether pasture is more efficient than fodder production. It certainly depends on what is to be protected (physical land and rainforests or other resources such as enclosed pastureland). However, what is indisputable is that the demands for decreased beef consumption, as suggested in our scenario, is questionable and that an implementation of scenario SD-4 will be met with hesitation and disapproval from the powerful interests involved in global beef production (Rifkin 1992:93ff, 125-131). Furthermore, these interests can base their arguments on a large group of experts, who argue that increased beef production is more sustainable than a transition to pork and chicken.

(5) Steering the production. When we discussed competition for land, we concluded that fodder prices might advance when demand for animal food increases. This is a strong incentive for farmers to change production from e.g., vegetarian food, to fodder. Up to a certain level, such increases are required for scenario SD-4 to be realised. However, beyond that (indefinite) level, additional fodder production may cause scarcity in food of more vital importance. Furthermore, in reality, the competition for land is more complex. In Section 6.1.1, I pointed out the potential competition from the energy sector, and contended that such competition might advance food prices and cause additional starvation largely because of unequally distributed purchasing

power. From our point of view this means that if competition for land increases while scenario SD-4 is being realised, it will become necessary to manage national and global agriculture in such a way that the prime objectives of scenario SD-4 are ensured even if such management results in competition with more high-yielding demands within other sectors.

If the global population is to consume animal food at the consumption rate of the Western world, or at least at a much higher rate than today, international co-ordination of an unprecedented degree is implied mainly for two reasons. First, animal food must be produced where it is most favourable and resource efficient. Second, food will not necessarily be distributed to those who are paying the best price, but to those who need it the most, or are entitled to a certain amount of animal food. Also advances towards scenario realisation (or the Brundtland Commission's requirements for that matter) probably require significant international co-operation. A minimum requirement must be that everyone has sufficient food, even if vegetables constitute the major part. However, even such a significantly lowered ambition can be ensured only if the food flows are regulated or steered in one way or the other.

> *Summary:* Bearing in mind the political impact on, e.g., US and EU farmers, a political attempt to implement scenario SD-4 would certainly be met with strong resistance. Regardless of any contextual changes made around our scenario, the objectives of the scenario adamantly require powerful political steering and value priorities, where the welfare of people in developing countries is seen as having priority over Western world farmers.

6.2.4   Other Interests Affected by an Implementation of Scenario SD-4

Consumers and producers are perhaps the most obvious among the many interest groups affected by the transitions implied by scenario SD-4. Throughout Chapters 5 and 6 I have touched upon at least some of these, with interests linked to (1) tourism and aesthetics and (2) the protection of rainforests, biodiversity, and also future generations. Let me complete this chapter by also reflecting briefly on these groups.

(1) Tourism and aesthetics. The transition from cattle to pork and chicken implies comprehensive changes in how animal food is produced. It is no longer a matter of freely grazing animals, but of a production largely characterised as agricultural industry. Consequently, the landscape will also change. Much of today's 'vivid countryside' around the world will change to arable land where fodder production is the main business. For anyone who cares about the present use of land, or for whom it is perhaps even a livelihood, scenario SD-4 will come as a disappointment. However, for scenario SD-4 to be realised, the

wishes of these interest groups must be disregarded or at least given a lower priory.

(2) *Protection of rainforests, biodiversity* and consequently *future generations.* Even if it proves difficult to conclude that there is not enough land to realise scenario SD-4, I would still be of the opinion that if additional land is required, some of it may currently host rainforests (cf. Section 5.1.1). Thus, complete protection of those forests and the biodiversity found there cannot be offered. This implies that the interests of people living in those forests and all others concerned with preserving them may be set aside for the benefit of a scenario realisation. This also means that future generations may lose important resources as global biodiversity is diminished. The latter may sound paradoxical since one of the outspoken aims of scenario SD-4 is to preserve key resources for future generations. However, unless we believe that sustainable development will start working from one day to the next, some resources probably have to be sacrificed before any global balance becomes achievable. In fact, if scenario SD-4 is not realised, or not achieved under controlled conditions as implied in this study, even fewer resources will be left for future generations. This is either because people cannot afford to save resources for the future, or because short term profits 'force' landowners and other interests to exploit resources too quickly.[52]

Summary: A range of interests will be affected by an implementation of scenario SD-4, of which only a few can be considered unquestionable 'winners'. The scenario obviously implies a systematic ranking of interests, where priority must be given to those who are supposed to gain from the idea of sustainable development, who are first and foremost the world's poor population and future generations - precisely those with the least power to ensure that the scenario is implemented.

6.3 Conclusions

Table 6.2 Categories of challenge derived in Chapters 5 and 6

- *Global co-ordination and resource logistics in order to attain the quantum of animal food production assumed in scenario SD-4 with the least possible demand on resources.*

- *Production of technological development as well as adaptation of available technology to local conditions, aimed at achieving the required production as indicated in scenario SD-4.*

- *Transference and (re)distribution of both technology and social and economic means, globally, in order to attain the demands for a global welfare and efficient resource use.*

- *Priority given to rank certain interests and values before others, in order to fulfil scenario SD-4.*

Notes:

1 This is an example of the kind of problem that arises when I apply an 'astronaut-perspective' (cf. Chapter 2) on a discussion about goods, services or resources *sporadically distributed* across the globe. The total amount of potential resources is one thing, and the total amount of available resources quite another.

2 When comparing scenario SD-4 with today's figures, we find that the total amount of biomass produced on grazing land is reduced by about 40%. When comparing the BAU-scenario and scenario SD-4, we see that the former presupposes 300% more biomass produced on pasture land.

3 Cities are expanding on cultivatable land while new ones are arising. Large numbers of people are moving into cities thus leading to their growth and the use of cultivable land for purposes other than cultivation. Another problem, generally considered, is that urbanised people tend to adopt a 'city-diet', which is considerably more resource demanding than the diet typically found in the provinces. There are two main explanations for this. First, the city-diet is composed of far more animal food, and second, the resulting urbanised diet is much more wasteful (Popkin 1993). Infrastructure is another example, e.g., the global transportation sector is highly land demanding (Steen et. Al. 1997). In short, it competes for the world's useable land areas, and the more society is developed, and the larger the world population becomes, the more this competition will increase.

4 Their forecast of future competition is based on and calculated for global wheat production, but the same way of reasoning ought to be valid also for the whole agricultural sector.

5 I.e., the 'independent' part of the target of social and economic development in the Brundtland Commission's report (cf. Sections 4.1-4.2)

6 This discussion is one of principle. It can be applied to present conditions too, i.e., what may happen to people living in countries already economically 'behind', if current global economic and development trends in animal food consumption continue (read the BAU-scenario).

7 Between countries, this may not be the case, and furthermore, this kind of reasoning is not valid for drinking water.

8 Cf. Table 6.1. Several countries are currently completely dependent on imports.

9 See De Soto (2000) for an illuminating analysis of what is needed for poor (and former communist) countries to generate capital and financial resources on their own. What is principally missing is legally enforceable property rights, something we in the Western world take for granted.

10 Let us take China as an example. China's economic growth is in absolute terms among the largest in the world today. The population is enormous. Furthermore, even if China is a geographically large country, it is forced to import large quantities of grain. Because of its relative wealth, China can afford such imports even during years when global grain surpluses are small (e.g., the year of 1994). i.e., even if the price increases, China can afford to maintain local demand through imports. This is not the case for many other countries. If the grain price increases, then many marginalised people cannot afford to buy enough food. For many reasons, the need for grain imports increases in China every year. First, animal food consumption is steadily increasing as a consequence of the constantly improving economy (Brown 1995), a development that will result in an even larger need for imports in the future. Second, Chinese industry is growing dramatically, leading to an increased demand for water (which is challenging the already relatively scarce access to water) (cf. Brown & Halweil 1998; Engi 1998; Brown 1996)

11 At least in those cases where the self-sufficient countries manage to generate surpluses that can be sold on the international market and where this market has responded to the shortage by price increases (cf. Brown & Halweil 1998).

12 Not a development where prices are increasing (since an increased demand reasonably increases the prices) but rather a *development where some are left without any food* because they cannot afford to buy it.

13 In the longer run, however, also the use of fertilisers and land must become more and more efficient for those resources to last for the future.

14 This figure is disputable. According to the World Health Organisation (WHO), 1000 m^3 of water per person per year is considered to be the minimum level below which most countries are likely to experience chronic shortage on a scale will impedes development and harms human health (Cunningham & Saigo 2001:433).

15 For example, some countries with extremely low water figures per capita, such as Egypt, do not need to import as much grain as, e.g., Oman, which has about 30 times as much water per capita. This shows that import dependency is not exclusively a matter of water access. Other conditions for growing must exist as well. For example, if a country is devoid of cultivatable land, then it also becomes import dependent. Other countries are located at such altitudes, or experience severe climatic conditions, that only certain crops can be grown. If these crops are not an integral part of the human diet, then imports must be used.

16 It is expected to more than *triple* in large areas of Africa and Asia until the year 2050 (FAO 1990).

17 By the year 2025, another ten African countries are expected to be added to the list. The same is the case for India, Pakistan and several other Asian states. According to current population forecasts (PRB 1995), the total number of people living with severe

water stress (in Africa, Asia and the Middle East) will increase more than sixfold from today's 470 million to about 3 billion by the year 2025 (Postel 1998:635).

18 These figures are kept down by our scenario assumptions such as increased technological development.

19 It is often maintained that access to water (and accordingly the price of water) is the major mechanism pushing development of more efficient water technology. "The single most important step here is to begin charging the full cost of supplying water, abandoning the subsidies that lead to wasteful use." (Brown 1995:124). Such a course of action can certainly lead to a more efficient use of water. At the same time, even if a market is created for water, it cannot (by itself) realise this part of the scenario. Considerable economic support from rich to poor is probably required to avoid either unsustainable use of water, or to avoid some people being excluded from enjoying water.

20 The most common way to distribute a good is through a market, i.e., distribution according to merit or purchasing power. As we saw in Chapter 5 there is not yet a working market or pricing mechanism for water for agricultural purposes. Thus, to be able to distribute water with any of the methods described below under supervision of a market mechanism, the first thing that must take place is to establish such a market. In this particular case, however, we might mistrust the market's capacity. If we return to the information gained from reading *Our Common Future*, we are forced to view 'access to water' in a way that makes no sense if we proceed from a market situation. The demand for social and economic sustainability refers to *ensured* needs and abilities—at least for our most basic goods in life (and water must reasonably be considered one of them). Correspondingly, scenario SD-4 is (in theory) supposed to illustrate a situation where needed water *is* ensured for everyone. However, the market does not distribute it according to need. What kind of market would that be? Thus, to be able to use any of the methods described below in order to meet human needs, we must move away from the market as the primary distribution mechanism. If we do that, then all three redistribution methods are plausible and workable—but they still generate very difficult questions when it comes to implementation.

21 Furthermore, redistribution of grain may have side effects such as relocation of labour.

22 See Alvstam & Jordan (1997) for an illuminating discussion.

23 However, whether water shortage *is* a major cause of conflicts is disputable. Some scholars instead maintain that scarcity rather tends to lead to increased *co-operation*, and prospective conflicts are only seen around the negotiation table: "In this context 'co-operation' should not be defined narrowly as mere absence of conflict. It should refer to a situation where conflicts are settled through negotiations and by political means, rather than through the use of armed force." (Rönnfeldt 1997a:77). Those involved realise that they gain more from mutual efforts to find an agreeable solution—even if it means that certain sacrifices have to be made (Stålgren & Swain 1998; Rönnfeldt 1997b; Dudney 1990). This line of thinking links up with *CPR-theory* and the range of prospects for creating *effective regimes* (Ostrom 1990; Ostrom et al. 1994). The aim of such regimes is to manage a *common resource*, e.g., a river or a lake, such that all interests involved can utilise the resource without causing any appreciable long term harm. The projects Ostrom studied were, however, all local. Thus, whether the CPR-logic is applicable on a national and international level, as in our case, is yet unexplored (Ostrom et al. 1999). If we join this school of thought instead, arguing that water scarcity can lead to co-operation, then less external support and involvement *might* be needed. Mutual efforts to be economical with the shared water resources then reduce the costs needed for

advanced irrigation and transportation systems, while at the same time making sure that each and every one is ensured a sufficient amount of water. Even if the introduction of such regimes may not reduce international involvement completely, it can perhaps be kept to a minimum. For example, even if support is required for meeting the *initial costs*, the organisation and maintenance of the system can be managed locally.

24 Compare, however, this reasoning with De Soto's (2000) analysis in which he argues that the reason why people are poor and remain poor in the developing and less developed world is not because they lack markets or entries to the markets, but rather because of absence of appropriate institutions. Without being able to show on (a legitimate and official) paper that you own the resources (and savings) you have at your disposal, these resources cannot be transformed into capital, but instead remains "dead capital" (2000:30ff).

25 An increased demand (in this case from a world population of 9.4 billion people) must be met by highly improved production.

26 Cf. the literature on "collective action" (e.g., Olson 1965). There are (good) reasons for individuals not to change their behaviour, but to take a 'free ride' on the efforts of others. This logic has a deceptive likeness with Hardin's (1968) "Tragedy of the Commons" (cf. Section 1.1.1) in that rational individual decisions may lead to collectively bad outcomes—which of course affects the free rider as well. Also see Ostrom (1990) on how equally rational individuals, collectively, can overcome this dilemma.

27 Riks-SOM 1997 (SOM-institutet, Gothenburg University).

28 We should keep in mind that our diet may change vountarily, not the least for health reasons. While this book was being written, the BSE disease was raging in Europe. If such diseases continue, then demand for animal food may decrease. Another health related reason is that too much animal food has been shown to be *unhealthy*. For a long time, dieticians and health medicine practitioners have warned of the damages and costs arising from excessive animal consumption in the developed world. Studies show that people in industrialised countries consume up to 50% more animal food than is considered healthy. In this context beef and other products from cattle are considered far more damaging than lighter meat such as chicken and pork (Engelhart & Hagman 1998; Popkin 1993:138f). The corresponding figure for Sweden is about 40% (SEPA 1996:27). If these warnings gain increased support and become publicly accepted, then the dietary changes assumed in scenario SD-4 might be more easily and (even) voluntarily implemented. Furthermore, if health in the Western world turns out to be generally improved because of such changes, then people in other parts of the world may start aspiring to less than the 30% indicated in Chapter 4, and also vary their animal food intake. Some studies indicate that people do *have* a certain desire to change their diet towards less meat. In one study, the Swedish National Food Administration (1996) investigated whether Swedish citizens were willing to change their habits towards a more healthy diet. More than 30% answered 'yes, absolutely', and an additional 35% answered 'yes, perhaps'. Between 1961 and 1988 the total per capita intake of animal food decreased from 29% to 23% in Norway (Milio 1991). This reduction is mainly explained by the conscious food politics and the high number of policies simultaneously carried out by the Norwegian government (Milio 1990). The fact that people may be harmed by excessive animal food consumption may thus facilitate a realisation of the dietary changes assumed in scenario SD-4. It is interesting that this environmentally favourable adjustment would then take place not because of any global resource scarcity, or of solidarity, but rather because people care about themselves (cf. Bender 1994).

29 On the other hand, this can be compensated for by a more intense consumption of chicken.

30 Fjaestad & Ohlsson (1997) make greater distinctions. When studying attitudes to biotechnology, they distinguish among several different groups dividing them on a five-grade scale from 'most positive' to 'least positive'. People in Spain, Portugal, Greece and Finland are most positive, while people in Austria are least positive.

31 This is, by the way, the only application Swedes can (partly) support.

32 However, biotechnology applied to animals receives a degree of support *if it is used for medical purposes* (Frewer 1997:140 my italics; also see Sparks et al. 1995).

33 They have conducted an extensive survey covering "most of all available research" done in this field.

34 Cf. also the discussion we had about biotechnology in Chapter 5 and the contributions of Morris & Bate 1999 (esp. Wilson, Hillman & Robinson [1999] who argue that the advantages of using biotechnology widely exceed the detrimental effects and risks; "Arguments against GMOs offer little scientific evidence, relying on shock and alarm to carry their case" [1999:59]).

35 Recall that many of the objections I present here apply to several non-biotechnological production methods already used today. E.g., many methods to produce animal food can be questioned for moral reasons. If viewing the food sector as almost a mechanical system without a second moral thought, then cows, chickens and pigs tend to become production machines. "They are reduced to their functions, which we are trying to maximise." (Schroten 1997:152) Evidently, values such as *efficiency*, *ecology* and *ethics* tend to conflict with each other here. To produce as much animal food as implied in scenario SD-4 without damaging the *environment* too much, it is important that the production is highly *efficient*. Included in the endeavours to increase efficiency is the objective of animals yielding the greatest possible return with the least possible use of resources. Thus, we have good reason to ask if the potential conflicts among efficiency, ecology and ethics may obstruct a realisation of our scenario. Obviously, the image of the future provided by the scenario implies significant changes to the living conditions of animals. Furthermore, if these changes are for the worse, while animals continue receiving stronger and stronger legal protection, then the political prospects of realising the scenario are probably circumscribed. The ethical-ecological-efficiency discussion becomes yet more complicated if we include biotechnology.

36 Cf. the discussion in Kungl. Skogs- och RSAAF (1997) where it is said that "It can never be in the interest of any pig to become something else than a pig".

37 "../..religions such as Judaism and Islam that stress dietary codes will have special questions about acceptability of transgenic foods." (Thompson 1997).

38 A control that may become difficult if, for example, a gene from a pig is transplanted into a crop to give it new and for certain purposes better qualities, and this modified crop is eventually mixed with other crops.

39 There are already examples of such mixing. American farmers started to grow genetically modified soya beans in 1996. In the worldwide trade with American soya, genetically modified beans are often mixed with non-modified ones. The only way to find out if a certain soya-based product contains modified raw material is to know the full history of the finished product, since it is practically impossible to find traces of the modified gene in e.g., soya-oil or lecithin (RSAAF 1997).

40 Cf. Rifkin 1998:41ff

41 For example because such crops are (in one way or another) better *suited*, and thus have a higher propensity for survival. Another reason is that genetically rich vegetation

may be cut to clear land for growing genetically modified crops instead (Frisvold & Condor 1998). The uncertainty appears to be comprehensive, e.g: "will fishes with extra growth-genes become a threat to marine biological diversity by crowding out wild salmon?" (RSAAF 1997:11). An uncontrolled application of biotechnology and products based on such technology *risks* being contrary to the signed convention.

42 "Naturally occurring plants and animals are not considered patentable inventions" (Frisvold & Condon 1998:552).

43 The term 'biopiracy' goes back a long way and principally refers to injustices connected to the fact that private interests have free access to the natural gene carriers (the plants) while they can charge for 'elite variants' descended from the original carrier. Since farmers in developing countries often have spent thousands of years preserving and developing particularly suited species, these farmers are of the opinion that they have contributed to the genesis of the attractive genes (cf. Shiva 1998, Mooney 1993, Brush 1992) and accordingly ought to have the right to share the profits.

44 Or they have to lower their prices, something that may not be possible because of large investments made earlier.

45 Cf. Rifkin's (1992) discussion on the impact and power of European and US meat producers.

46 Admittedly, future *production* will look completely different to that of the average farmer of today.

47 An increased demand (in this case of a world population of 9.4 billion people) must be met by highly improved production.

48 They would probably be compensated for such redistribution. Yet, it can be argued that it would limit their freedom of choice.

49 As I intimated earlier in this chapter, the attitude towards beef and cattle production is often quite opposite to the one we proceed from in this study, i.e., it is ecologically sounder to produce cattle and other ruminant animals, than pork and chicken. "Meat from cattle and lamb, mainly breeding on non-fertilised natural enclosed pasture-land demands less contribution of energy to fodder and breeding, compared with meat coming from grain-eating animals such as pork." (SEPA 1996:29 *my translation).* This view is interesting if we view it from our own point of departure (namely that there might be non-agricultural future competition for land) and the kind of cattle production SEPA is advocating is probably very land demanding.

50 The two reports 'Omvärlden år 2021' (The World Around Us in the year 2021) (1997a) and "Det framtida jordbruket" (The Future Agriculture) (1997e) are both integral parts of the agency's great future study called 'Sverige år 2021' (Sweden in 2021).

51 Worth noticing is that this goal is to be realised while at the same time global forest production ought to increase (in order to absorb 20% more carbon dioxide globally than today). How these two (competing, we have learned) goals are to be practically feasible is not discussed in the report.

52 I do not wish to adopt a moral dimension to this discussion. Yet, what has been said so far may intimate a future where practically everyone is less well off than they are today. Admittedly, the most obvious 'winners' by a scenario realisation seem to be the world's poor and possibly also future generations while all the rest of us appear to end up as losers. However, one should not forget that scenario SD-4 implies a fabulous market where people in general enjoy fairly strong purchasing power, indicating both great economic profits and consequently also welfare in the future. Furthermore, a fairly sound global environment and a decent living standard *in general* may also be considered a rather attractive reward worth striving for.

Chapter 7

Implied Policies

Having identified changes and challenges that society has to manage to achieve the goals expressed in scenario SD-4, I can now develop the last piece needed to accomplish a type-four compatibility analysis, which is to discuss the *policies* required for the social changes to take place. Even if much of what I develop here has been touched upon in the two previous chapters, it is only when the challenges are specified that I can outline the consequential policies. Certainly, I cannot tell *exactly* what specific *legislation*, *taxes*, *subsidies*, and *information* are presupposed by scenario SD-4. What measures to select and apply in practise is largely a *political matter*. Furthermore, it is beyond my scope to establish the 'appropriate' or 'desirable' measures. My objectives are thus rather modest: I emphasise what I perceive to be the most likely *direction* of policies needed to meet the challenges implied in scenario SD-4.

7.1   Global Co-ordination and Resource Logistics

7.1.1   Land Use

As shown in Chapter 5, several things are required to bring about optimal use of every individual unit of land. First, countries must delineate their individual land-use and co-ordinate it according to productivity. Second, this also means that countries must accept that present land uses may have to be changed into more productive ones not only in the short run, but also in the long term. All this must be done to make sure that the greatest possible global yield is guaranteed, using the least amount of land. If not, the relatively small need for extra land resources indicated in scenario SD-4 will not be reached. Third, global co-ordination furthermore implies that co-ordination has to take place not only within countries, but most likely also among them.[1]

Implied policy: Governmentally imposed or encouraged co-ordination of global land use on a national as well as on international level.

7.1.2 Water Use

With a growing world population, global use of water will have to be organised more effectively than today. Increases in animal food production indicated in the scenario demands not only land for forage, but also water (and land) for cattle food. There are still relatively large areas of land theoretically available for this. However, several countries in the world suffer from water shortage, and the number increases every year (cf. esp. Sections 6.1.3 and 6.1.4). Many of the countries most exposed to water shortage are found in the developing world. Without access to additional water, or to methods of utilising it more efficiently, the amount of water needed for food production will not be met. Furthermore, a prospective increase in such production may lead to an increased shortage of household water. Thus, also the shortage of water infers that a global realisation of scenario SD-4 presupposes global co-ordination of water use.

Implied policy: Governmentally initiated or encouraged co-ordination of the global use of water, ranging from a national to an international level.

7.1.3 Use of Phosphorus

Although phosphorus in not a scarce resource in urgent need of being conserved *per se*, this study shows that there is still every reason to be cautious about its use. There are large amounts of phosphorus in the Earth's crust, but *pure* phosphorus is relatively rare. In addition, cheap phosphorus is difficult to separate from the deadly toxic *cadmium* that often goes along with it. If poor countries are to stop using that cheaper and perilous fertiliser to increase their agricultural production, there is a need for phosphorus distribution according to efficiency rather than to price or purchasing power, which may prove to be a formidable challenge.

Also, using phosphorus is problematic. Leakage from the agricultural industry leads to increasing eutrophication of lakes and coastal zones, with negative effects on marine plant life and fishery. Moreover, leakage of phosphorus is often an international phenomenon affecting neighbouring countries. Both these factors provide reasons for (1) being cautious with the use of phosphorus and (2) finding ways to use it globally without risking any damage to human beings or other life forms.

Implied policy: Governmentally initiated co-ordination and sanctioned control systems both within and among countries to extract pure phosphorus in order to avoid the use of poisonous bi-products, to use phosphorus efficiently and to distribute it *not* according to purchasing power, but according to where it is required the most (in order to fulfil the productivity goals implied in scenario SD-4).

7.1.4 Food Logistics

Under scenario SD-4, it is not only natural resources that must be co-ordinated, but also commodities at the end of the production chain. It is unlikely that all countries will be self-sufficient in food production. In many countries only a limited range of foods can be produced, either because of climatic circumstances, or because of the size of the population in relation to the amount of necessary resources like land and water. For example, one of the largest countries in the world, China, has to import a large amount of food each year. Without this import, the Chinese people would perhaps not starve but their opportunities to choose a varied diet would certainly diminish. To offer people a relatively rich diet on a global scale, including a daily intake of 30% animal food, requires that products are distributed to where they are wanted/needed, which does not necessarily coincide with where they fetch the best price if we see to scenario SD-4.

Implied policy: Free trade on its own does not seem to be enough in order to distribute globally produced food in line with the requirements suggested by the Brundtland Commission. For such distribution to happen, additional (inter) governmental support and initiatives are required to make sure that food actually reaches groups with weak or perhaps even no purchasing power.

7.2   Technological Development

This paragraph refers more to the promotion than to the invention of new technology, e.g., by offering a sound business environment. In Chapter 5.2 we discussed several demands for more efficient techniques. We also found that these techniques are required especially in poor regions of the world if scenario SD-4 is to be realised. Although a market system is said to be the ideal environment for the invention of new technology, we concluded that it is difficult to imagine a global spread of these techniques if there is not enough global purchasing power. This is because we cannot expect these technologies to be developed and distributed unless there are economic benefits to be reaped. Since the necessary purchasing power often does not exist, we concluded that the market system alone may not be able to propel, and certainly not safeguard, adequate development and a global spread of these techniques. Scenario SD-4 requires development of partly new technologies and adaptation of existing technologies to local circumstances. If the locals cannot afford to pay for it, someone else must cover the cost of implementation if the scenario is to be realised. This appears to hold for each of the three cases of water, phosphorus and biotechnology.

7.2.1   Water

In Chapter 5, I gave several examples of where governmental support may become required. First, we have the problem of *transporting water*. Often this takes place by open canals. It is not difficult to calculate the losses arising from such methods in general, and in warmer countries in particular. Pipelines are the most obvious solution, but this technology is costly, particularly for an underdeveloped farming community. Second, there is the problem of *storing water*. Many regions of the world experience irregular precipitation. To get a steady supply of water for growing crops, surplus water must be stored and distributed appropriately throughout the year, as well as from year to year. The cheapest and most inefficient method (but today the most common one) is to store surplus water in open basins, exposed to seepage and evaporation.

Third, there is the issue of *recycling water*. There is competition for the use of water among households, agriculture and industry. Fresh water is used by businesses that do not require it, and much water could be re-used if kept within closed systems. To rely on natural circulation in regions with severe water scarcity is insufficient if biomass production is to be expanded as implied in scenario SD-4. Recycling water often requires expensive constructions. Fourth, *optimisation* of water is also demanded, because water is not only lost through evaporation during transportation, but also in irrigation. Several often highly advanced systems for efficient irrigation are available, but they are all associated with large investment costs. If scenario SD-4 is to be realised, these costs have to be subsidised for those who could otherwise not afford them.

Implied policy: Unless support is given on a voluntary basis by the rich water users or by other wealthy groups, governments have to initiate support for technological development within the water area. Furthermore, adaptation and distribution of such technology are needed, not only domestically but also internationally.

7.2.2   Phosphorus

To expand global biomass production in the way we assumed in scenario SD-4 without bursting the physical limits for land, implies that considerable amounts of fertiliser must be added to many existing areas of cultivated land. Phosphorus, one of the main sources for artificial fertilisation, is not scarce, but much of it contains large amounts of toxic cadmium and thus requires purification. Purified phosphorus is expensive and is often not affordable by the poor. To reach the scenario goal without poisoning people who cannot afford to buy purified fertilisers, cheap techniques for purification have to be developed. Also, phosphorus recycling will be needed since extensive use tends to cause environmental damage like eutrophication. To date no comprehensive solution is known.

Implied policy: Support for, and if required, initiation of the development of technology and methods to diminish eutrophication and for purifying phosphorus, both nationally and internationally.

7.2.3 Biotechnology for Animal as well as Crop Production

When examining scenario SD-4 we found reasons to assume that the required volumes of animal food can only be attained with methods that include biotechnology. The ethical challenges associated with this scenario will be discussed later. Here I will only discuss the arguments based on efficiency. First, the biomass demand inferred in scenario SD-4 requires large volumes of water and phosphorus, and consequently requires considerable technological development. With biotechnology, however, the mechanical challenges *may* be less demanding since it seems to be possible to improve the intake of nourishment and water in many crops.

Second, by improving the productivity of crops, less land is required to meet the biomass demand. The same holds for genetically modified animals, in the sense that they are able to convert/turn over crops more efficiently. It has been argued that such modification may come to decrease the demand in *every* preceding stage—at least if we view the food sector as a closed biophysical system. Most biotechnological research and development takes place in the industrialised world, while many of the benefits from it may come to be most significant when applied in the poor world. Thus, it seems important that such development is encouraged, even if the benefits from it may not always be expressed monetarily.

Implied policy: Support for biotechnological research, which offers a favourable environment for production, but also *ensures* that the products of the technology reach the required groups identified in scenario SD-4.

7.3 Transferring and (re)Distribution

I now proceed to policies implied by the socio-economic challenges derived in Chapter 6. First, I discuss the economic and distributional challenges. I argue that active governmental involvement is required to manage most of these challenges globally, whether we speak of (1) financing the initial costs of technological development, (2) transferring technology or (3) redistributing economic and social development. A rather interesting exception concerns (4) changes to import duty and subvention policies.

7.3.1 Take the Initial Costs

The policies discussed here resemble those discussed in Section 7.2.3 on biotechnology. A new technology is always more expensive to the consumer in the initial stage of a product's lifecycle. This means that those who can afford the early expensive versions subsidise those who need the technology, but cannot afford it at the initial stage. The same reasoning is applicable in the case of scenario SD-4. For example, new irrigation technology is expensive, and can perhaps not be applied globally without economic support of some kind. The rates of distribution will increase as the price decreases. This logic is not controversial in it self, but becomes problematic when a particular technology has to be *specifically designed* for poor regions where there is an urgent need for such technology. This also holds if the current technology is not *desirable* for those who can afford to cover the initial costs. For example, adaptation to local circumstances may be very expensive and may not be covered by initial costs. Another relevant example is biotechnology.[2]

Implied policy: If the market does not absorb the initial costs, this can, and has to be done by governmental policies and measures.

7.3.2 Transferring Technology

If countries are in urgent need of, but are not able to pay for, the best available irrigation technology, then this technology must become accessible anyway in order to realise scenario SD-4. This situation indicates transferring or subsidising technology. The question is *who will pay for it*? In this book (which of course could be far more detailed) the answer has been 'those who can afford it'. 'Those who are obliged' is an alternative, but would probably be difficult to bring about successfully[3] (that is not to say that it would be politically much easier to make those who can afford it pay).

Implied policy: Both points of departure imply (or presuppose) distribution of technology, or the economic means with which to finance the required technology. With the global achievement of scenario SD-4, this distribution will quite likely be required not only domestically but also internationally.

7.3.3 (Re)Distribution

One of the greatest political challenges comes from the distributional demands indicated in scenario SD-4. This demand for distribution of social and economic means is motivated by two partly different goals: *efficiency* and *social justice*. Even if it is argued that because of their low living standard, people in developing countries contribute less to environmental degradation (which is assumed to be a result of over-consumption rather than inefficient resource use), it is equally reasonable to argue the other way.[4] People in poor regions are desperate and forced to use resources on a day-to-day basis, without any environmental or long-term considerations. Furthermore, they are incapable of financing the efficiency measures necessary for sustainable production methods. The more people who live under such conditions, the harder the strains on the environment.

In the scenario analyses I pointed to several areas where new technology (read increased efficiency) is required, but where payment most likely must come from others than the direct beneficiaries of that technology. This is of course valid on the supply side (selection of technology), but actually also on the demand side (selection of product). By this I mean that if people lack a decent standard of living, there is always a risk that they will be forced to continue choosing products produced with cheap but environmentally unfriendly technology.

It might be tempting to *dismiss* the demand for social and economic development in scenario SD-4. Indeed there are probably strong reasons for doing so. It can be considered unrealistic, unattainable, or even an unfounded requirement (for example because we believe that the ecological parts of the Brundtland Commission's report, call it *ecological sustainability,* is the only thing that really counts). We then, however, disregard that the demand for social and economic development is also imposed by the objective of *social justice* (cf. Section 4.2).

Social and economic development is at the core of the Brundtland Commission's report. Thus, besides the fact that social and economic development may be important in order to solve environmental problems and reach sustainability, according to the commission, it is also a goal in itself. We can allow ourselves to separate social and economic sustainability from a corresponding ecological one (cf. discussion in Dobson 1998:3-11), but there is no way we can come around the demand for global social and economic development *per se.* Whether we view them as interdependent, or as two separate goals, a scenario based on the report has to pay attention to this demand. In our analysis of scenario SD-4, this attention results in a frequently repeated demand for redistribution of economic, social and technological means to certain regions of the world. This is because they (1) lack purchasing power to invest in efficient technology, (2) are devoid of a living standard which allows for selecting products being produced with such technology or (3) lack the economic and social means to enjoy a decent and worthy life.

Implied policy: Both the demand for social and economic development, and for more efficient technology, point in the same direction: a demand for *governmentally initiated redistribution* of the means required to create stability and improvements in areas of need. Examples referred to in Chapters 5 and 6 are food, financial resources, education, but also, and not least important, the means required to create and support appropriate institutions with which to manage and generate social goods, capital and financial resources.[5] Obviously this demand is not only a national or domestic matter, but to a considerable degree of international and global concern, i.e., one of border-crossing welfare measures.

7.3.4   Import Duty and Subvention Policy

Our discussions in Sections 6.1.2 and 6.2.3 imply that *deregulation* of the food market may facilitate greater opportunities for food production in developing countries. This could make it easier for them to procure funds with which to invest in more efficient agricultural technology. Today, many countries are practising highly sophisticated methods in order to secure their domestic agricultural sectors. A dismantling of EU's present agriculture policy would thus hit the sector significantly. From a strict market perspective, deregulation is probably desirable. From a political perspective where agricultural interests need to be considered, such a policy is extremely challenging—not the least if it threatens the whole of a sector. It should be added that any suggested interference in the food market is highly controversial.[6]

Implied policy: Provided that scenario SD-4 requires a deregulation of the food sector in order for the developing world to get the capital needed to develop their food production, one important implication is that governments in developed countries withdraw from import duties and from subsidising their agricultural sectors in the food market.

7.4   Giving Priority to, and Ranking Interests and Values

Sustainable development has often been understood as striking a balance between economy and ecology. Social and economic development does not go beyond ecological limits, and does not jeopardise the possibilities that future generations can meet their needs. There is, however, one further question: What *consequences* would attempts to implement sustainable development have, not only in specific terms of political action but also in how such action would affect different interests? We discussed the possible effects for some interests in Chapter 6.2.

Among 'ecological modernists' it is popular to think of sustainability in terms of 'win-win solutions'. It is questionable how realistic that conception is when we view sustainability as a global and intra-generational project.[7] According to our discussions in Chapter 6.2, it appears difficult to implement the requirements imposed by scenario SD-4 without being forced to give priority to certain interests before others, presumably leaving some groups less well off than before. Even bringing up the most obvious interests affected by a realisation of scenario SD-4 is enough to point to the principal conflicts of interest that a realisation of scenario SD-4 would engender.

7.4.1   *The Consumers*

There is always the possibility that individuals will change their attitudes, customs and thus their behaviour *voluntarily*. That is not to say that there will actually be changes in people's diet in the near future. There seems to be a lack of general willingness to change diet in a direction favourable from a sustainability perspective.[8] Individual freedom of choice is challenging both the physical environment and the rest of the world's possibilities to eat more animal food, and in the worst case, *to eat at all* (cf. Chapter 6.1.1-6.1.2) We did assume a certain change in diet, however, insofar that some sort of animal food is substituted for beef. We assumed, perhaps incorrectly, that this could take place using methods such as information rather than legitimate political force. Health information could play an important role in such a dietary transition. The present intake of animal food in the Western world is larger than dieticians generally recommend (about 50% more). If more coercion is required, like taxes or even rationing, then little choice is left for individuals. On the other hand, if a certain level of global animal food consumption is to be ensured, and everyone is to have the opportunity to eat an equal amount of animal food, then some use of force is presumably required.[9]

Implied policy: Unless individuals change their diets voluntarily and 'potential animal food consumers'[10] adapt their increased animal food intake in line with the proportions assumed in scenario SD-4, then governmental involvement and political steering is required, according to the scenario analysis. It is impossible to establish the degree of force required.

7.4.2 Interests Linked to Biotechnology

Today biotechnology is an explosive issue. The general public is apparently critical of such research and campaigning against biotechnology is common, particularly in the Western world. In Chapter 6, I presented several (ethical and biological) arguments raised against biotechnology. On the other hand, if world food production does not become radically more efficient, enormous land areas must be exploited in order to fulfil the future demand for food implied in scenario SD-4. Certainly there are other business interests such as energy, infrastructure, urbanisation and tourism that also require land, which increases the demand for land even more.

In scenario SD-4 some elements of biotechnology are taken for granted, since it would otherwise not be possible to reach the production numbers indicated in the scenario. This is especially so if no more land area than estimated in scenario SD-4 is to be exploited. Now, this issue requires that priorities are made no matter what choice is made. The ethical problems with biotechnology and its threats to sustainable development (in biological and physical respects) should be weighed against its potential for sustainable development (in social and economic respects). Scenario SD-4, however, points in an unequivocal direction.

Implied policy: Measures are required that promote biotechnological research (and a global distribution of developed products), rather than interests that are against such technology, or may come to suffer from it. If governments decide to follow the will of the public, not by prohibiting biotechnological research but by making sure that as few as possible of the fears regarding biotechnology ever occur, then regulation is still needed; not against the public, however, but against the powerful corporations that are developing much of such technology today.

7.4.3   The Producers

Scenario SD-4 requires changes in current global agricultural practises. The transition from grazing to crop production is required whether farmers like it or not.[11] This creates perhaps a less desirable image of the future for them. If the demand for animal food rises as indicated in scenario SD-4, then this transition might take place without governmental involvement. The increased demand for animal food increases the price of crops for fodder, which is a strong incentive for farmers to change their business. Still, we cannot exclude the possible use of some kind of politically imposed *force*—if necessary—to *make sure* that the outcome in scenario SD-4 is realised.

Another challenge to (some) producers is the possible deregulation of the food market discussed in the previous section. In order for Third World farmers to be able to produce the amount of biomass indicated in the scenario, economic support might be needed to make their production as efficient as possible. Most likely, however, external subsidies are neither enough, nor desirable. In order not to place those farmers in a never-ending dependence on economic support from the rich world, efforts to create a natural market must be made. As we saw earlier, an obvious way of doing this would be to deregulate the international food market. This may, however, turn out to be quite problematic and also politically unpopular among, e.g., EU and US farmers. Thus, old markets ought to be opened up to new actors to create domestic capital in order not to become dependent on the rich world, but also in order to create effectiveness in the long term. Besides these challenges, I also pointed to additional regulation and imposed dietary changes as plausible policies that may be required, although they affect producers negatively.

Implied policy: Unless achieved through the market or in combination with regulations, a governmentally initiated *transition* from grazing to crop production is required. This means to set some producers' interests before others, by making them change their business. A deregulation of the food market, redistribution of crops and food, and governmentally imposed dietary changes are other policies that may strike hard on certain producers while being favourable for other groups such as Third World farmers and future generations.

7.4.4   Aesthetics and Tourism

It is by now quite obvious that scenario SD-4 does not exactly provide us with an image where calves are freely grazing on enclosed pasturelands. The 'country-side idyll' must be changed if the scenario is to be implemented. One alternative, which we have already discussed several times, is an almost zero consumption of animal food. Against this, we can argue that to produce no animal food at all is inefficient, because there are areas that cannot be used for anything else. This is perhaps correct if the world is only appreciated for its capacity to produce food. However, the world provides other values that are threatened by such thinking. If we accept an expansion of animal food production with the argument that animal food is a necessary part of a complete diet, or if we argue that large areas of the world are not useful for anything else, then we are looking only at certain human desires.

There *are* other valuable applications of land. Sometimes they cannot be expressed in monetary terms, but may still be far too valuable to be lost. One such example is the aesthetic value of nature, or the *value of wilderness*. Although aesthetics may be difficult to price, other more industry-like activities may also suffer economically from such losses. Tourism is one example. To find equilibrium between different land-use interests is an arduous task, and priorities must be made. But the question is by whom they should be made and according to what criteria? As we know, the market has its own methods of dealing with this issue. The interest that pays best wins. If we turn to scenario SD-4, however, priority will be given to projects that safeguard the most satisfactory outcome as defined by the scenario. In our case that means that interests like aesthetics and tourism may have to be overturned.

Implied policy: National and international planning is required to make some interests and businesses representing more exclusive needs and wants, stand back for the benefit of others presumably representing more basic needs. This planning is a result of governmentally imposed policies rather than market forces.

7.4.5 Rain Forests and Biodiversity

As with aesthetics and tourism, the values of rain forests and biodiversity may become threatened by the increased demands for biomass expressed in scenario SD-4. Large areas of still untouched land are covered by rainforest. Continued expansion of uncontrolled animal food production will result in a reckless clearing of such forests, although this seems to occur regardless of scenario SD-4. When adding four billion people to the world population of today, more land will be required, whether we assume today's distribution of animal food or the one suggested in scenario SD-4. Furthermore, even if global economic development will not reach the growth assumptions made in the scenario, but stays at the average growth rate since the 1960s (approx. 1% per year), this growth will lead to the exploitation of additional areas of land.

The choice between forcing people to change their diet, and allowing a further decrease of rainforests and biodiversity is not straightforward. Still, if scenario SD-4 is to be realised, and we believe that an extensive encroachment on people's 'household preferences' is illegitimate, then there is only one answer. Some additional rainforest must be sacrificed for the benefit of a continued human consumption of animal food.

Implied policy: Scenario SD-4 implies policies that both allow for, and may even *support* an expansion of land use, at the expense of other values and interests.

7.4.6 Future Generations

Obviously several factors give us reason to reflect upon why and how society needs to be considerate to future generations. To reach a future balance in the food sector, which in itself would be favourable for future generations, large quantities of resources such as land, water, and phosphorus must be exploited. The faster the present generation transforms the foundations of the food sector in the direction of SD-4, the more resources and choices will be left for future generations. However, since the transition is so comprehensive, it will take a long time. Meanwhile large quantities of resources will be devastated. A far quicker method is to change the global diet. To do so by force would require a global authoritarian body for food policy, an idea that we cannot possibly assume will ever gain global political legitimacy. A milder and more attainable alternative is national policies mainly in the high consumption countries aimed at encouraging or forcing consumers to change their diet (cf. Section 7.4.1). To only rely on exhaustive change through free will is an even more attractive alternative, but would probably not at all be likely (cf. Section 6.2.1).

In scenario SD-4 we are therefore largely relying upon technological development. There are obvious potential negative effects for future generations that occur because we are trying to avoid resource outputs that are too extensive. Biotechnology is perhaps the best example. If we assume that the most likely centre for biotechnological development continues to be the Western world, a sceptic public there (cf. Section 7.4.2) might prevent this industry from developing techniques which, if subsidised and redistributed, could make life more endurable for people in other parts of the world. Perhaps this would help future generations, e.g., because the currently assumed negative effects from using these techniques would then not occur. On the other hand, if today's poor populations cannot afford a tolerable diet (read scenario SD-4) without having to abuse a wide range of natural resources, then also the *absence* of biotechnology might produce threats to future generations. Even if scenario SD-4 to a great extent is aimed at improving or ensuring tolerable conditions for future generations, this is difficult to do—and even to imagine—unless present generations enjoy a decent life.

Implied policy: Concerns for future generations are assumed in scenario SD-4. Paradoxically, for any such concern to be given, scenario SD-4 implies measures and policies that may affect future generations negatively. However, unless such measures are implemented, then future generations may be even less well off. Who is actually prioritised in this situation is difficult to tell. Rather, it seems as if sustainable development requires some sacrifices by people of today in order for people of tomorrow to live decent lives.

7.5 Conclusions

We can now summarise the implied policies. Table 7.1 should be read as follows. To the left are the challenges identified in Chapters 5 and 6. In the right column the outlined policies aimed at managing these challenges are shown. I bring these policies with me to Chapter 8. By now the analytical framework is fully operational.[12]

Table 7.1   Implied Policies

Specified challenges	Implied policies
Global co-ordination and resource logistics in order to attain the animal food production assumed in scenario SD-4 with the least possible demand on resources	National and international planning for organising the use and production of: • Land • Water • Phosphorous • Food
Production of technological development as well as adaptation of available technology to local conditions, aimed at achieving the production numbers indicated in scenario SD-4	Giving support to and implementing development of improved technology regarding: • Water • Phosphorous • Biotechnology
Global transferring and (re)distribution of both technology and social and economic mean, in order to attain the demands for global welfare and an efficient resource use	Transferring and redistribution of technology and social and economic means, which requires: • Acceptance of initial costs • Duty- and subvention policy • Redistribution of economic and social goods for social justice and efficiency
Allocation of priority to and ranking of certain interests and values, in order to fulfil scenario SD-4	Policies and decisions with potentially negative effects for interests such as: • The producers • The consumers • Aesthetics and tourism • Rain forests and biodiversity • Bio-ethics • Future generations

Notes:

1 I must admit that this, fairly simplistic 'solution' can be questioned. See for example Ostrom et al. (1999) who, when discussing how to deal with global commons, draw on experiences from studying local resource management arrangements, so called 'common-pool resources' (CPR). They argue that rather than the kind of resource 'socialism' (1999:278) I might be blamed for suggesting here, the particular CPR logic may be applicable to global issues as well. Perhaps the CPR logic would be more appropriate. That is not to say it is more applicable though, because to implement any such global regimes a range of challenges must be overcome, such as: what happens when the environmental problems are *scaled up* from local to global level, how to cope with *cultural diversity*, and *accelerating rates of change* (1999:281-282), i.e., largely the kinds of issues we have struggled with throughout Chapters 5 and 6.

2 Subsidising adaptation of technology may also be controversial if it is specific to local conditions in *other* countries.

3 For example, what criteria should have been used for picking out some groups as being more *obligated* than others?

4 Empirically, the relationship is rather that poor living conditions contribute significantly to environmental degradation, not per capita but in total. This is because resource use is highly inefficient, and since so many people in the world live under poor conditions, the total degredation is significant. Now, in the opposite situation (those living in excellent economic conditions), the reverse applies. Still, the environmental effects are severe. In rich countries, in general, production takes place with relatively efficient methods. Consumption, however, is so comprehensive and deep, that the total effects are disastrous. Thus, the environmental impact figure (for some commodities anyway) is negatively curved (i.e., the Environmental Kuznets curve); low income means less efficiency but low per capita consumption, while high income guarantees relatively efficient production, but also high consumption (cf. Ekins 2000:182-214 for a critical examination).

5 E.g., laws (particularly property rights), courts and lawyers (cf. DeSoto 2000).

6 Usually, governmental interference with the market is considered undesirable. It prevents the market from working perfectly, and it challenges the right to hold private property and enjoy the fruits of it. In Europe (among others), the food sector is principally privately owned (Lang 1999:202ff). In spite of that, to actually enjoy the fruits of the privately owned land seems to require subsidies, i.e., a significant interference with the market.

7 Cf. Langhelle (2000a:42-45 and 2000b) on this matter.

8 I.e., the 'collective action' problem.

9 What could legitimise such use of force? First, it may be legitimised because excess consumption is destroying the environment and its preservation is considered so fundamental that environmentally disturbing individual preferences can be disregarded. Second, such force could be legitimised because the basic needs of other individuals cannot be satisfied unless some people's excessive behaviours are changed. Here different interest groups are opposed to each other and some choice must be made. If this is the case, then sustainable development cannot be an evolution in which everyone is a winner.

10 I.e., those who are not yet, but according to scenario SD-4 will be practising the Western world diet in the future.

11 How to actually realise such a transition is another question, and only speculations can be offered on my part. However, economic control instruments and incentives may

be a winning approach. If farmers are forced to undertake this transition, for example by imposing taxes, some kind of compensation or liquidation support is a minimum, I suppose.

12 Cf., the introduction of Chapter 8.

Chapter 8

Compatibility Between Policies for Sustainable Development and Liberal-Democratic Core Values

In Chapter 7, I specified the policies required to realise scenario SD-4. Together with the compatibility criteria elaborated in Chapter 3, I can now turn to an analysis of whether these assumed state-imposed policies can be considered compatible with the policy restrictions that each of the two liberal-democratic models contains. In other words, it is time to go back to the analytical framework that was established in Chapter 2, although it is now fully operational and ready to be used for conducting a type-four compatibility analysis.

In Section 8.1 I examine the relationship between protective liberal democracy (PLD) and sustainable development by comparing the suggested policies with the policy restriction specified for the PLD ideal-type. I argue that practically none of these policies can be considered compatible with PLD, largely because scenario SD-4 calls for governmental action so comprehensive that it violates several of the key premises of PLD.

In Section 8.2 I compare sustainable development policies with the policy restriction specified for the developmental liberal-democratic ideal-type (DLD). I contend that, contrary to PLD, few of the policies *must* violate the DLD policy restriction. To firmly conclude so, we need information that goes beyond the scope of this study.

Table 8.1   The Operational Analytical Framework

Sustainable Development Policies	PLD Policy restriction	DLD Policy restriction
National and international planning for organising the use and production of: • **Land** • **Water** • **Phosphorus** • **Food**	(-) / (+)	(-) / (+)
Support and implementation of improved technology: • **Water** • **Phosphorous** • **Biotechnology**		
Transference and redistribution of technology and social and economic means require: • **Support of initial costs** • **Duty and subvention policy** • **Redistribution of economic and social goods for social justice and efficiency**		
Prioritising and ranking with potentially negative effects for: • **The producers** • **The consumers** • **Aesthetics and tourism interests** • **Rainforest and biodiversity** • **Future generations**		

Comment: On the left hand side of the table, the different policies are presented. On the two right columns of the table the two policy restrictions (PLD and DLD) are represented. In the forthcoming analysis, *incompatibility* will be represented by (-) and *compatibility* by (+). By the end of the chapter, the table will be complete (cf. Table 8.2).

In Section 8.3 I analyse the global aspects of the policies. Since the DLD ideal-type originally is *nation-state bound* and the policies have a global reach,

In Section 8.3 I analyse the global aspects of the policies. Since the DLD ideal-type originally is *nation-state bound* and the policies have a global reach, this calls for specific examination. To investigate if the global reach of the policies constitutes a violation of any of the DLD premises, I use two different approaches. First I adopt a Rawlsian 'veil of ignorance' perspective to see if there are differences in principle between the national and the global level of scenario SD-4. Second I re-examine the *DLD premises* to see if they presuppose a specifically limited geographical territory. *Finally* I challenge my conclusions from the two first tests by examining if the (asymmetrical) relationship between rights and obligations (O'Neill 2000) may constitute an argument for why the policies ought to be considered incompatible with DLD. In Section 8.4 I examine the intergenerational aspects of the policies. The role of future generations in democracy is not specified in my DLD model, thus to analyse this issue I have to use the help of other theorists. First I start from Rawls' (1972) saving principle and Wissenburg's (1998) restraint principle. Thereafter I add the idea of equal opportunities to the analysis. In Section 8.5 I summarise the conclusions of my study.

8.1 The Compatibility Between Sustainable Development Policies and Protective Liberal Democracy

I argued in Chapter 3 that the protective liberal-democratic ideal-type is founded on a set of premises which must not be violated if a policy is to be compatible with PLD according to our criterion. This criterion was formulated as shown below.

Figure 8.1 Compatibility Criterion Derived from the Idea of Protective Liberal Democracy

Premise 1.	The 'good life' is exclusively an individual matter.
Premise 2.	Individual liberty shall solely be understood negatively.
Premise 3.	The individual's right to hold and enjoy property is absolute.
Premise 4.	Equality only comprises legal and political standing.

Policy restriction: Thus, in order not to violate premise 1, the protective liberal-democratic state must be neutral in regard to an individual's life plans, and passive in all respects other than those presupposed in premises 2-4.

Compatibility criterion: Any sustainability policy presupposing a violation of this policy restriction is to be considered incompatible with the core values of protective liberal democracy.

8.1.1   National and International Planning and Organisation

In the analysis of scenario SD-4, we identified the requirement of policies aimed at co-ordinating the use of natural resources such as land and water. Another demand was to get a general view of and control over global food production in relation to where the food is produced. This implied a *global co-ordination system* to which all, or at least most, states in the world must conform. Its decisions would determine what is to be produced, where, by whom and how much, all in order to reach the desired outcome in scenario SD-4. Such co-ordination conflicts with most, but not necessarily all, of the PLD premises.

Let us begin with land. Most of the land already cultivated and available for cultivation is privately owned (Lang 1999:200-202). Under premise 3 it is solely a matter for the landowner to decide how his or her land ought to be managed. The state should *not* intervene under any circumstances. The co-ordination and regulations needed to attain scenario SD-4 would be an intrusion on an absolute right. A similar argument can be made about *phosphorus.*[1] Today's market-determined system that distributes phosphorus tends to over-exploit and extract toxic forms. This is against the objectives in scenario SD-4 and therefore requires preventive regulations. Such regulations, however, are in opposition to PLD premises 2 and 3, since they both reduce individuals' liberty and their right to enjoy their property.[2]

Water is an interesting exception, because water is mostly a *common* good— although more and more water assets are becoming privatised (not least to price them more adequately). To control and influence the use of water on a global scale would thus have greater prospects of implementation. Still, this is not enough for us to conclude that a co-operative and mutual control system aimed at satisfying the human needs for water would be an appropriate policy according to PLD. At least from the point of view of economic effectiveness, but most probably also from a philosophical PLD viewpoint, water ought to be privately owned. However, privatisation ruins the prospects for co-ordinating and controlling the uses of water, and thus for realising scenario SD-4. This is because such policies would violate premises 2 and 3 on negative liberty and on holding property. Thus, PLD recommends private ownership of water. If this privatisation where implemented, however, it follows from premise 3 that it ought to enjoy immunity from governmental involvement.

Co-operation, planning and steering measures for global food production are also contrary to the fundamental dogmas of PLD. Like all other commodities, food ought to be distributed according to demand and solvency, not according to 'need' or 'legitimate aspirations' as presupposed in scenario SD-4. The only legitimate governmental interference is that aimed at securing premises 2-4. This excludes co-operation or any regulation of food production, as well as any political control over the global extraction of water or phosphorus.

Conclusion: Policies such as global co-ordination and resource logistics cannot be considered compatible with PLD because they presuppose an *active state*. This, in various ways, violates premises 2 to 4, and thus also premise 1.

8.1.2   Support and Implementation of Improved Technology

In Chapter 7, I suggested that scenario SD-4 presupposes governmentally initiated promotion of technology within several areas. I concluded that unless support is given on a voluntary basis, then public policies supporting development, adaptation and diffusion of technology are required for scenario SD-4 to be realised. Furthermore, this demand is not only valid at the state level but also internationally. Second, we found a similar demand for governmental involvement in the development of technology and for methods aimed at diminishing eutrophication and for purifying phosphorus. A third area concerned the demand for additional research and the distribution of biotechnology. I concluded that governmental initiatives to provide a favourable environment for research and production appeared necessary. Fourth I pointed at a demand for policies *ensuring* that the products and the technology actually reach the groups that require them.

In principle, we can assume that the requests for new water and phosphorus technologies required by scenario SD-4 are legitimate from a PLD point of view, and even that the business environment provided by such a political system is favourable. A demand for new or adapted technology is not in opposition to any of the PLD premises 1 to 4. Thus, in this respect we have no reason to argue that the increases in technological development, which are required in scenario SD-4, would contradict the PLD model.

There is just one problem. We find little reason to believe that the required technology for water and phosphorus use will be developed and distributed to where it is required or needed, just because it *is* required (cf. Chapter 5.2). Besides a strong wish, factors such as *purchasing power* are important to attract real interest in any such development. As we have learned, purchasing power is often missing. This motivates governmental intervention, according to scenario SD-4 (cf. Sections 7.2 & 7.3.2). We found some different motives for state intervention in biotechnology (cf. Section 7.4.2). Although there are several factors of uncertainty connected to biotechnology—for example a sceptical public and the actual potential of this technology—that may moderate a continued development in a free market, these factors should not be allowed to prevent progress in such research. Obviously this calls for governmental interference in the market.

If we now examine our established policy restrictions and premises, none of the suggested governmental policies can be interpreted as examples of what the PLD state could actually do. On the contrary, the only legitimate powers that the state has recourse to are the authority to uphold an equal distribution of negative liberty and the right for individuals to hold property, i.e., premises 2 to 4. Thus, even if we could expect the requirement for (1) *new and more effective technology* to be successfully attained by the market, the demand for (2) *local adaptation, distribution and development of (uneconomic) technology* still calls for governmental initiatives that break the restrictions of PLD.

Conclusion: If (1) market demand on its own is presupposed to support scenario SD-4, i.e., new and more effective technology is attained by the market, then we cannot exclude conceivable compatibility between scenario SD-4 and PLD. However, since (2) governmental initiatives are required, the policy restriction is violated and compatibility will not reign.

8.1.3   Transference and (Re)Distribution

When discussing transference and redistribution in Chapters 5 and 6, different degrees of distributional challenges were discussed. The mildest form is (1) the demand for covering the initial cost of the introduction of a new product. Another issue is free trade. Provided that scenario SD-4 requires deregulation of the food sector for the developing world to get necessary capital to develop its food production, one important policy implied by scenario SD-4 is (2) possible governmental withdrawal from the international food market. A policy that is perhaps even more challenging is (3) redistribution of either technology, or the economic means with which *to* finance required technology, something we just touched upon (in Section 8.1.2). Most challenging, however, is the demand for social and economic development derived from the Brundtland Commission's report. Both the demand for social and economic development for providing access to more efficient technology and the requirements *per se* (cf. Sections 4.2.1 & 4.2.2) pointed in the same direction, i.e., (4) a demand for governmentally initiated redistribution of the means to create stability and improvements in areas of need. Obviously this demand is not only a national or domestic matter, but also an international and global concern, i.e., it implies transnational welfare measures.

Let us begin with (1) the initial costs. At first glance this idea is not very challenging from a PLD point of view. That the economically wealthier absorb the initial cost of the introduction of a new product is pure market logic. Those with strong preferences and strong purchasing power can always afford to pay a higher price for that product. In the long run this will benefit those who cannot afford the initial production costs and the additional costs to get the production going. When the price gradually decreases, the demand increases correspondingly and so does availability. Thus, so far the idea of initial costs does *not* interfere with any of the PLD premises 1 to 4. It should, however, be noted that I designated these kinds of measures as supporting distribution. This infers an active role for the state—at least in cases where the price does not decrease to a level that is affordable by those who require such technology to obtain their share of scenario SD-4.[3] Such state subsidies are a violation of premise 2 on negative liberty, since the state would in this case support substantial objectives, and are in violation of premise 3 on holding property, since substantive objectives require economic means that will most probably have to be taken from private capital.

(2) *Governmental withdrawal* from the international food market is not particularly challenging from a PLD perspective. Cutting public subsidies must be asserted as a *strengthening* of PLD. The only way a deregulating policy may violate any of these premises is if the present expenditure aims at upholding any of the premises 2 to 4. In our case current regulations do not uphold equal negative liberty (2 *and* 4). They do uphold possession of property though. Recall, however, that premise 3 refers to the *negative* right to hold property, i.e., the government, or others, are not allowed to take the property from someone, although he or she may very well 'lose' it in competition with others. Thus, a governmental withdrawal from the international food market ought to be considered compatible with PLD.

What about (3) redistribution of technology and (4) redistribution of social and economic development? The principal rule says that such policies are under no circumstances legitimate from a PLD point of view.[4] The reason is very simple. Any governmental initiative aiming at something more than safeguarding premises 1, 2, 3 and 4, is in corresponding violation of one or several of these premises. For example, if we argue that liberty means something more than absence from interference, then for the government to assist such liberty means that someone else must give up something he or she possesses. Thus, if the government is supposed to redistribute social and economic means according to the demands imposed by scenario SD-4, these means must be *taken* from others who then must cease to enjoy (parts of) their property, which of course violates premise 3. Such redistribution can only be legitimised if it is done *voluntarily* by property holders. As I argued in Chapter 3.2.1, according to several protective liberals, to *receive* economic or other politically determined support violates PLD (in particular premise 2), since one then becomes *dependent* on someone else, and thus becomes 'unfree' or even 'enslaved' as some protective liberals argue.

Finally, there is an international or global aaspect of scenario SD-4, which is also worthy of attention. While developmental liberal democracy (DLD) is often accused of being geographically bound to the nation state (see further below), PLD's defence of negative liberty and the right to hold property is quite easily applied on an international level. This is because to fulfil the obligation of leaving someone alone is far easier than to manage an international political organisation charged with transferring social and economic goods to those who are entitled to them. Furthermore, the distributional tool that PLD is advocating, i.e., the market, is not tied to any geographic areas. Therefore, as long as we accept the *market* as a fair and efficient distributor, the international dimension of sustainable development is not problematic under PLD. However, it is questionable whether the market is 'efficient' and 'fair' in terms of implementing scenario SD-4.

Conclusion: In principle, both (1) bearing the initial costs and (2) governmental withdrawals are to be considered compatible with PLD. An exception from the rule is if the government imposes the covering of initial costs. Neither the global aspects of scenario SD-4 nor its implied policies are very problematic from a PLD viewpoint. However, neither (3) redistribution of technology, nor (4) redistribution of social and economic means can ever be considered compatible with the core values of PLD.

8.1.4   PLD and Prioritising and Ranking Interests and Values

When analysing scenario SD-4 in Chapters 5 and 6 we found that in order for this scenario to be realised, several measures and policies appear to give rise to priorities and rankings of interests. These priorities are assumed to be established by the government. One such policy was (1) a governmentally imposed transition of crop production, which inevitably places certain producer interests before others. Furthermore, unless some consumers voluntarily adopt (2) the dietary change that contributes to scenario SD-4, governmental *forcing* measures have to be used against these consumers, for the benefit of others. (3) National and international planning policies force certain interests representing more 'exclusive' needs and wants (like aesthetics, tourism and saving of rainforests) to give way to other presumably more 'basic', needs like food and water. Scenario SD-4 also presupposes (4) the use of biotechnology and that any resistance against the use of such technology must reasonably be met with governmental measures.

These forcing measures (1 to 4) are all examples of policies that cannot be legitimised by the PLD model. To (1) impose transition of crop production and (2) force individuals to change their diet are evident violations of premise 2 regarding negative liberty. There is perhaps an exception here, however. If a diet adopted by some actually prevents others from exercising their negative liberty (premise 2), then a forced dietary change may be legitimate. However, since negative liberty only presupposes political opportunities, the 'affecting others'- argument probably fails (again we see the power of sticking to negative liberty). Also the third example above may well be rejected for the same reasons. To consciously set aside some interests before others implies a state that, at best, does not fulfil its obligations under PLD premises 2 to 4, and at worst not even under PLD premise 1.[5] Only in a competing market can one interest be set aside for the benefit of another without violating the PLD policy restriction, because it is not a result of governmental action but reflects the relative strength of the current preferences of individuals and consumers.

The example of (4) biotechnology may also be an exception from this rule. At least in theory any liberal viewpoint holds that it is up to the individual to decide whether to use a technology or not. If enough people demand a technology, it will be developed and distributed. Most certainly, the state ought *not* to promote or prevent any such development, since that would violate both premise 2 (only individuals themselves ought to decide what is best for society) and premise 3 (such collective promotion costs money and thus presupposes limitations on individual property). Instead, the competing market should be the arbiter, i.e., what citizens/consumers want is what citizens/consumers get.

This discussion can be more finely tuned. An example is the religious aspects of biotechnology mentioned in Chapter 6.2.2. Today there is a gradually globalised distribution of genetically modified food, sometimes more or less uncontrolled. Soya protein is a good example. In a few years, we will not be certain whether a product containing soya protein also contains genetically modified soya. Meanwhile some religious groups require complete information about what they eat. In order to be able to practise their religion in a proper manner. Unless people are (a) fully informed about this modification, and/or (b) the spread is completely under control, and/or (c) there is a 'pure' substitute offered, this particular commodity can no longer be included in the diet of the relevant religious group members, which would be a restriction on their liberty.

What is the proper role of the PLD state in this matter? If it is agreed that freedom to practice religion belongs to the rights encompassing political equality, then governmental intervention to protect this right should occur in accordance with premise 4, and thus be fully legitimate even if it constitutes market interference. As a matter of fact, it would violate the policy restriction if the government *did not* interfere. If freedom to practice religion is not among the liberties encompassing PLD equality, or is considered inferior to, e.g., freedom of trade, then the religious aspects should not be considered by the PLD state.

Finally, there is concern for *future generations*. The PLD standpoint on this issue is clear. The premises 1 (regarding the 'good life'), 2 (negative liberty) and 3 (holding property) are the focal points. Under these premises, an individual's liberty to determine what to do with his or her life and how to manage his or her property is exclusively a matter for the individual to decide. This axiom certainly affects future generations as well. If I have an unreserved right to decide over my property, it follows that a preceding generation will always either (a) be given priority over the following generations, and/or (b) be benefited at the *expense* of future generations.[6] The reason is that the right to decide over a resource or a property is connected to ownership, a capacity that the unborn cannot exercise.

As we have seen, scenario SD-4 requires policies that involve present *and* future human demands, and that also work in accordance with those demands. That is the main motive for increasing efficiency and striving for decreasing resource use. Such a policy would violate premises 1 to 3, however, and can thus not be considered compatible. Since the PLD model obviously cannot legitimise any welfare programmes within present generations (as became obvious earlier in this chapter), neither can it legitimise any such programmes for the benefit of *future* generations.

Conclusion: Although there are *conceivable* exceptions to the rule, it is quite clear that the governmentally initiated priorities identified here are incompatible with PLD. Any such action would presuppose a violation of at least premises 2, 3 and 4.

8.1.5   *Conclusions Regarding PLD and Scenario SD-4*

Based on our examination of the four core premises of PLD and the policies implied by scenario SD-4, we can conclude that *few* such policies can be considered compatible with PLD. If sustainable development is also defined as 'the good life' or understood as a superior social goal, which is probably the case if seen from a PLD perspective, then obviously also premise 1 is violated as well. The main reason is that unless we have reasons to believe that it will be implemented voluntarily, scenario SD-4 requires *governmental* action. This means forcing power of a kind that I have shown would be in violation mainly with the last three premises, i.e., it presupposes that the state goes beyond its fundamental policy restrictions. However, action initiated by the state *must not* be contrary to the PLD policy restriction. This restriction established that the state should stay *passive* in all respects other than those that are presupposed for safeguarding the right to individually interpret the meaning of the good life, and to enjoy negative liberty and property. Those rare occasions where the suggested policies could be considered compatible, are explained by the fact that scenario SD-4 implies deregulation of the market rather than regulation, or that the market appears to produce limitations on individuals' *negative* liberty (as with biotechnology).

8.2   The Compatibility Between Sustainable Development Policies and Developmental Liberal Democracy

Chapter 3 showed that the developmental liberal view of the democratic state differs significantly from the protective liberal view. According to DLD, the state ought to not only protect its citizens, but also to *make sure* that they are given opportunities to realise their individual life plans. Access to at least some of these opportunities should be distributed equally. This is often referred to as 'equality of opportunity'. The range of opportunities, and the purposes of these opportunities, are restricted/regulated by the principle of state neutrality to individual life plans. Furthermore, there is no single conception of the good life; there are many. This view of the state is a consequence of a specific understanding of liberty and equality, with evident effects on the conception of property. Consequently, the right to hold property is not defended as an absolute right. Neither is liberty understood solely as negative, but also as positive in terms of autonomy. Equality does not only refer to political rights, as in PLD, but also to *social and economic rights*. This means that the idea of having the right to hold property, and to enjoy the fruits of it, must be weakened. The reason is that opportunities often refer to material and economic resources that have to be financed with incomes derived from the fruits of the use of the property.

Reasonably, there are *limitations* on the objectives related to which individuals can or should enjoy equal opportunity. One extreme example is when all individuals have *exactly the same* means and opportunities.[7] This communitarian view indicates a society where the freedom of choice is limited to only one alternative. The other extreme is when individuals have an infinite set of choices, but no means to realise these choices. DLD finds itself somewhere in-between these extremes although it is unclear exactly where. As was argued earlier (Section 3.3.2), this can not be solved, but it can be illuminated by theoretical argument. Rather it is an ideological and/or empirical issue. The way I understand it, the nature of these opportunities and the extent of the equality of access for individuals to these opportunities, are matters for citizens to decide through the democratic process. From this way of reasoning we have the following compatibility criterion:

Figure 8.2   Compatibility Criterion Derived from the Idea of Developmental Liberal Democracy

Premise 1.   The 'good life' is exclusively a matter for the individual to define.

Premise 2.   Individual liberty shall be understood as autonomy (opportunity to fulfil one's life-plans).

Premise 3.   Equality comprises opportunities to choose and fulfil life plans.

Policy restriction: Thus, the developmental liberal-democratic state must be neutral with regard to individual life-plans, active in the respects presupposed by premises 2 and 3, but must never end up in a majority violating neither a citizen's negative liberty, nor the principles of harm, ECR and autonomy.

Compatibility criterion: Any sustainability policy presupposing a violation of this policy restriction is to be considered incompatible with the core values of developmental liberal democracy.

In Section 8.1, we concluded that one main reason why scenario SD-4 cannot be considered compatible with PLD is largely because PLD only offers highly *limited possibilities of state action.* We thus have valid reason to investigate if the policies suggested in Chapter 7 can be considered more compatible with DLD. The crucial restriction is that while providing opportunities, the state must remain neutral to individual life plans. At the same time, this restriction should not be understood too rigorously. If the right to hold and enjoy the fruits of private property is not absolute, and the state actually has the right to distribute parts of it to other citizens, this consequently means that already a large number of life plans have been modified (i.e. 'comprehensive neutrality'). Thus, the state ought to be *actively* neutral to individual life plans.

I will split up my analysis into three different parts. In much of presently known liberal theory, DLD is bound to the nation state. Furthermore, when we add *positive* liberty to the agenda, the symmetry between rights and obligations becomes less straightforward, not only from an international point of view, but also regarding future generations and other species.

I thus begin this part of the chapter by first analysing SD-4 policies and their relationship to the DLD premises *in principle*, without paying any particular attention to the global dimension of scenario SD-4. I then approach the global aspects, and end the chapter by discussing priorities between present and future generations[8]

8.2.1 *National and International Planning and Organisation*

Admittedly, it is impossible to argue authoritatively that a 30% level of animal food in the human diet (the level we assure in scenario SD-4) is a *prerequisite* for people to fulfil their life plans. At the same time, such a level of animal food consumption can be argued on both empirical and normative grounds. We know that economic development is accompanied by increased animal food consumption. The slope of the curve flattens out at around 30%, long before reaching the average GNP per capita in the Western world. If the Brundtland Commission's norms for economic and social development are accepted as prerequisites for individuals to fulfil their life plans, and if these norms are implemented, then the consumption of animal food must rise. Whether realistic or not, such an increase in human consumption of animal food forces us to pay considerable attention to the groups of people presently lacking purchasing power. An increase in animal food consumption is followed by greater competition for land and food. If there is no global increase in economic and social wealth, some groups may be severely threatened by such development (cf. Chapter 6.1.1 & 6.1.5). This also points to the need for increases in production efficiency, and is also important for future generations. Thus, even if we do not consider the animal food consumption assumed in scenario SD-4 as a sustainability goal *per se*, we do assume it to be a consequence of the social and economic demands of sustainability.

The examination of PLD with regard to *co*-ordination and resource logistics made it obvious that changes are required in state-initiated planning and co-operation with regard to water and land, as well as food and phosphorus. Decisions should be made not on the basis of individuals' preferences, but on the basis of global efficiency. This we found violates both premise 2 on negative liberty and premise 3 on holding property.

In contrast to PLD, however, DLD has been defined as a system where liberty in premise 2 means 'autonomy' and where we cannot determine a strict premise for property, since it is not considered an *absolute* right.[9] That is not to say that DLD allows for *complete* expropriation of property. Still, whenever some restriction on private property is permitted, planning and steering is a valid consideration, without necessarily jeopardising the principle of private property or premise 2 on autonomy. Thus, unless we can establish that the co-ordination and logistic policies require too many limitations on liberty and individual property that violate premise 3 (i.e., that prevents the majority of people from enjoying the opportunities to fulfil their life-plans), we cannot conclude that such policies would be a violation of DLD. Since I understand this to be the case, then I must conclude that some other factor forces us to disqualify the mentioned policies.

The aim of the assumed sustainable development policies is to make sure that economic and social development, crucial to human life both now and in generations to come,[10] can take place without impoverishing natural resources crucial to human life. Since this development is supposed to benefit everyone, obviously the *scope* of such policies must be wide. Certainly, when we consider large scale, and indeed very intrusive planning, we approach the very antithesis of liberalism (cf. Kenny & Meadowcroft 1999:1-9). If planning and co-ordination is considered legitimate according to what we just concluded above, and we continue claiming that large scale planning *is* illegitimate, then the *scope* of policy must be the disqualifying factor.

However, can we dispatch the idea of planning as a violation of DLD by referring to scope? This is the case *only if* the matter of scope violates any of the core premises. From what we learned in Chapter 3, however, DLD is principally concerned with the *aim* of governmentally implemented planning. According to the policy restriction, if the aim of state action is not to fulfil premises 2 and 3, but to fulfil a *superior goal* formulated by the state itself, then all the DLD premises 1 to 3 are violated. However, none of the premises actually refers to, or imposes restrictions on *scope*. Certainly we can come up with several practical arguments for disqualifying these policies by referring to scope, such as administrative difficulties or lack of concern beyond a certain geographic area. Still, we cannot do it exclusively by arguing that any of the DLD premises 1 to 3 are violated.

Conclusion: The policies derived from scenario SD-4 regarding long term resource planning and co-ordination cannot be considered a violation of the compatibility criterion of DLD.[11] This can only be concluded by defining the actual *content* of premises 2 and 3 (i.e., *exactly* in what respects individuals ought to be given equal opportunity)—something I have claimed is hardly a theoretical issue, and certainly beyond the objectives and scope of this book. Furthermore we cannot argue that the state, by implementing this planning and co-ordination will violate any of the harm, ECR and autonomy principles. Rather on the contrary, since avoiding these measures may cause severe harm to large groups of people.

8.2.2 Support and Implementation of Improved Technology

All the policies regarding support for development, adaptation and distribution of technology that are required for scenario SD-4 to be realised fall under this heading. The policies I brought up previously were governmental involvement in the development of technology and methods aimed at diminishing eutrophication and purifying phosphorus. Also, methods for efficient water use and for promoting additional biotechnological research and the diffusion of its results were dealt with. We also discussed governmental initiatives to provide a favourable environment for research and production, and pointed to a demand for policies *ensuring* that a product or a technology actually reaches the groups that require it.

If technological development is supported with the aim of providing individuals with equal opportunities to choose and to enjoy an autonomous life, it is difficult to prove that state support goes beyond the DLD policy restrictions. Certainly, there are limits as to how extensive that support should be, especially if we deal with technologies that would never be developed unless subsidised. *Where* to draw this limit is a delicate issue. The three DLD premises provide *some* guidelines and so do the harm and ECR principles. Formal as they are, however, they do not offer us much information regarding precisely within which area support is legitimate. Thus, what is actually appropriate and relevant to investigate here is whether governmental support for technological development can be considered at all compatible with the DLD perspective.

The conditions are similar for all the areas implied in scenario SD-4. Take water technology as an illustrative example. Obviously some people already suffer from water shortage. In countries where the price or the institutional organisation allows for it, people help each other by redistributing water from rich areas to poorer ones, and by sharing the burdens resulting from this distribution (cf. Sections 5.1.2 & 6.1.2). All this is done to fulfil primary needs among all citizens or stakeholders. In economically poor, and/or demonstrably unequal 'opportunity countries', such policies are not always implemented, or even considered.[12] The reason is not necessarily that such policies are illegitimate from a liberal perspective, but rather that the willingness and the money to pay for the policies are missing.

Thus, the lack of water—and the consequent lack of opportunities to fulfil life plans—gives the state reason to support the development of adequate technology. Furthermore, the lack of purchasing power gives rise to motives for allowing governmental support to make sure that such technology is adapted and spread to where it is required and needed. While such policies were considered incompatible with PLD because they violate both the premises on individual liberty (2) and property (3), the corresponding guiding principle in DLD (premise 2) says nothing explicitly about property. Instead it establishes that liberty ought to be understood as autonomy (i.e., to enjoy opportunities to choose and fulfil one's life plans).

Provided that, e.g., water is a prerequisite for enjoying autonomy, and that this resource ought to be distributed equally (according to premise 3), governmental support for the development of water technology (aimed at providing individuals with equal opportunities to access water) is thus fully in line with the policy restriction that the state must be *active* in regard to what is demanded in premises 2 and 3.[13] A crucial issue then is whether equal opportunity to access water is a prerequisite for individuals to enjoy an autonomous life. According to the Brundtland Commission and also along with scenario SD-4, access to water certainly is. Without access to water it is difficult to imagine any life at all.

Against this we can claim that the increased demand for water is partly, or even *mainly,* a result of the assumed huge increase in global animal food consumption.[14] Without this increase, less water would be required. Furthermore, the large amount of animal food that was assumed in scenario SD-4 is perhaps not a prerequisite for an autonomous life. *If not*, then obviously we cannot claim that all the required water is a prerequisite for an autonomous life. Consequently we must also conclude that some of the technology distribution is less important, and that the state should not support all the implied policies according to DLD. This is because under the DLD policy restriction, only the goods and technologies that are deemed necessary for *autonomy* are legitimate targets for state policies.

The autonomy objective forces us to think and speak in terms of degrees—something that, for obvious reasons, is beyond the scope of this book. It is simply impossible to tell exactly how much water is required for an individual to enjoy autonomy.[15] Additionally, it appears as if the basic problem remains: *there is, and will be, a regional shortage of water that requires governmental policies and measures.* Furthermore, the Brundtland Commission holds that social and economic development *is* required in the poor regions of the world, both in and of itself and as for sustainability reasons. Economic and social development brings increases in animal food consumption. Consequently, the need for water correspondingly increases with social and economic development.[16]

Conclusion: We have questioned both scenario SD-4 and the policies from several different angles. The conclusion is that we cannot *eliminate* the assumption that a certain amount of water, phosphorus and land directly *or* indirectly required in scenario SD-4 are prerequisites for individual autonomy. Thus, we cannot claim that the policies aimed at supporting technological development, adaptation and distribution are incompatible with DLD, according to our criterion. Instead, as long as technological policies aim at providing individuals with equal opportunities to enjoy an autonomous life, then premises 1 to 3 *are* fulfilled, and the policy does not go beyond the specified policy restriction. Should the state choose not to ensure these resources, the majority could even be accused of violating the harm, ECR and autonomy principles.

8.2.3   Transference and (Re) Distribution[17]

Here we focus on distribution or cost transfers in terms of (1) *covering initial costs*, (2) a possible governmental withdrawal from the (international) food market, (3) redistribution of either technology or economic means, and (4) a demand for governmentally initiated redistribution of the technological and economic means required to create stability and improvements in areas of need. As long as these measures aim at satisfying legitimate basic needs enabling the citizens to enjoy equal opportunities to attain autonomy, it is difficult to dismiss them as incompatible.

When we understand liberty as 'autonomy', we can gradually move from the negative focus on external hindrances towards possibilities to actually do what is otherwise impeded by those hindrances. It is, however, very difficult to deduce theoretically deduce what these possibilities are. Liberal theorists have all suggested quite similar vaguely expressed minimum sets of goods as necessary to enjoy some kind of autonomy (cf. Section 3.3.2). Gewirth's (1982) list, for instance, bears a resemblance to the UN list of human rights. This minimum standard is supposed to be the very minimum of goods that people need to enable them to live according to their life plans. The list is reasonably comprehensive and also contains objectives such as the right to education and work. If these rights are fundamental for individuals to enjoy autonomy, then there is also a governmental obligation to ensure that they are fulfilled, according to premise 3.

A certain ecological standard is presumably necessary for people to realise even the most basic elements of their life plans, i.e., to enjoy autonomy (cf. the Brundtland Commission report, WCED 1987:392). To view a reasonable ecological standard as a basic need may be a 'given' in Sweden and Norway ot in other countries that are ecologically relatively sound. However, for people living next to badly maintained nuclear power plants, in dioxin-infected Bhopal, or near the Exxon Valdez ecological disaster, the physical standard of the environment is a crucial issue.[18] Thus, scenario SD-4 *can* be seen as an expression of the resources required by individuals to enjoy autonomy not only via an assumed global social and economic development, but also through the ecological concerns it reflects.   Let us glance at the measures that were suggested under the heading of transference and redistribution.

To give support by (1) bearing the initial costs (for example for the water and phosphorus technology market, as well as for the biotechnology necessary to overcome some of the biophysical scarcity) is no more problematic for DLD than for PLD. The market for a commodity grows as the price decreases. Contrary to PLD, however, if the free market does not reach the groups in need through market based 'initial cost-taking', DLD may allow for governmental involvement to ensure such a distribution. For example, if wealthy groups do not accept the initial costs of important biotechnology required for poor regions,[19] then state subsidies may be legitimate as long as the aim of the subsidised product is to promote the satisfaction of basic needs, and not to force people to succumb to a superior, substantial goal. Although we can see situations where such state involvement is an apparent violation of DLD, the three premises require us to define the aim of the policy. Unless we have specified exactly what 'autonomy' actually requires, then any policy aimed at providing equal opportunities to enjoy autonomy can be considered compatible, according to the DLD compatibility criteria. As long as the suggested technologies contribute to the realisation of scenario SD-4, and scenario SD-4 can be viewed as an expression of equal opportunities, then the policies for subsidising such technologies do not violate any of the premises 1 to 3.

A (2) governmental withdrawal from the (international) food market is a most straightforward governmental initiative, according to the compatibility criterion of PLD. However, the same strategy is somewhat more questionable in view of the DLD compatibility criterion. The purposes of subsidies and taxes are, among other things,[20] to make sure that a country's farmers are able to earn enough income from their business. Without such policies, cheaper producing foreign farmers may drive them out of the market. Such a consequence is fully compatible with PLD. According to the DLD premises, however, a withdrawal of governmental support is solely legitimate if the domestic farmers will have at least their basic needs for autonomy secured in some other way, as demanded by premise 2.[21] Furthermore, such a withdrawal must be shown to provide foreign farmers with more means to enjoy autonomy than before, again in accordance with premise 2. Their expected gain must also reasonably be larger than the losses of the domestic farmers—simply because otherwise such a policy produces less resources and especially fewer *opportunities* than before. I cannot estimate whether these demands would actually be fulfilled if, for instance, Sweden would adopt such a withdrawal. Most certainly Swedish farmers would be able to enjoy some basic *autonomy* anyway, although perhaps not related to farming.

Thus, as long as economic arguments for free trade as a way to *increase* global welfare and sustainability are considered valid, we cannot condemn such a policy as incompatible with the DLD criterion. This holds at least as long as the aim of the policy is to increase economic and social welfare, and we have not defined the *geographical area* within which the policy restriction is valid (cf. the next Section 8.3).

(3) *Transferring technology* coincides with what was concluded about technological development under the previous heading. Scenario SD-4 requires that those who need the best available techniques in order to achieve their share of the scenario should have them. This claim is valid, regardless of whether people have enough purchasing power or not. Thus, scenario SD-4 implies re-distribution policies. According to our DLD premises, a re-distribution policy can be considered compatible with the DLD criterion, *provided* that its objective is to give individuals equal opportunities to realise their life plans; a lot speaks in favour of such an interpretation of scenario SD-4.[22]

A similar way of reasoning is relevant for (4) the *economic transfers* indicated in the scenario analysis. Even if the sole purpose of such a (re)distribution is to secure *every* person's capacity to live an autonomous life, there are no logical reasons for DLD *not* to allow for such policies. Again it can even be argued that by deliberately neglecting such transfers, the state actually violates the harm principle. The crucial relevant restriction is the requirement that the state preserves its neutrality to the individual's choice of life plans, and that the state acts only to produce equal opportunities for people to enjoy autonomy. A difficult balance is faced here. On the one side DLD accepts the idea that liberty may require substantial means (although it is unclear which ones and how many of them), according to premise 2. On the other hand, it does not allow for this extension of means to transform into a substantial end, which is a reflection of an underlying conception of 'the good life', according to premise 1.

Can it be theoretically determined whether scenario SD-4 is such a 'substantial' end or goal? Focusing on the *scope* of scenario SD-4, the answer is most certainly yes. A project like that has never before been seen in the budget of any existing liberal democracy. Nor have the international implications been considered yet. As I claimed before, however, only the objective, but not the scope of action, is a theoretically valid objection under the premises—provided that the harm, ECR and autonomy principles are not violated. Furthermore, there is a lack of an absolute criterion for when a governmental goal turns into a 'superior' or 'substantial' goal (cf. Section 3.3.2).

Conclusion: Even though scenario SD-4 may imply *far-reaching* aims, I cannot conclude that the redistribution policies that were implied by scenario SD-4 actually have to go beyond the policy restriction and thus be considered incompatible according to the DLD compatibility criterion. This is due to the fact that the *scope* of state intervention is not a legitimate objection; only *intents* are.

8.2.4 DLD on Giving Priority to and Ranking Interests and Values

Many of the identified policies imply that the state must actually rank competing interests. Such a process is was legitimate for the PLD state only if one individual's interests constitute a threat to another individual's rightful *liberty*. As seen already, DLD is more generous on this matter. The clearest example is that DLD allows for restrictions on private property for the purpose of securing equality of opportunity.[23] This means that those life plans that presuppose full access to the revenues from private property may be subordinated to the benefit of other interests. Furthermore, via the idea that everyone has equal rights to an (indefinite) set of basic goods, it was concluded that some interests (more precisely those that jeopardise an *equal* distribution of basic goods necessary to enjoy autonomy) can be legitimately restricted under the DLD ideal type.

The priorities to be dealt with are: (1) Governmentally initiated transition from grazing to crop production[24] which puts the interest of certain producers before those of other producers, by making them change their business. (2) Governmental policies aimed at changing individuals' diets place the needs and wants of not yet animal food consuming individuals ahead of those with an unacceptable diet according to scenario SD-4. (3) National and international planning, as well as the support for the expansion of land use, forcing interest groups and businesses representing more exclusive needs and wants (like aesthetics, tourism and the keeping of rainforests) to stand back in favour of interests representing more basic needs, like food production. (4) Measures that promote biotechnological research benefiting producers of such technology, as well as those who can physically gain from it, while largely disregarding those who are against such technology or who may come to suffer from it.[25] Such priorities are problematic from any liberal-democratic point of view. I argue, however, that as long as the aim of the policies can be seen as confined to only maintaining individuals' equal opportunities, then there are no theoretical reasons for dismissing these priorities as 'incompatible' with any of the DLD premises.

The compatibility problems imposed by the last priorities, biotechnology and future generations, cannot be completely examined until I in Section 4 of this chapter have discussed the principal stand of DLD on matters relating to the future. I do, however, outline what I consider to be the main problems of biotechnology.

To examine whether (1) governments giving active priority to a producer to grow a particular crop is considered compatible with DLD, it is necessary to consult the policy restrictions and the premises. If none of the premises is arguably violated, then it can be claimed that such a priority may be compatible. The first premise can hardly be violated since the aim of scenario SD-4 is not to arrive at a *superior goal*, but to ensure that individuals can enjoy certain basic goods. Provided that the policy produces more opportunities than before, then premise 2 cannot be violated either. According to scenario SD-4 (which is the only available yardstick), more opportunities can be produced if productivity is increased.[26] Nor can the third premise be violated, i.e., the demand for equal opportunities, since the aim of the policy is precisely to equalise opportunities for individuals to choose and fulfil their life plans. Thus, it cannot be concluded that this state-imposed policy presupposes action beyond the policy restriction.

In the same way there can be an argument about priorities which set aside (2) certain consumer preferences[27] and (3) aesthetic, tourism and rainforest interests. As long as the aim of the policies is to provide individuals with equal opportunities to enjoy autonomy,[28] then the state-imposed policies work in line with the policy restriction and can be shown logically as compatible with the DLD criteria.

The first premise cannot be considered violated since the aim is not to impose a particular life-plan, or to achieve a superior goal. The second premise is not violated since the aim is to increase and not to reduce liberty (understood as autonomy). The third premise can hardly be seen as violated, since the aim is to *bridge* and not increase the gap between individuals' opportunities. Thus, as long as our deduced premises from Chapter 3 are not violated, it cannot be concluded that the policies are in conflict with any of these premises.[29]

The way I present the function of (4) biotechnology and its effects makes it obvious that it can both gain and harm sustainable development. It depends partly on the definition of sustainability, and what certainties there are regarding positive and negative effects. Since biotechnology is not yet used on any large scale, it cannot be stated with any certainty whether the benefits from its use are large or small (cf. Section 5.2.3). Also, there is only fragmented knowledge about the risks. Biotechnology was assumed to be favourable insofar as it creates opportunities—mostly for groups presently enjoying, at best, a marginal diet. Thus, from a *social* and perhaps also an *economic* sustainability perspective, biotechnology can be beneficial. At the same time, biotechnology is assumed to be a threat mostly to physical and ecological aspects of sustainability.[30]

If the introduction of biotechnology increases the chances for people to have their basic needs satisfied, i.e., it contributes to the equalisation of people's opportunities, then it is legitimate for DLD to support such technology, according to premise 3. If it can be shown that biotechnology has a negative effect on the physical environment in the sense that human beings, in the longer run, will have their prospects for fulfilling basic needs diminished, then a conflict arises between social and economic sustainability on the one hand, and ecological sustainability on the other.

Obviously, there is a conflict both between short term social and economic interests, and the interests of future generations. In the short run, social and economic development may gain considerably by such technology. The day the ecological system is about to collapse, however, it will also have negative implications on social and economic conditions. Thus, there are actually two arguments against implementing biotechnology today. First, it may eventually destroy the ecological environment. Second, it may come to undermine the opportunities of future generations to fulfil their life plans. Whether this is a violation of any of the DLD premises I cannot conclude until I have defined the DLD stand in relation to the future. I therefore return to this issue in the conclusions of Section 8.4.

8.2.5 *Conclusions Regarding Sustainable Development Policies and DLD*

According to my examination based on the DLD compatibility criterion, it is difficult to conclude logically that the policies derived from scenario SD-4 violate any of the premises, and thus the compatibility criterion. As long as (1) the suggested measures and policies are aimed at meeting basic needs, and they (2) are distributed equally in order for (3) the state to supply individuals with equal opportunities to fulfil their life plans (not to achieve some particular authoritatively imposed conception of the good life) and (4) none of the harm, ECR and autonomy principles are violated, then the conclusion is that the policies can be considered compatible with the core values of DLD. Any other conclusion presupposes information that cannot be derived from our approach. Thus, if our compatibility criterion is fulfilled, or not violated, and we have reason to believe that scenario SD-4 will be realised, it seems as if the state can remain neutral to individuals' life plans and still be active in the work of redirecting society towards sustainable development.[31]

Two issues have not yet been examined: The international dimension of scenario SD-4 and the matter of future generations. Both are most crucial to the idea of sustainable development.

8.3 The Global Aspects of the Sustainable Development Policies and Developmental Liberal Democracy

In the following two Sections I do not re-examine all the suggested policies, since that is not necessary for my purposes. I take the results from the DLD examination so far as given, and analyse if that conclusion is valid also when applied to these new dimensions. Could the policies aimed at providing an equal distribution of basic goods/resources/capacities (opportunities) also be extended in *space* and *time?*[32]

There is an ever-growing literature on democracy and international and global issues. The economy is becoming more and more global, as is communication and the characteristics of many of the most malignant environmental problems. Most of the liberal theorists I referred to in defining my ideal types in Chapter 3 take their point of departure at the national level. I think this is reasonable, since the liberal democracies as we know them are strongly attached to the nation state.

More recently, a range of scholars (for instance Low & Gleeson 1998; Held 1997; Altwater 1999; Dahl 1999; Hardin 1999; O'Neill 2000) have argued that liberal democracy is inadequate when it comes to *international* issues. Several factors explain the limitations, many of which can be characterised as institutional (cf. Sections 1.3 and 2.1). There are no liberal-democratic parliaments that cover the same geographic area as the border-crossing problems at hand. There are few, if any, international *laws* that restrict countries, industries and individuals from doing harm outside the nation state. Nor are there any really effective *sanctions* in the cases where such laws, conventions, protocols or international agreements exist. One of the few exceptions is the UN declaration on human rights, which has a legal system, a judicial power and the right to impose penalties. Thus, liberal democracies *have* difficulty upholding their own cherished values beyond their geographically defined borders.

Although aware of this fact, I do not regard these statements as a reason not to investigate whether or not liberal democracy can in principle *legitimise* the global scale measures and policies implied by scenario SD-4. My research question is not whether a particular form of democracy is *going to* realise scenario SD-4, or *earn the required powers* to do so. Instead, my concern is confined to whether or not we, when proceeding from all the assumptions made in this study, can logically conclude that the environmental policies derived from scenario SD-4 can be considered compatible with liberal democratic core values.

As far as I can see, there are at least two ways to analyse whether the *global dimension* of the policies aimed at realising SD-4 makes any difference to our (national) conclusions in Section 8.2. Either there needs to be an analysis of the prerequisites for scenario SD-4, or the DLD premises need further scrutiny. To examine the first approach, I proceed from John Rawls' (1972) 'original position' where, when we have 'placed' ourselves behind a 'veil of ignorance', it can be discussed whether a national or international focus on scenario SD-4 makes any difference in principle. Thereafter I analyse if there are any assumptions within the DLD premises that force (DLD) to be limited within national boundaries. I argue that regardless of starting point, I cannot unconditionally conclude that the policies are incompatible just because they have a global reach—a quite provocative conclusion considering the fact that it is precisely here that many scholars argue that liberal democracy and sustainable development move apart. To confront my conclusions, I therefore challenge them with what I understand to be one of the trickiest objections being directed to the relationship between liberal democracy and international issues (justice), i.e.: Onora O'Neill's (2000) assertion that (liberal-democratic) rights and obligations have an *asymmetric relationship* when applied at the international level.

8.3.1 Prerequisites for Scenario SD-4

In his *A Theory of Justice* (1972), John Rawls derives two principles of justice on a 'rationalistic' platform. Rawls argues that these principles are the most rational for individuals to comply with in order to experience as much justice as possible, individually as well as collectively. This he does by assuming an original position where sensible individuals do not have any substantial information about what sort of life they will experience. In this situation Rawls argues that the most rational choice for them is to agree with his two principles of justice (118-192):

(1) Each person is to have an equal right to the most extensive total system of equal basic liberties compatible with a similar system of liberty for all.
(2) Social and economic inequalities are to be arranged so that they are both (a) to the greatest benefit of the least advantaged and (b) attached to offices and positions open to all.

These two principles are a 'special case' of a more 'general conception' of justice saying that all social values should be distributed equally, unless an unequal distribution of any or all of these values is to everyone's advantage.

According to Rawls, there are certain primary goods that must be distributed such that they are of the greatest advantage for everyone.

Now, someone who does not have any access *whatsoever* to those primary goods is arguably the most extreme example of a deviation from the two principles, and would allow for an adjustment of the circumstances to benefit the least advantaged individual. Reverting to scenario SD-4 it was considered that particular resources ought to be provided in such a way that each citizen enjoys 'equality of opportunity' to choose and attain his or her life plans. Only if human beings have a certain amount of these resources do they have such opportunities. It was found that this legitimises political action so that all members of a society attain a level where they can enjoy certain opportunities, or certain 'social and economic goods' (Rawls' term is 'wealth', cf. p.62). There is a clear resemblance between the resources discussed in the former section and the ones that Rawls refers to.

Thus, if Rawls presupposes that a certain general 'wealth' must be provided for the special case (the two principles of justice) to be valid and applicable, then the assumptions about an equal distribution of opportunities can reasonably be placed in an analytical framework similar to the one Rawls defines and uses; i.e., the veil of ignorance.

In the original position there were persons who had no idea about themselves in terms of capacities or personal preferences. They also lacked the knowledge about where they will live.[33] Since these people lack all this important knowledge about their lives, Rawls argues that they will conclude that the two principles of justice will be chosen as the guiding principle for distribution of liberty. They will also conclude that certain social and economic resources (wealth) are prerequisites for enjoying such liberty. These principles are not bound to a nation state or any other geographical border, but are universal (although it is likely that Rawls was mostly thinking of United States when he published his book [cf. Wolff 1998]). If this is the case for Rawls' two principles of justice, and especially with regard to the primary goods he is defending, then it is reasonable to claim that the basic goods in scenario SD-4 have the same universal or global status.

On the national level, scenario SD-4 measures and policies could claim compatibility to DLD thanks to the idea of equality of opportunities and the distribution of basic goods. If we follow a Rawlsian method of legitimising basic goods, it appears difficult to argue that the basic goods covered by scenario SD-4 only ought to concern individuals within a particular geographical unit. After all, what rational reason would someone who does not know where he or she will live possibly have for claiming that the right to equality of opportunity to enjoy autonomy should be limited to, for example a certain state or group? These resources are basic and fundamental no matter where in the world someone lives.[34] Theoretically, the demand for an equal distribution of these opportunities cannot possibly be confined to a particular area or country.

Conclusions: Even if liberal democracies so far have been nation-bound, my analysis implies that the fundamental *political philosophy* behind liberal democracy must not necessarily be geographically bound. From this follows that the measures and policies implied by scenario SD-4 cannot be considered incompatible with DLD just because they have a global reach and a global aim.

Let me now turn to the second approach for testing whether the global dimension of scenario SD-4 should be considered incompatible from the perspective of the compatibility criterion, i.e., whether any of the DLD premises requires geographical limits.

8.3.2   The Geographical Limitations of the DLD Premises

Because of the character of the analysis that follows, allow me to start the exercise by refreshing our memories a bit. DLD is constituted by three core elements: a democratic state, liberty and equality. The state is supposed to execute the will of the people, and has distributive power. Further, the state is limited by its claims to guarantee individual liberty and equality. Liberty, then, is the idea that individuals ought to enjoy a space within which they are released from external obstacles, so that there are no hindrances for them to do what they find worth doing, i.e., negative liberty. This liberty ought to be sustained by the state, as long as one individual's liberty does not restrict another's. Negative liberty is not enough for individuals to be *really* free, however. They also require capacities and powers to be *able* to do what they consider worth doing. Without certain means, individuals do not have any real opportunities to have or do even the most basic things, even if they are actually not prevented from doing them. They have no positive liberty (read 'autonomy').

In addition to liberty and the (liberal-democratic) state is also a universal element. Individuals are regarded as being of *equal* value, and therefore having equal rights to certain things. Except for an equal status in the pure political sense, individuals have an equal right to some resources that give them the opportunity to choose the lives they would like to live—life plans. In line with several liberal theorists there is a vaguely suggested set of 'basic goods'. With reasonable certainty, food, water and shelter are considered such basic goods, as is a quantum of social and economic wealth (cf. Rawls 1972; Dworkin 1977; Gewirth 1982; Sen 1982; Arneson 1989 and Cohen 1989). I have also suggested that a certain level of a sound physical environment is probably needed. Without these goods, there will not be many choices available to the individual. Thus, equality (of opportunity) is an entirely vital element of DLD. By accepting a more substantial understanding of liberty, DLD departs from PLD, which only acknowledges the negative side of liberty.[35] Awarding liberty a positive feature facilitates arguments for the welfare state. At the same time, this creates difficulties regarding how to deal with and uphold the universalistic element of liberalism, including in the international arena.

Understanding DLD the way I have outlined here does not mean it has to be applied simply on a national level, although it is easier to imagine an effective welfare state within national borders. However, none of the liberty, equality or democratic elements of DLD *presupposes* a particular geographic unit. The first known democracies were practised within 'city states' only. Direct democracy presupposed a limited number of people in order to work effectively. Any other forms of democracy and of geographical boundaries were inconceivable or not effectively staked out before the Peace of Westphalia approximately two thousand years later, when the first nation states were defined. In the long run, this has given rise to the geographical units that are associated with liberal democracies today. These units are thus not primarily a product of the three core elements of DLD, but rather of the fact that until recently there has been no other geographical unit than nation states *available* for the liberal-democratic 'experiment'.

Is it possible to imagine the three liberal-democratic components being pursued across a wider geographical territory? Quite likely. None of them holds any geographically limited content, nor do any other liberal core values such as impartiality and universalism. The reasons for associating liberal democracy with nation states seem to be mostly historical and functional. Thus, designing a 'New World Order' with border-crossing liberal democracies ranging over several nation states is not logically *impossible* (cf. Low & Gleeson 1998: ch. 6-7), although evidently very difficult in practise.

Conclusions: With respect to what geographic territory the three core values of DLD constitute, I only found historical and functional arguments for why I should attribute liberal democracy to a specific geographic and demographic area, such as the nation state. Nothing in the compatibility criterion of DLD gives me any explicit theoretical reference to such a spatial delimitation. In the same way as it is found difficult to dismiss any of the SD-4 policies when the analysis is limited to the national level, it is difficult to claim incompatibility between the scenario SD-4 policies and the core values of DLD when the analysis is broadened to a global reach.

8.3.3 Border-Crossing Rights and Obligations—A Critical Test

Onora O'Neill (2000) suggests that liberal democracies are particularly unable to deal with international distributional justice since redistribution requires an identification of both someone's right and someone else's corresponding obligation to live up to this right—something a liberal democracy cannot identify beyond the nation state. If she is correct, then DLD should have difficulties legitimising or at least realising policies that require such border-crossing redistribution. Let us confront the sustainable development policies with this declaration.

Although this 'asymmetrical' argument is both relevant and hard to cope with, I cannot see how it would contribute to scenario SD-4 violating any of our three DLD premises. Rather, this is yet another empirical objection that points to the incapability of present liberal democracies to deal with international environmental and social issues.

An individual's right to enjoy a certain space of liberty infers an obligation on the state and on other individuals to not intrude on that space. To reason in terms of space, on the one hand, and privacy from interference on the other, is in fact applicable from the individual level up to a global level. Thus, if the focus is solely on negative liberty, then this very simple relationship between right and obligation is valid. All it takes to uphold a negative right and a corresponding obligation is to leave other individuals alone where they have the right to be left alone. The relationship between right and obligation is fairly symmetric, and the causal link is obvious. As long as you not interfere with me, I enjoy my right, and you enjoy yours.

However, considering any form of positive liberty, like in DLD and scenario SD-4, the relationship between a right and an obligation becomes far more problematic. Within the national boundaries of a sovereign state, the liberal-democratic state can identify those who have the obligation to provide someone else with the means necessary to enjoy the basic goods to which he or she has the right. There are different criteria for obligation. For example, those who can afford it have an obligation to set aside means for the benefit of the least advantaged. Another is those who have contributed to the existence of the disadvantaged. The state has the distributive power, and can make redistributions in order to secure a basic standard for all its citizens. As long as the state has constitutional support, it can direct any citizen to pay the costs of providing individuals with equal opportunities to choose the good life. Thus, although less symmetrical than in the case of only negative rights, *within* DLD liberal democracies it is possible to point out those who should pay for the provision of basic goods for the collective in general, and for those in need in particular.

To point out needy individuals on an international level is not difficult either, especially in terms of individuals in need of basic goods – it is usually quite obvious who they are. Thus, it is not particularly challenging to identify whose 'basic' rights ought to be maintained. It is, however, extremely difficult to point out whose responsibility it is, or whose obligation it is to *provide* these individuals with the means necessary to enjoy equal access to basic goods and opportunities. Within the present global system, there is no authority that can redirect a particular individual's wealth to someone else across national borders, and declare that it is this person's obligation to make sure that a particularly needy person is guaranteed a certain set of basic goods. O'Neill's observation is thus valid. This implies that as long as liberal democracy's sphere of influence and authority is limited to the nation state, then SD-4 policies cannot be realised other than *within* countries. Does, however, the fact that current liberal-democratic states cannot legitimately identify obligations of individuals beyond its borders constitute an argument that is *inconsistent with the rest of this analysis* and thus questions scenario SD-4, and therefore also its compatibility with DLD?

The 'asymmetric' argument, put forth by O'Neill, is certainly both adequate and difficult to refute. Still, I cannot see that it would necessarily refer to something 'intrinsic' or 'inherent' in liberal democracy (cf. Section 1.1). Rather, the asymmetric argument is yet another empirical objection that points out the incapability of present liberal democracies to deal with international environmental and social issues and where institutional factors often explain why liberal democracies fail.[36] However discouraging O'Neill's assertion may be, it is relevant to reason that just as democracies once were transformed from city-bound to nation-bound systems, a similar transformation from nation-bound systems to, e.g., federation-bound systems can be imagined. For example, what does it take in terms of additional integration before the EU can be considered a liberal democracy—at least according to the three DLD premises? Equality of opportunity is certainly a guiding principle in the EU already—both within and across national borders.

8.3.4 Conclusions Regarding DLD and the Global Aspects of Sustainable Development Policies

In practice there are severe problems that have to be dealt with in order for a liberal-democratic state to actually implement the policies implied by scenario SD-4. This particular dilemma, however, points to the need for liberal democracies to update their ways of functioning rather than to any inherent antagonism between sustainability policies and liberal-democratic values. The question in this section is whether it might be logically concluded that the environmental policies derived from scenario SD-4 must be considered incompatible with the liberal-democratic core values just because they have a global reach. The answer is that with the policies I have identified, and the criterion being derived, I find no convincing evidence that any of the premises would be more violated when the policies are applied on the international level than on the national level. Again, this is partly because *scope* is not a relevant general premise, given our analysis throughout Chapter 3. The premises constituting DLD are by no means theoretically bound to the nation state, and if we cannot conclude that the SD-4 policies are incompatible within a country, then we cannot conclude incompatibility when they are applied at the global level.

8.4 The Intergenerational Aspects of the Sustainable Development Policies and Developmental Liberal Democracy

In this final Section I investigate if the intergenerational dimension of scenario SD-4 gives rise to any violation of the three core premises of DLD. Since no reference is made to future generations in our DLD model, I have to consider the work of other liberal theorists who have analysed the challenges imposed by the concern for future generations. I argue that none of the DLD premises constitutes principal hindrances for showing concern for future generations. However, for the premises not to be violated we have to presuppose a *ranking order*, where present generations have precedence over future generations.

Although perhaps a bit difficult to derive, scenario SD-4 does contain an intrinsic consideration for future generations, in its radical assumptions about efficiency.[37] These cannot be motivated only with reference to the needs of the current generation, for which few assumptions about efficiency have to be made—although some of the redistribution arguments also appear to be valid in a short-term perspective. There is enough land to exploit for a long time to come. Water is so far only scarce in some regions where it often will be possible to continue pumping up ground or fossil water for quite a while. Phosphorus will be available for at least another 175 years with the present levels of extraction. Furthermore, we assume a gradual increase of efficiency in production. Thus, consideration for future generations is built into the scenario. Whether this is *enough* is another issue that can hardly be answered unless the size of future generations and their particular needs and wants are known, and/or their specific rights have been determined.

I have placed the matter of future generations to the end of the analysis for the reason that there is no *explicit obligation* to future generations in DLD. That is not to say that there is no concern for future generations in liberal political philosophy. On the contrary; the liberal philosopher Brian Barry has written most extensively on the matter (e.g. Barry 1996). Another example is John Rawls whose saving principle (1972:284-293) is a logical consequence of his reasoning on the original position (cf. Section 8.3). Since nobody is able to control what generation he or she will be born, everyone will rationally agree that resources ought to be saved over time so that one may secure one's own welfare. However, each generation has a kind of moral obligation to at least the next two generations—but not to a bloodline's "entire life span in perpetuity" (Rawls 1972:287). This version of the saving principle has been roundly criticised.[38] In his *Political Liberalism* (1993), Rawls adjusts his principle by stating that "society is a system of co-operation between generations *over time*" (1993:274). This is an important amendment. After the first generation is born, new generations are added while the first generation is still alive. This means that the two principles of justice are not only valid for one generation, but at least for a couple more at the same time. When the first generation becomes old and needy, it wants to hand over a well-managed society in order to be helped, which also benefits the generations to come. The 'new' saving principle is therefore not only a matter of self-interest and/or moral obligations, but of mutual advantage as well.

Marcel Wissenburg (1998) has shown that the saving principle can be generalised to all liberal theories and not only to those that depart from an 'original position' (Wissenburg 1998:127-131), thus including our ideal-types as well. Even if Rawls saving principle does consider future generations and, interestingly enough, actually forces *every* preceding generation to do so, one important problem with the principle prevails. It "allows us to sacrifice the well-being of one generation to a perhaps minute gain for others in cases where all generations could perhaps be very well of." Wissenburg (1998:136).

Wissenburg therefore formulates a 'restraint principle' with traits from the saving principle, that can only be overruled by the quest for *survival*.[39] This means that if there is no other way to preserve a present life ('worth living', p. 136) other than by harming a future generation, then this must be accepted. The same holds for animals. The principle is formulated as follows:

> "No good shall be destroyed unless unavoidable and unless they are replaced by perfectly identical goods; if that is physically impossible, they should be replaced by equivalent goods resembling the original as closely as possible; and if that is also impossible, a proper compensation should be provided." (Wissenburg 1998:123)

While Rawls' saving principle allows for an inter-generational 'jump' between—at least—two generations, the restraint principle ties each and every generation to a *chain* of responsibility. The purpose of the principle is to safeguard basic human goods, and to do this with the least possible damage to the physical environment, which means saving resources for future generations. Notice that this is not a rule that *guarantees* a particular outcome; it is rather a filter through which decisions ought to pass, in order to remove decisions that would *needlessly* damage the environment for future generations.[40]

What can the restraint principle bring to this analysis? Disregarding for a moment the content of the principle, and instead focusing on the main reasom behind its formulation—i.e., that several generations are interwoven, extending governmental obligations and the time frame for governmental policies—it is easily found that the restraint principle has important implications on the DLD policy restriction. Provided that the DLD policy restriction, which states that equality of opportunity must be the guiding principle for the state in national and international/global environmental politics (cf. Section 8.2 & 8.3) is valid, then logically this premise is valid also between generations—since apparently there are no 'between' generations. In any case, the restraint principle certainly does not command present liberal governments *not* to consider future generations. Rather, the fact that generations are woven into each other implies that a policy that *disregards* future generations is a violation of the DLD policy restriction. This is because premises 2 and 3 would then not be properly observed during the time that the policy is effective.[41]

Thus, the policies deduced from scenario SD-4 meant to provide basic goods for both present and future generations must not be in violation to any of the core premises, for the same reason as why the restraint principle can be considered a valid liberal principle for more than one generation: *successive generations are interwoven*. If the rights and corresponding obligations within one generation can be identified (as in premise 3), then these rights and obligations are reasonably valid for the next generation to come, and so on.[42]

This must not and does not imply that present and future generations enjoy the same status. The restraint principle works as a filter only. Nothing in the formulation implies any welfare guarantees for future generations. If the next generation has to exploit the entire global environment, in order to survive, then the restraint principle cannot prevent this from happening. All it can do is persuade that generation to reflect on the consequences of its actions and perhaps encourage it to use resources more efficiently. If such an efficient use of resources is not adequate to ensure an assumed future population the resources required for everyone to enjoy equality of opportunity, then a liberal democracy cannot do anything about that under its premises.

This, I would like to assert, is a conclusion that requires elaboration. If we cannot make our resource use efficient enough to fulfil our basic needs and at the same time leave enough for future generations to have their basic needs fulfilled, there is still one option left. However, we must keep in mind that this is an option that is *solely* imaginable in the most comprehensive form of DLD.[43]

The argument goes like this. Wissenburg elaborates with what he calls 'Population policy', i.e., that the government, just like in China, determine the size of the population. He correctly concludes that this policy is not legitimate from a liberal-democratic point of view. However, if the restraint principle were applied in combination with an outspoken policy for equality of opportunity,[44] I would say that a double protection for future generations emerges. The first protection, the restraint principle, has already been discussed.

If society is not able to secure the provision of resources required for future generations to attain equal opportunities to enjoy autonomy, the number of people within future generations may be pre-determined; *not* by practising some kind of state imposed draconian population policy, but by actively practising policies aimed at providing present generations fairly equally with a certain amount of welfare. Without such welfare, people will do everything in their power to survive from one day to the next, regardless of any negative environmental consequences. This was one argument for ensuring all currently living human beings certain fundamental basic goods, according to the Brundtland Commission, since then they would at least be given a choice not to needlessly destroy vital environmental resources. Moreover, while enjoying these resources they also get a choice and an opportunity to decide the size of future generations. If the current generations have reason to believe that the coming generations will not be able to live a life worth living, they, by free will, can affect this sad condition by deciding to give birth to fewer children, or by not having any children at all. To be able to make such a decision, a certain standard of living is probably necessary.

We can give a valid argument against this by saying that there are religious limitations this suggestion. No less valid is, however, the correlation between number of births on the one hand, and income and general welfare on the other.[45]

If a liberal state not only practises the restraint principle, but also actively works in accordance with the DLD policy restrictions and in line with the three core premises, I thus suggest that the probability for future generations to have the resources required for enjoying equal opportunities will increase even more than Wissenburg maintains. *However*, this may not be *sufficient* protection.

The results of this investigation must be painful for anyone who places present and future generations on an equal footing in all respects and argues that for the earmarking of resources for the future (resources that the present generations will have no access to). Nevertheless, it is difficult for me to see how a liberal democracy, no matter how comprehensive in scope, could legitimately range over more than morally based filters through which present decisions ought to be put before they are implemented. A state that withholds crucial resources from its current citizens, making them unable to enjoy equal opportunities for the benefit of future generations, must *inevitably* violate both premises 2, 3 and the harm principle.

It seems that the DLD premises presuppose that present generations always have precedence over future generations. Nothing in the DLD can avoid this, or require the opposite. Thus, Wissenburg is totally correct when asserting that if there is no way to preserve a life today other than by sacrificing future generations, then that must be accepted. This statement becomes intelligible if the third premise is applied. If the state is to actively practice a policy aimed at providing equal opportunities to enjoy autonomy, such a policy will be resource demanding. Perhaps even so demanding that it will jeopardise the prospects for future generations to enjoy those same opportunities. To avoid this, present generations (assumed to enjoy the resources required to have equal opportunities) can apply certain measures. For example, by leading to people giving birth to fewer children, such a policy will not[46] violate any of the premises and will thus not go beyond the policy restrictions. However, the reverse would not be legitimate according to the DLD premises. If the state practices a policy aimed at setting aside resources to provide future generations with equal opportunities to enjoy autonomy, and this means that (at least some of) the present generation will not have their fundamental resources met, then this policy violates the DLD policy restriction since the state would then not actively practice policies in accordance with premise 2 and 3.

Conclusion: Sustainable development policies aimed at preserving resources for future generations can be considered compatible with DLD, *if and only if* the resources required for present generations to attain equal opportunity to enjoy autonomy are *simultaneously* ensured.

8.5 Conclusions

Table 8.2   The completed Analysis

Sustainable Development Policies	PLD Policy restriction	DLD Policy restriction
National and international planning for organising the use and production of:		
• Land	(-)	(+)
• Water	(-)	(+)
• Phosphorus	(-)	(+)
• Food	(-)	(+)
Support and implementation of improved technology:		
• Water	(-)[i]	(+)
• Phosphorous	(-)[ii]	(+)
• Biotechnology	(-)[iii]	(+)[vi]
Transference and redistribution of technology and social and economic means require:		
• Support of initial costs	(+)[iv]	(+)
• Duty and subvention policy	(+)[v]	(+)
• Redistribution of economic and social goods for social justice and efficiency	(-)	(+)
Prioritising and ranking with potentially negative effects for:		
• The producers	(-)	(+)
• The consumers	(-)	(+)
• Aesthetics and tourism interests	(-)	(+)
• Rainforest and biodiversity	(-)	(+)
• Future generations	(-)	(+)[vii]

Clarifying notes:

[i-iii] These conclusions are valid, provided that the market alone is incapable of globally supporting new and effective water technology, phosphorus technology and biotechnology (cf. Section 8.1.2).

[iv] This conclusion is valid, given that it is not the government that has to bear the initial costs (cf. Section 8.1.3).

v) This policy is legitimate seen from a PLD perspective, and if anything, should be considered a *strengthening* of PLD. (cf. Section 8.1.3).

vi) Governmentally initiated support for biotechnology is legitimate given that the technology is aimed at providing individuals with equal opportunities (cf. Section 8.2.2)

vii) According to the ranking order established in Section 8.4, if e.g., the use of biotechnology is required for present generations to survive or enjoy equal opportunities, then future generations must stand back. This means, if required, such a priority is legitimate (cf. concluding discussion Section 8.4).

An adequate answer can now be given to the priority issue in the discussion on biotechnology that was not fully dealt with above (cf. Section 8.2.4). I then concluded that it is doubtful whether DLD can legitimise policies promoting biotechnology since short term advantages are put against longer-term disasters or disadvantages. However, according to the analyses of future generations, the answer now becomes quite straightforward. If the choice between using and not using biotechnology literally is a matter of life and death, or at least concerns equal opportunities to attain autonomy *for present generations*, compared with imposed risks on future generations and ecological values, then to give priority to the needs of present generations is legitimate from a DLD point of view. Admittedly, the restraint principle forces us to reflect on all the options, but if biotechnology appears to be the only alternative, then it will be used. Thus, since biotechnology is assumed to be a prerequisite for the realisation of scenario SD-4 and the objective of scenario SD-4 cannot be disqualified on the basis that it is in violation with any of the core premises, such technology cannot be considered logically incompatible with DLD.

Our type-four compatibility analysis is now complete. First, compatibility between sustainable development policies and *Protective Liberal Democracy* (PLD) was analysed. With few exceptions I conclude that as long as the implied societal transitions presuppose *state-implemented* policies, they can not be considered compatible with that ideal-type. The analysis of compatibility between the policies and D*evelopmental Liberal Democracy* (DLD) basically ends in the opposite conclusion; it has proved difficult to argue that any of the policies are incompatible with, or must violate, the core values constituting that ideal-type. In Table 8.2, my main conclusions are specified.

Notes:

1 Almost, anyway. Phosphorus and phosphate rock is mainly located in the Earth's crust, and the right of extraction is therefore partly dependent on each individual state's distribution of, and rules for making use of, resources located there.

2 One exception is conceivable. If people were actually forced (by external forces such as extreme weather conditions) to use toxic phosphorus, then perhaps governmental intervention to prevent this would be appropriate and legitimate from a PLD perspective. This is, however, hardly the case here (cf. the discussion about natural and intentional coercion in Section 3.2.1).

3 This is not an unlikely scenario if we think of local adaptation, for example. To distribute and effectively make use of water in extremely poor regions of the world, highly advanced and often costly methods are required. Some of these (adjusted) technologies might not be required anywhere else in the world, and the price would therefore not decrease sufficiently to make the product economically available.

4 When studying individual protective liberal theorists, there might be exceptions to the rule, e.g., Nozick's (1974) discussion about 'moral catastrophes' and the government's ability to prevent such events.

5 This is reasonably an empirical question, i.e., 'Does anyone have a life plan that would be violated if the state puts some interests before others?'

6 Having priority over someone else, in this case the unborn, does not mean and must not imply that I will take advantage of that.

7 There is, of course, an important restriction on the idea of opportunities. There is always an upper limit to how many opportunities can possibly be offered and to how equal access is to them. Not least this is a matter of economic capacity within a country. If the GNP per capita is low, then the taxation base is low and that limits the citizens' opportunity to equal welfare, for example. This is a fact no matter how liberal-democratic the constitution is in all other respects.

8 Such priorities are a prerequisite for a society to reach the level of efficiency assumed in scenario SD-4. If we do not bother about the future, then we do not have to attain scenario SD-4, but can keep on living as we do today until we cannot live any more—or until we have found an alternative way of living. Thus, even if concern for future generations is not an explicitly defined variable in scenario SD-4, a concern for future generations is taken for granted in the construction of the scenario—the scenario is supposed to illustrate some kind of resource output equilibrium (which of course can be disturbed if a few more billion people are added to the picture). At any rate, the main issue is whether concern for future generations is legitimate from a DLD perspective.

9 That is not to say that demand for private property does not exist. But the premise would have to be formulated as 'property ought to be held and enjoyed privately unless premises 2 and 3 require something else', which means that what and how much property ought to be kept privately is answered through these premises, although theoretically indeterminable (cf. Section 3.2.2). As long as premises 2 and 3 are not violated, the right to hold property is not violated.

10 Either, to uphold welfare which here is assumed to include animal food consumption, or such consumption will be a consequence of increased welfare.

11 I am fully aware that the issue of basic goods and needs is crucial here. We would need a *standard* which defines what basic goods are needed by everyone (to enjoy equal opportunities), and furthermore a comprehensive and coherent acceptance of that standard to legitimise the planning needed to realise the outcome in scenario SD-4. Such a standard cannot be established here. All I am claiming is that if we accept that a certain amount of welfare (basic goods) is required for everyone to enjoy equal opportunities to realise life plans, as is done in the DLD ideal type, and if we accept the idea that providing equal opportunities is a legitimate target for the developmental state, then planning for securing such basic goods *can* be legitimised by DLD. For reasons presented earlier (cf. note 45 in Section 3.3.2), this kind of reasoning cannot be extended to any goods that people may want. e.g. eating pheasant every day can hardly be argued as a main component of autonomy. Still, while we stick to fundamental needs such as food, and a certain quantum of economic welfare (that obviously gives rise to an increased demand for animal food), we cannot dismiss the demand for planning indicated in scenario SD-4.

12 As became clear in Chapter 5 on water shortages.

13 As a matter of fact, provided that water is a key resource for autonomy, it would be a violation of both premises 2 and 3 as well as the harm, autonomy and ECR principles not to support such technology.

14 Not only though. Already today at least 25 countries in the world are suffering from 'severe water shortage' and 30 more will reach this level with an additional 4 billion people born within 50 years (cf. Section 5.2)

15 To solely *survive* is something different.

16 It certainly would also happen without the assumed animal food consumption. A socially and economically stable society is not possible unless the basic need for water is fulfilled.

17 These measures and policies are to a considerable degree also international and global matters. Nevertheless, I will not pay attention to the global aspect here, but will instead deal with it in the next Section on the international aspects of scenario SD-4.

18 Not least is the ever-expanding literature on *ecological justice* a sign of the importance of this matter (see e.g. several contributions in Gleeson & Low 2001).

19 For instance because the product in question is not required in the Western world, where it would otherwise be developed.

20 Such as to uphold a certain degree of self-sufficiency in a country.

21 Presumably in the form of some kind of compensation.

22 Certain needs must be fulfilled for an individual to enjoy autonomy. Provided that the needs expressed in scenario SD-4 coincide with the 'autonomy need', then a realisation of scenario SD-4 is legitimate where the government bears the initial costs. Both the ecological and the socio-economic demands in scenario SD-4 refer to basic needs that individuals probably require to enjoy such autonomy. We cannot claim that this policy is illegitimate according to any of the DLD premises as long as we cannot claim the contrary.

23 To be able to understand liberty as autonomy, forced through this reduction. A continued defence of an absolute right to hold property, while at the same time allowing for a positive understanding of liberty, would be a contradiction, or *extraordinarily* naïve. There is certainly a striving to keep property as intact as possible, but if *needed*, this has to be reduced. There is an effort to keep as much as possible intact. Still, the more 'opportunity for autonomy' is satisfied with an economic and social content, the more the right to hold property has to be cut. This is not to say that a *complete* eradication of private property is legitimised. To standardise the whole of society is, naturally, unacceptable in all liberal respects. However, as soon as an exclusive negative understanding of liberty is left behind, there are analytical problems in finding a limit beyond which no more private property is allowed to be used for public expenditure.

24 See addition examples in Section 6.2.3.

25 Recall from Section 6.2.2 that governmental regulations and political force might be needed either against a *sceptical public* or against the producers of such technology—to meet the demands from the sceptical public. The principal problem is, however, the same: governmentally initiated priorities are required.

26 It goes without saying that in the case where the producers are required to change their production and lose their ability to enjoy autonomy, some kind of compensation must be paid.

27 In Sections 3.1.2 and 3.3.2, I brought up John Stuart Mills' harm principle. When I did that, I said that the formulation of this principle became a starting point for developmental liberal thinking. The idea of avoiding harm, if possible, is a fundamental idea behind thinking in terms of opportunities. This infers that a defence of the

opportunity idea is also justification for actions to prevent harm. Especially if none of the measures suggested in the scenario analysis is realised (including the assumption of a 30% animal food diet), it can easily be concluded that harm may be experienced in the future. In the most extreme case, those who can afford it continue to eat animal food at the same rate as now. With gradual economic growth in densely populated regions, the number of animals required will increase over time and may come to create a competive situation between animal fodder and food. This is a harmful scenario, at least for the poorest (not to speak of future generations), and I doubt that this cannot be considered a fundamental matter. If it is fundamental, then I see no reason why restrictions on an individual's diet would not be legitimate. Excessive dietary requirements must then be placed against an empty diet. In such a situation, I suggest, it is both the no-harm principle and the three DLD premises that are relevant.

28 Of course this equalisation must not result in others ending up with a *deficit* of basic opportunities.

29 It is certainly so that the idea of equality of opportunity creates a theoretical space in which the state may and is even *expected* to act more actively and intrusively then is the case with a thinner understanding of liberal democracy. This role of the state results in a reduction in the number of life plans that are actually achievable for people. This is a necessary consequence caused by the positive understanding of liberty.

30 Something that certainly can have both social and economic consequences.

31 This conclusion does not imply that the state is allowed to impose, e.g., 100% income taxes in order for all citizens to enjoy equal opportunities. The simple reason for this is that such taxation would both remove people's ability to enjoy autonomy, and most likely also cause them harm.

32 Putting the explicit policy examples aside inevitably results in an even more theoretical analysis than what we have experienced so far.

33 If this is *not* assumed, it is no big deal to add this to the list of missing knowledge.

34 As pointed out in Section 3.3.2, there is an ongoing debate regarding whether any such resources can be identified objectively. See Douglas et al. (1998) for an illuminating summary of this debate.

35 By understanding liberty and equality this way, a partial fusion occurs between the two elements. The result is the idea of equality of opportunity.

36 The discussion also shows the importance of keeping the institutional and philosophical aspects of liberal democracy apart—actually all four aspects of liberal democracy that I suggested in Section 1.1.

37 Perhaps not in exactly the same way as green political theory in general, where future generations are sometimes placed as equal to present generations.

38 See for example Wissenburg (1998:127ff).

39 This is not indisputable. I suggest they are valid *at least* for every DLD theory. For example, if the protection of private property is very strong, as in the PLD model, I would say that the restraint principle may be overruled by this right, whether we are speaking of survival or various other life conditions. The same argument goes for the often referred to 'Lockean Proviso' which is sometimes suggested as an inherent liberal protection for the environment and for future generations (cf. Wissenburg 1998:83; Dobson 1998:145-148). However, I believe that it overlooks Locke's proviso, which was mainly founded in humanity's obligations to God; not on any obligations to future generations. That is, privately owned property was to be managed properly because humankind had borrowed Earth from God. When God was eventually 'defined away' to another galaxy by latter liberal theorists, they also passed the former protection for the environment and future generations out into the heavens. Remaining of the proviso is

now only the (more or less *absolute*) right to hold property among PLD theorists—a right that has been shown to offes little protection for future generations (cf. Section 8.1.4).

40 Is it possible for the state to remain neutral if it is to decide what is needless and what is not? Although we are confronting a difficult balancing act here, the fact that generations are interwoven requires that the currently available resources needed to attain equal opportunities to enjoy autonomy, must also be enjoyed by future generations—*if possible* (the latter amendment explains 'needless').

41 Again we are confronting the risk of non-neutrality, i.e., that the policies are turning into substantial goals. However, as we learned in Chapter 3, for any of the policies to be considered 'substantial', or constituting a violation of any of the DLD premises, we have to show that the *aim* of the policy is illegitimate—not that it is directed towards a specific group of people, whether living today or tomorrow. To show that this is the case without having access to a precise framework has proved difficult (cf. Section 8.2).

42 I must *emphasise* that from this assertion it does not necessarily follow that future generations are guaranteed the same opportunities as current generations, or are ensured the basic goods required to fulfil their life plans.

43 An extension I do not believe Wissenburg would accept as liberally legitimate—according to how he defines the framework within which the policy is legitimate. His concept of liberalism is 'thinner' than that allowed for in my approach.

44 Cf. Barry 1996:242ff).

45 I.e., the theory of 'demographic transition' (cf. Tietenberg 1994:80-95). Recall that this theory is not my main point. Instead I wish to capture that the set of choices (such as how many children we wish to give birth to) increases with welfare. Thus, this argument should not be viewed as opposed to Wissenburg's principle, but as a compliment.

46 Ideologically it can, of course.

Chapter 9

Sustainable Development and Liberal Democracy: Insights and Conditions for Compatibility

This book emanated from a political-theoretical debate on the relationship between sustainable development and liberal democracy. This debate has evoked scholars to argue that these two entities are *incompatible*; alternative political systems are required to deal successfully with the comprehensive and perhaps insoluble issues of sustainable development. I asserted on four grounds that this debate can be improved both theoretically and methodologically: (1) there is no such thing as a uniform liberal democracy, (2) liberal-democratic practice and its philosophical foundation ought to be kept apart, (3) we are far from seeing any green liberal democratic theory, and (4) sustainable development can be viewed either as a set of values or policies.

These grounds or 'motives' supplied the reasons for me to carry out what is to date a unique analysis, largely based on interdisciplinary research and with the particular aim of determining whether sustainable development *policies* can be considered (in)compatible with liberal democratic *core values*. In this final chapter, I discuss the implications of the results from that analysis and from the book in general.

9.1 Conditions for Compatibility Between Sustainable Development Liberal-Democratic Core Values

The short version of my conclusions is the following: Yes, given the assumptions and postulations provided in this study, sustainable development policies are—*logically*—compatible with the core values of DLD but not with those of PLD. Yet, this conclusion needs to be additionally elaborated and especially, we need to discuss what implications this conclusion has for the overall compatibility debate introduced in Chapter 1.

When viewed in light of our DLD ideal-type, many of the sustainability policies laid out in Chapter 7 become more attainable than is the case with the PLD ideal-type. The premises and policy restriction in the compatibility criterion of DLD are not only more flexible, but also more vaguely and generously defined than those of the PLD. However, concluding that the DLD ideal-type is the same as 'anything goes' would, as shown throughout Sections 8.2-8.4, be a fundamental misinterpretation. It is true that starting from developmental liberal theory makes it difficult to derive any absolute limits for what sustainable development and equality of opportunity ought to comprise, and thus to reject consistently many of the sustainability policies suggested in this study. Nonetheless, there *are* limits also to what the DLD state is allowed to do with respect to sustainable development policies. In this study I have mainly pointed out four such limitations, of which the third is a combination of four different principles. The first three limits were introduced in Section 3.3.2. while the fourth was derived in Section 8.4 on future generations.

(1)   The *aim* of a sustainable development policy must be limited and must not be formulated or considered to be an over-arching 'communitarian' goal presupposing the DLD state to transgress its (active and comprehensive) neutrality. This also means that no substantial outcome can be *guaranteed* by a developmental liberal democracy. Consequently, in the final analysis this means that whether a certain goal *will* be realised or not is principally a practical political issue.

(2)   Limitations on *equality of opportunity*. This matter concerns what resources should and can be made available to everyone for equality of opportunity to arise. By accepting a positive understanding of liberty in the DLD ideal-type, we open the door to a (still limited) room within which more or less comprehensive social and economic redistribution is possible. The precise size of the room, i.e., an exact specification of which resources and what amount of these resources are legitimate, has proved difficult to deduce from developmental liberal theory. Among other factors, ideology and the harm-principle (see below) contribute to define the quantum of resources that can be distributed legitimately.

(3)   When redistributing the resources required for citizens to enjoy equal opportunities to autonomously choose and attain their life plans, the state must never violate any individual *negative rights*, and *the harm, ECR* or *autonomy principle*. Thus, if the implementation of any of the sustainable development policies presupposes such a violation, it cannot be considered compatible with the core values of developmental liberal democracy. But is it possible to argue that any of the policies *would* violate these principles? According to how the Brundtland Commission report has been interpreted in this book, the discussed resources are considered fundamental for humanity to flourish and enjoy autonomy. This has brought me to the conclusion that a DLD state would violate these principles unless it endeavoured to distribute the resources properly.

(4)   DLD establishes a strict *order of precedence.* If required, present generations ought to be put before future generations within the developmental liberal perspective. Furthermore, human beings always have precedence over all other animals and species. This ranking order certainly implies policy limitations. However, since this order does not *exclude* other interests, but only ranks them differently, this limitation is relative and dependent on factors such as the total amount of resources available.

Thus, there are certainly limits when we discuss the DLD ideal type a well. However, except from a semantic point of view, i.e., in case the aim of a sustainable development policy is actually formulated as a communitarian goal, the precise range of these limits can be neither theoretically nor logically derived from studying developmental liberal theory. They must be considered personal ideological matters.

In fact, the aim of a policy, the range of equality of opportunity and whether harm is caused by the majority, the ECR principle is violated, the autonomy principle is disregarded or the specific ranking order is properly executed, all are among the issues that citizens in liberal democracies regularly vote on—and *should* vote on if sustainable development is to be realised within a liberal democracy worthy of the name.[1]

What I have shown in this book is that our particular type-four compatibility is principally a matter of delimitation. Unless we *specify* the above limitations too narrowly, the implementation of our sustainable development policies can logically be regarded legitimate from a DLD point of view and thus *compatible* with the core values of DLD. Any other conclusion requires that we have an exact list of which resources and what quantum of resources should be distributed for the citizens to enjoy equal opportunities to autonomously choose and attain their life plans. This brings us to the following conclusion:

In order to arrive at the conclusion, or even to legitimately proceed from the assumption that sustainable development policies are *incompatible* with liberal-democratic core values, it is necessary to specify:

- What is the explicit *aim* of sustainable development policies?
- What is the legitimate *scope* of equality of opportunity?
- What are the *precise limits* for the harm principle, the ECR principle and the autonomy principle?
- What is the legitimate *order of precedence* between present and future generations as well as other species?

Unless the answers to these four questions are such that they clearly violate the core values of liberal democracy, it makes little sense to talk about incompatibility between sustainable development *policies* and liberal-democratic core *values*.

9.2 General Insights

Let me now continue this concluding discussion by re-examining my four motives. Have I brought any 'order' into the green debate? I argue that even if the particular type-four analysis is limited to only one of the research fields in the matrix, the overall reasoning in the book has generated theoretical and methodological material valid for the debate as a whole.

9.2.1 Liberal-Democratic Practice and its Philosophical Foundation Ought to be Kept Apart

I argued in Section 1.1 for further specification of the set of 'intrinsic' or 'inherent' features of liberal democracy, stated by both non-democratic and democratic theorists as reasons for incompatibility and serving as arguments for suggesting alternative political systems. Unless we keep the different features apart, most of the incompatibility arguments make little sense. I suggested as a minimum requirement, that it is necessary to distinguish between the institutional/practical dimension and the philosophical foundation of liberal democracy. In Chapter 3 I 'applied' this way of reasoning by leaving out the institutional and procedural aspects of liberal democracy and solely focusing on its core values, i.e., democracy, liberty and equality.

By making, and systematically observing this distinction, I tried to formulate stringent criteria against which sustainable development policies can be tested.[2] In terms of analytical precision, much was gained by practising this separation, since it forced the separation of the different arguments for and against compatibility. This way of thinking is valid for all the four plausible compatibility analyses implied by the matrix introduced in chapter 1, because quite clearly there are several critical arguments against compatibility. However, all these arguments are not necessarily applicable simultaneously. One illuminating example of this was when O'Neill´s (2000) 'asymmetrical argument'[3] was applied to the issue of sustainable development (cf. Section 8.3.3). Had my analytical framework been based on, or contained elements of the institutional dimension of liberal democracy,[4] then O'Neill's objection, unfoundedly[5] I would say, would have remained valid, or even would have made no sense at all. However, by consistently sticking to the philosophical foundation of liberal democracy, i.e., the core values, we could establish that O'Neill's argument misses the target in this particular case.

9.2.2 There is No Such Thing As a Uniform Liberal Democracy

In Section 1.2, I summarised the arguments that have been put forth against compatibility between sustainable development and liberal democracy. When examining these arguments,[6] I found that two things stand out rather clearly: it is necessary (1) to distinguish between different forms of or *ideal-types* of liberal democracy, and (2) to make use of *criteria* to facilitate a consistent and transparent compatibility analysis. Let me summarise these conclusions:

(1)   *Liberal ideal-types.* There are several suggestions for defining liberal democracy as different ideal-types. However, I have found no compatibility analysis where this distinction has been systematically dealt with in earlier research. Whether applying this distinction has proved profitable needs no further discussion—my conclusions speak for themselves. There are significant differences between the ideal-types, and they have important effects for my conclusions. Hardly any of the sustainable development policies are compatible with the protective understanding of liberal democracy, and virtually every policy *can* be argued to be compatible with developmental liberal democracy.

(2)   *Determining compatibility by using explicit criteria.* Also my suggestion that the use of criteria would facilitate future compatibility analysis has gained support. This is not only the case when the purpose is additional clarification, but also from the viewpoint of *inter-subjectivity*; anyone who so wishes can re-examine my conclusions and the way they are drawn. The use of criteria and policy restrictions also allows me to draw stringent, transparent and most importantly, conclusions that allow for scrutiny, since all the steps preceding the analysis have been clearly presented and discussed.

9.2.3 A Green Liberal Democratic Theory is (Still) Far Away

In Section 1.3, I argued that surprisingly few theorists have made any thorough tests of the environmental qualifications of liberal democracy. Furthermore, most attempts have focused on some specific issue, such as whether the liberal list of rights can be broadened to include future generations or other species, and whether the ideas of some particular liberal theorist could be extended to cope with environmental issues. Given that such a theory is at all plausible, I therefore asserted that no consistent theory of a green liberal democracy exists. Whether this study brings us much closer to a plausible theory of green liberal democracy is also questionable. Yet, there are three elements of this book that I would say constitute important contributions to such an attempt: (1) the matrix, (2) the 'type-four' analysis of liberal democratic values and sustainable development policies, and (3) the explicit specification of what is required to conclude (and consequently to avoid) incompatibility between sustainable development policies and liberal-democratic core values.

(1)   *The matrix* serves as a useful tool for mapping and understanding the green debate and for relating to other compatibility analyses. It allows categorisation of a particular compatibility analysis as belonging to any of the four variants in the matrix. Furthermore, it provides an insight into the comprehensive work required to actually design a *consistent* green liberal democracy, i.e., a theory that is considered consistent in all four squares of the matrix.

(2)   The poorly investigated square 4. I argued in Chapter 1 that liberal-democratic values and sustainable development policies make up the most poorly analysed and investigated research field within the compatibility debate. One of the few examples that I brought up was Achterberg (1993) (De Geus:2001 was another) who proceeds from John Rawls (1972) and the Netherlands's Environmental Policy Plan (NEPP) and who suggests that his approach is at least 'heuristically useful'. The conclusions in this book support Achterberg's results. However, by proceeding from more general liberal-democratic ideal-types and environmental policies with global and intra-generational scope, my conclusions should be seen as more far-reaching, thorough and more generally valid.

(3)   Is a green liberal democracy possible? The conclusions from my type-four analysis are interesting in relation to the prospects of a green liberal democracy. This is because they suggest that as long as (a) the *aim* of sustainable development is not expressed as and meant to be an over-arching goal, (b) the *scope* of equality of opportunity is not required to be too comprehensive, and (c) the *order of precedence* established in Chapter 8 is not considered illegitimate—all three of which I argued are individual normative matters—it is difficult to say there are no prospects for such a theory to be formulated.[7] Furthermore, there are good reasons to argue that these arguments are valid also in square 2 of the matrix (liberal-democratic values/sustainable development values). As long as the normative/philosophical foundation behind sustainable development is not absolute, i.e., as long as the Brundtland Commission's objectives are not to be seen as an over-arching communitarian goal, then sustainable development values can be considered compatible with liberal-democratic core values. To establish whether the Brundtland Commission's objectives should be considered as such a communitarian goal, we must not proceed from the *scope* of the implied revolution (which by necessity is enormous), but from the normatively/philosophically justified aim of that goal.

9.2.4 Viewing Sustainable Development as a Set of Values or a Set of Policies

I argued in Section 1.4 that most analyses of the relationship between sustainable development and liberal democracy have so far proceeded from a philosophical understanding of sustainable development, i.e., as a set of mainly environmental values. One category of compatibility analysis is missing, i.e., one proceeding from sustainable development *policies*. Although such policies *have* been dealt with here, the most distinguished characteristic of the study is still the *method* being used to outline and specify these policies.

This book did not start out from the rather vague guidelines implied in the Brundtland Commission's report. Neither did it proceed from a single country's established plan for implementing sustainable development. Instead *environmental science* constituted the foundation for determining the policies.

These scenarios were used to translate the Brundtland Commission's guidelines into more specific and analysable scenarios. By then viewing these scenarios from a 'back-casting' perspective, I was able both to identify the societal changes required to realise scenario SD-4, and to outline the policies required to 'implement' these transitions. Ideally, scholars from other disciplines should have interpreted the scenarios. Yet, already our limited attempts have proved fruitful and worthy of further elaboration.

I applied this method to the particular research question found in the fourth square of the matrix, i.e., liberal-democratic values vs. sustainable development policies. However, my approach is just as valid and useful when dealing with the issues in square 3, i.e., if we wish to say something further about the liberal-democratic *institutions* required to implement sustainable development on a global scale. This is because here we also need to know what policies are required to realise sustainable development.

It is certainly correct to claim that liberal democracies have, or would have, difficulties implementing something like sustainable development. However, this is not necessarily because of the core ideas constituting such political systems, but rather because of the institutions and procedures that have been developed within them. Thus, John Stuart Mill's words will also be valid in the future:

"No great improvements in the lot of mankind are possible, until a great
change takes place in the fundamental constitution of their modes of thought".
(J. S. Mill 1873: *Autobiography*)

Notes:

1 Cf. the presentation of the Aristotelian political theorist M. Nussbaum (Section 3.3.2) who suggested a very long list of resources that the state ought to provide citizens, not necessarily with the purpose of ensuring equality of opportunity to choose and attain their individual life plans, but rather in order to make them able to live a paternalistically decided good life.
2 Recall that the aim of this division was not to make sustainable development more or less compatible with liberal democracy. The pupose of this discussion was to contribute with clarifications enabling more stringent analyses.
3 E.g., why liberal democracy cannot cope with international justice.
4 Cf. my examination in Section 1.1.3 where I argue that some theorists have mixed philosophical and practical arguments.
5 Given that our intention was to analyse the relationship found in square 4 of the matrix.
6 Cf. Section 1.1.3
7 That is not to say that such a theory *can* be formulated. To get an idea of how much more work would be required, I return to the matrix. To be able to formulate a theory of green liberal democracy, i.e., one that is both theoretically consistent *and* functioning, the theory ought to range over (and compatibility must reign in) all four squares of the matrix. To get there would be quite a task. A less ambitious project would be to only formulate a *theoretically consistent* theory, i.e., one where compatibility reigns in both

square 2 and 4, or a *functioning* green liberal democracy, i.e., one where compatible reigns in both squares 1 and 3.

Bibliography

Achterberg, W. 1993: "Can Liberal Democracy Survive the Environmental Crisis? Sustainability, Liberal Neutrality and Overlapping Consensus." In Dobson, A. & Lucardie, P. *The Politics of Nature. Explorations in green political theory.* London, Routledge.

Achterberg, W. 2001: "Environmental Justice and Global Democracy." In Gleeson, B. & Low, N. 2001: *Governing for the Environment. Global Problems, Ethics and Democracy.* New York, Palgrave.

Alderman, H. 1986: *The effect of food price and income changes on the acquisition of food by low-income households.* Washington (D.C) International Food Policy Research Institute.

Alexandratos, N. 1995: *World Agriculture: Towards 2010.* Published by: Food and Agriculture Organisations of the United Nations (FAO) Chichester, John Wiley& Sons .

Allison, R. 1992: 'Environment and water resources in the arid zone, in Cooper, D.E & Paler, A. (eds) *The Environment in Question. Ethics and Global Issues.* London, Routledge.

Altvater, E. 1999: "The democratic order, economic globalization, and ecological restrictions – on the relation of material and formal democracy." In Shapiro & Hacker-Cordon *Democracy's Edges.* Cambridge, Cambridge University Press.

Alvstam,C. G. & Jordan, T. 1997: "Råvaruförsörjningen" In Jervas,G. et al. *2000-talets stora utmaningar. Aktuella resurs- och miljöproblem i ett konfliktperspektiv.* Stockholm, SNS förlag .

Andersson, C. & Wahlberg, K. 1996: "Gentekniken och framtiden" *Vår Föda,* 5/96 Temanummer om den nya maten.

Arblaster, A. 1994: *Democracy.* Buckingham, Open University Press.

Arneson, R. 1989 'Equality, and Equality of Opportunity for Welfare'. *Philosophical Studies, 55.*

Arneson, R. 1990: "Primary Goods Reconsidered". *NOUS* 24.

Ascher, W. 1979: *Forecasting. An Appraisal for Policy-makers and Planners.* London, The John Hopkins University Press.

Avnon, D. & de-Shalit, A. 1999: *Liberalism and its Practice*. London, Routledge.

Azar, C. & Berndes, G. 1999: "The Implication of Carbon Dioxide Abatement Policies on Food Prices." In Dragun, A. K. & Tisdell, C. (eds) *Sustainable Agriculture and Environment. Globalisation and the Impact of trade liberalisation*. Cheltenham, Edward Elgar Publ.

Baker, J. 1987: *Arguing for Equality*. London, Verso.

Baker, S., Kousis, M., Richardson, D. & Young, S. 1997: *The politics of sustainable development. Theory, Policy and Practice within the European Union*. London, Routledge.

Banerjee, S.B. 2001: "Who Sustains Whose Development? Sustainable Development and the Reinvention of Nature." (forthcoming) *Organisation Studies*.

Barber, B. 1984: *Strong Democracy*. Berkeley, University of California Press.

Barns, I. 1995: "Environment, Democracy and Community", *Environmental Politics*, vol 4, no 4.

Barry, B. 1996: "Circumstances of Justice and Future Generations" in R.I. Sikora & Barry B. *Obligations to Future Generations*. Cambridge, White Horse Press.

Barry, J. 1999a: *Rethinking Green Politics*. London, Sage.

Barry, J. 1999b: *Environment and Social Theory*. London, Routledge.

Barry, J. 2001: "Greening Liberal Democracy: Practice, Theory and Political Economy". In Barry, J & Wissenburg, M. 2001: *Sustainable liberal democracy. Ecological Challenges and Opportunities*. Basington, Palgrave.

Barry, J & Wissenburg, M. 2001: *Sustainable liberal democracy. Ecological Challenges and Opportunities*. Basington, Palgrave.

Benbrook, C. 1991: "Introduction." In National Research Council *Sustainable Agriculture Research and Education in the Field: A Proceedings*. Washington (D.C.), National Academy Press.

Bender, W.H. 1994: "An end use analysis of global food requirements". *Food policy*, vol. 19 no 4.

Benn, S.I. & Weinstein, W.L. 1971: 'Being free to act and being a free man' *Mind*, 80.

Bennulf, M. 1997: "Miljöengagemanget i graven?". In Holmberg, S. and Weibull, L. (eds), *Ett missnöjt folk?*, SOM-rapport nr 18 (Samhälle - Opinion - Media). Göteborgs universitet.

Bennulf, M. 1999: "Medborgarna och den hållbara utvecklingen". In Holmberg, S. and Weibull, L. (eds), *Ljusnande framtid*, SOM-rapport nr 22 (Samhälle - Opinion - Media). Göteborgs universitet..

Berlin, I. 1969: *Four Essays on Liberty*. Oxford University Press, Oxford.

Bhagwati, J. 1993: "The Case for Free Trade", *Scientific American*, Nov 1993.

Biesiot, W. & Mulder, H. 1994: "Energy Constraints on Sustainable Development Paths". In Smith, P.B., Okoye, S.E, de Wilde, J. And Deshingerkar, P. (eds) *The World at the Crossroads. Toward a Sustainable, Equitable and Liveable World*. London, Earthscan.

Blackburn, S. 1994: *The Oxford Dictionary of Philosophy,* Oxford, Oxford University Press.

Bongaarts, J. 1994: "Can the Growing Human Population Feed Itself?" *Scientific American* March 1994.

Borgström, G. 1970: *Mat för miljarder.* Stockholm, LT.

Boström, B-O. 1988: *Samtal om Demokrati.* Göteborg, Doxa.

Brown, H. 1954: *The Challenge of Man's Future.* Viking Press, New York.

Brown, L. 1994: *State of the World, 1994.* New York, Norton.

Brown, L. 1995: "Who Will Feed China? Wake-up Call for a Small Planet". *The Worldwatch Environmental Alert Series.* New York, Norton & Co.

Brown, L. 1996: "Tough Choices: Facing the challenge of food scarcity". *The World Watch Environmental Alert Series.* New York, Norton & Co.

Brown, L. & Halweil, B. 1998: "China's Water Shortage Could Shake World Food Security." *WorldWatch Environmental Alert Series.* New York, Norton & Co.

Brown, L. & Kane, H. 1994: "Full House." *Worldwatch Environmental Alert Series.* New York, Norton and Co.

Bruch, S. 1994: *Providing farmers' rights through in situ conservation of crop genetic resources.* Report to the FAO Commission on Plant Genetic Resources. Rome, UN.

Bruhn, C.M. 1992: "Consumer Concerns and Educational Strategies: Focus on Biotechnology". *Food Technology,* March.

Carlsson, S & Kumlin, S. 1998: "Den bärkraftiga utvecklingen och det globala underskottet." In Holmberg, S & Weibull, L. *Opinionssamhället,* SOM-rapport 20 (Samhälle, Opinion, Media, Göteborgs universitet).

Carson, R. 1962: *Silent Spring.* Cambridge, MA, Riverside Press.

Clark, M. 1990: "Meaningful social bonding as a universal human need" in Burton, J. (ed) *Conflict: human needs theory.* New York, St Martin's Press.

Cohen, G.A. 1989: "On the Currency of Equalitarian Justice", *Ethics* 99.

Cohen, G.A. 1988: *Self-ownership, freedom and equality.* Cambridge, Cambridge University Press.

Copp, D. 1992: "The Right to an Adequate Standard of Living: Justice, Autonomy and the Basic Needs". *Social Philosophy & Policy,* no 1.

Crosson, P. 1995: "Future Supplies of Land and Water for World Agriculture". In Islam, N. (ed) *Population and Food in The Early Twenty-First Century: Meeting future food demands of an increasing population.* International Food Policy Research Institute (IFPRI), Washington.

Cunningham, W.P. & Saigo, B. 2001: *Environmental Science: A Global Concern.* Boston, MCGraw-Hill

Dahl, R. A. 1956: *A Preface to Democratic Theory.* Chicago, University of Chicago Press.

Dahl, R. A. 1998: *On Democracy.* New Haven, Yale University Press.

Dahl, R.A. 1999: "Can international organisations be democratic?" in Shapiro, I. & Hacker-Cordon, C. (eds) *Democracy's Edges.* Cambridge, Cambridge University Press.

Daily, G., Dasgupta, P., Bolin, B. Et al. 1998: "Food Production, Population Growth, and the Environment." *Science* Vol. 281, 28 August.

Daly, H.E. 1991: 'Elements of Environmental Macroeconomics, in Constanza, R (ed) *Ecological Economics*. New York, Colombioa University Press.

Dasgupta, P. 1993: *An inquiry into well-being and destitution*. Oxford, Oxford University Press.

De Geus, M. 2001: 'Sustainability, Liberal democracy, Liberalism', in Barry, J & Wissenburg, M. (eds) *Sustainable liberal democracy. Ecological Challenges and Opportunities*, Basington, Palgrave.

DeSoto, H. 2000: *The Mystery of Capital: Why capitalism triumphs in the west and fails everywhere else*. New York, Basic Books.

Demandt, I. 1999: *The world phosphate fertilizer industry*. Research project Environmental Regulation, Globalisation of production and technological change. Background report No. 10. Maastricht, united Nations University Institute for New Technologies (INTECH).

De-Shalit, A. 1995: *Why Posterity Matters. Environmental policies and future generations*. London, Routledge.

De-Shalit, A. 2000: *The Environment Between Theory and Practice*. Oxford, Oxford University Press.

De Vries, F.W.T., Rabbinge, R. & Groot, J.J.R. 1997: "Potential and attainable food production and food security in different regions. *Phil. Trans. R. Soc. Lond. B* 352

Dobson, A. 2000: *Green political thought* (3rd edition), London, Routledge.

Dobson, A. 1998: *Justice and the Environment. Conceptions of Environmental Sustainability and Dimensions of Social Justice*. Oxford, Oxford University Press.

Dobson, A. 1990: *Green political thought* (1st edition). London, Routledge.

Dobson, A. 1996: "Representative democracy and the environment." In Lafferty, W.M. & Meadowcroft, J. *Democracy and the Environment. Problems and Prospects*. Cheltenham, Edward Elgar.

Douglas, M. 1986: *How Institutions Think*. Suracuse, (New York), Suracuse University Press.

Douglas, M., Gasper, D., Ney, S & Thompson, M. 1998: "Human Needs and Wants" in , Rayner, S & Malone, E.L. (eds) *Human Choice & Climate Change, vol 1: The societal framework*, Columbus, Battelle Press.

Dreborg, K-H. 1996: "Essence of Backcasting" *Future*, Nov.

Dryzek, J.S. 1987: *Rational ecology. Environment and Political Economy*. Oxford, Basil Blackwell.

Dryzek, J.S. 1990: *Discursive Democracy: Politics, Policy and Political Science*, Cambridge, Cambridge University Press.

Dryzek, J.S. 1992: "Ecology and Discursive Democracy: Beyond Liberal Capitalism and the Administrative State", *CNS*, 3 (2), June p. 18-42.

Dryzek, J, S. 1995: "Political and Ecological Communication", *Environmental Politics*, volume 4, no 4 p.13-30.

Dryzek, J. S. 1996: "Strategies of ecological democratization." In Lafferty, W.M. & Meadowcroft, J. *Democracy and the Environment. Problems and Prospects*, Cheltenham, Edward Elgar.

Dryzek, J. S. 1997: *The Politics of the Earth. Environmental discourses.* Oxford, Oxford University Press.

Dudney, D. 1990: "The Case Against Linking Environmental Degradation and National Security." *Millenium*, Vol. 19, No. 3.

Dunn, J. 1969: *The Political Thought of John Locke.* Cambridge, Cambridge University Press.

Dunn, J. 1979: *Western Political Theory in the Face of the Future.* Cambridge, Cambridge University Press.

Dworkin, R. 1977: *Taking Rights Seriously.* London, Duckworth.

Dworkin, R. 1981: "What is Equality? Part 2: Equality of resources." *Philosophy & Public Affairs*, 10, no. 4.

Ebbesson, J. 1995: *Compatibility of international and national environmental law.* Uppsala, Justus.

Eccleshall, R. 1986: *British Liberalism. Liberal Thought from the 1640s to 1980s.* London, Longman.

Eckersley, R. 1992: *Environmentalism and Political Theory: Towards an Ecocentric Approach*, London, UCL Press.

Eckersley, R. 1995: "Liberal Democracy and the Right of Nature: The Struggle for Inclusion." *Environmental Politics*, volume 4, no 4

Eckersley, R. 1997: *Green Justice, the State and Democracy.* Paper presented at the Environmental Justice: Global Ethics for the 21st Century Conference at Melbourne University Oct 1-3 1997. p.169-199.

Edwards, J. 1988: "Justice and the Bounds of Welfare". *Journal of Social Policy*, vol 17, no. 1.

Edwards, P. (ed) 1967: *The Encyclopedia of Philosophy.* Vol 5, New York, Macmillan.

Ehrlich, P. 1968: *The Population Bomb.* New York, Ballantine.

Ehrlich, A.H. 1994: "Building a Sustainable Food System." In Smith, P. B., Okoye, S.E. m fl. *The World at the Crossroads. Towards a Sustainable, Equitable and Liveable World.* London, Earthscan.

Ekins, P. 2000: *Economic Growth and Environmental Sustainability. The Prospects for Green Growth.* London, Routledge.

Elinder, C-G. & Järup, L. 1996: "Cadmium exposure and health risks: Recent findings." *Ambio* 25, no 5, August.

Ely, D.G., 1994: "The Rule of Grazing Sheep in Sustainable Agriculture." *Sheep Research Journal*, Special Issue 1994.

Engelhart, H & Hagman, U. 1998: "Vad händer om vi minskar vårt intag av animaliska proteiner?" *Vår föda* 1/98.

Engelman, R. & LeRoy, P. 1993: *Sustaining Water. Population and the Future of Renewable Water Supplies.* Washington, Population and Environmental Program, Population Action International.

Engelman, R. & LeRoy, P. 1995: *Conserving Land Population and Sustainable Food Production.* Population and Environmental Program Population Action International, Washington.

Engi, D. 1998: "China Infrastructure Initiative", *Sandi National Labaratory, Albuquerque.*

Ewin, R.E. 1991: *Virtues and Rights. The Moral Philosophy of Thomas Hobbes,* San Francisco, Westview Press.

Ezekiel, M. & Fox, K.A. 1967: *Methods of Correlation and Regression Analysis. Linear and Curvilinear.* New York, John Wiley & Sons.

Fageria, N.K. 1992: *Maximizing Crop Yields.* New York, Marcel Dekker.

Falkenmark, M. 1997: "Vattenproblem som konfliktfaktor". In Jervas et al. *2000-talets stora utmaningar. Aktuella resurs- och miljöproblem i ett konfliktperspektiv.* Stockholm, SNS förlag.

FAO, (United Nations Food and Agriculture Organisation) 1990: *Agricultural Production Yearbook,* Rome.

FAO (United Nations Food and Agriculture Organisation) 1995: *Irrigation in Africa in Figures,* Rome.

FAO (United Nations Food and Agriculture Organisation) 1998: *SOFA Report 1998.* (www.fao.org/WAICENT/FAOINFO/ECONOMIC/ESA/sofa/sofa97e/w580 0e00.htm)

Fernie, J & Pitkethly, A.S. 1985: *Resources, Environment and Policy,* London, Paul Chapman Publishing.

Fjaestad, B. & Olsson, S. 1997: "Därför gillar vi inte gentekniken." *Forskning & Framsteg 6/97.*

Flathman, R.E. 1987: *The Philosophy and Politics of Freedom.* Chicago, The University of Chicago Press.

Frankenhuis, M. T. 1994: "Sustainability, more than just sustainable animal production." In Huisman, E.A. m fl. (eds) *Biological basis of sustainable animal production. Proceedings of the fourth Zodiak Symposium.* Wageningen, The Netherlands April 13-15 1993.Wageningen, Wageningen Press.

Freeman, M.A. 1991: "Valuing Environmental Resources under Alternative Management Regimes." *Ecological Economics,* 3.

Frewer, L. J. 1997: "Consumer Aspects of Public Understanding and Acceptance of Transgenic Animals." In *Transgenetic Animals and Food Production,*(Royal Swedish Academy of Agriculture and Forestry) Kungl. Skogs- och Lantbruksakademiens tidskift Årg. 136 Nr 20.

Frisvold, G.B. & Condon, P. T. 1998: "The Convention on Biological Diversity and Agriculture: Implications and Unresolved Debates." *World Development* Vol. 26, No. 4.

Galtung, J. 1990: "International Development in Human Perspective." In Burton, J. (ed) *Conflict: human needs theory,* New York, St Martin's Press.

Gardner, G. 1997: "Irrigated area up slightly." In Brown, L., Renner, M. & Flavin, C. *Vital Signs,* New York, W.W. Norton.

Gasser, C. S. & Fraley, R. T. 1989 "Genetically Engineering Plants for Crop Improvement." *Science,* No 244.

Gaull, G. E. 1997: "Regulatory and Policy Issues in Animal Biotechnology Viewed in a Cultural Framework: An American Perspective." In *Transgenetic Animals and Food Production,*(Royal Swedish Academy of Agriculture and Forestry) Kungl. Skogs- och Lantbruksakademiens tidskift Årg. 136 Nr 20.

GN 1997: *Konsumenterna och gentekniken.* Gentekniknämnden/ Swedish Gene Technology Advisory Board 1997–97-15), Gentekniknämndens utredningsserie.

GN 1998: *Genteknik, Livsmedel och Säkerhet.* (Gentekniknämnden/ Swedish Gene Technology Advisory Board 1998-07-15. Gentekniknämndens utredningsserie.

Gewirth, A. 1978: *Reason and Morality.* Chicago, Chicago University Press.

Gewirth, A. 1982: *Human Rights: Essays on Justification and Applications,* Chicago, University of Chicago Press.

Gleeson, B. & Low, N. 2001: *Governing for the Environment. Global Problems, Ethics and Democracy,* New York, Palgrave.

Goklany, I.M. 1999: "Meeting global food needs: the environmental trade-offs between increasing land conversion and land productivity." In Morris, J & Bate, R. (eds.) *Fearing Food. Risk, Health & Environment,* Woburn, MA, Butterworth Heinemann.

Goodin, R. E. 1992: *Green Political Theory,* Cambridge, Polity Press.

Goodin, R. E. 1996: "Enfranchising the Earth, and its alternatives", *Political Studies,* 44: 835-850.

Goudie. A. 2000: *The Human Impact on the Natural Environment,* (5th edition), Oxford, Blackwell.

Gray, J. 1983: *Mill on Liberty: a Defence.* London, Routledge & Kegan Paul.

Gray, J. 1989: *Liberalism. Essays in Political Philosophy.* London, Routledge.

Gray, J. 1993: *Beyond the New Right. Markets, Government and the Common Environment.* London, Routledge.

Gray, J. 1995: *Liberalism.* Buckingham, Open University Press.

Green, T.H. 1888: "Liberal Legislation and Freedom of Contract." Reprinted in Miller, D. 1991: *Liberty.* Oxford, Oxford University Press.

Greenpeace 1996: *Genvägar till en ekologisk katastrof? Genmanipulation och genetisk förorening.* Stockholm, Greenpeace Sverige.

Gruen, L. & Jamieson, D. 1994: *Reflecting on Nature. Readings in Environmental Philosophy.* New York, Oxford University Press.

Habermas, J. 1996: *Between Facts and Norms: Contributions to a Discourse: Ethics of Law and Democracy.* Cambridge, Polity.

Halldenius, L. 2000: *Liberty Revisited. A historical and systematic account of an egalitarian conception of liberty and legitimacy.* Lund, Bokbox Publications

Hardin, G. 1968: "The Tragedy of the Commons." *Science,* 168.

Hardin, G. 1993: *Living Within Limits: Ecology, Economics and Population Taboos.* New York, Oxford University Press.

Hardin, R. 1999: "Democracy and collective bads." In Shapiro, I. & Hacker-Cordon, C. (eds) *Democracy's Edges.* Cambridge, Cambridge University Press.

Harrison, P. 1993: *The Third Revolution. Population, Environment and a Sustainable World.* London, Penguin Books.

Hart, H.L.A. 1961: *The Concept of Law.* Oxford, Oxford University Press.

Hayek, F.A. 1960: *The Constitution of Liberty.* London, Routledge.

Hayward, B, M. 1995: "The Greening of Participatory Democracy: A Reconsideration of Theory." *Environmental Politics,* volume 4, no 4 p.215-246.

Hayward, T. 1995: *Ecological Thought: An introduction,* Oxford, Polity Press.

Hayward, T. 1998: *Political Theory and Ecological Values,* Cambridge, Polity Press.

Heilbronner, R. 1974: *An Inquiry into the Human Prospect,* New York, Harper and Row.

Held, D. 1995: *Democracy and the Global Order. From the Modern State to Cosmopolitical Governance.* Cambridge, Polity Press.

Held, D. 1997: *Models of Democracy.* Cambridge, Polity Press.

Hjort af Ornäs, A. & Strömqvist, L. 1997: "Jordförstöring och miljösäkerhet". In Jervas, G. et al. (eds) *2000-talets stora utmaningar. Aktuella resurs- och miljöproblem i ett konfliktperspektiv.* Stockholm, SNS förlag.

Hoban, T. J. 1997: "Consumer Acceptance of Biotechnology: An International Perspective." *Nature Biotechnology.* Vol. 15, March.

Hobbes, T. 1651: *Leviathan.* Reprinted 1955 by Basil Blackwell, Oxford.

Hobhouse, L.T. 1974: *Liberalism.* Oxford, Oxford university Press

Holden, B. 1995: *Understanding Liberal Dmocracy.* London, Harvester Wheatsheaf.

Holmberg, J, 1995: *Socio-Ecological Principles and Indicators for Sustainability,* Ph.D. Thesis, Institute of Physical Resource Theory, Chalmers University of Technology, Göteborg.

Homer-Dixon, T. F. 1994: "Environmental Scarcities and Violent Conflict: Evidence from Cases." *International Security, Vol 19, No. 1.*

Hurka, T. 1998: *Perfectionism.* Oxford, Oxford University Press.

Jacobs, M. 1991: *The Green Economy.* London, Pluto Press.

Jacobs, M. 1996: *The Politics of the Real World.* London, Earthscan.

Janelm, A. & Wahlberg, K. 1996: "Fackmyndigheterna". In Gentekniknämdens utredning *Om Märkning av Genetekniskt Modifierade Livsmedel.* Gentekniknämndens utredningsserie / Swedish Gene Technology Advisory Board 1996-10-15.

Jervas, G. 1997: "Översikt, slutsatser och rekommendationer. Råvaruproblem i ny belysning." In Jervas, G. et al. *2000-talets stora utmaningar. Aktuella resurs- och miljöproblem i ett konfliktperspektiv.* Stockholm, SNS förlag.

Jones, G. & Hollier, G. 1997: *Resources, Society and Environmental Management*, London, Paul Chapman Publishing.

Jones, P. 1994: *Rights*. London, The Macmillan Press.

Järup, L. & Berglund, M. 1998: "Health effects of cadmium exposure – a review of the literature and a risk estimate." *Scandinavian Journal of Work, Environment & Health* (1998:24 Suppl 1:52).

Karlsson, S. 1996: *Some reflections on the need for and possibilities of a material decoupling of society and nature.* Institutionsrapport 1996:06, Fysisk Resursteori, Chalmers.

Karlsson, T. & Pettersson, O. 1998: "Vegan, vegetarian, allätare." *Kungl. Skogs- och Lantbruksakademiens tidskift* Årg. 137 Nr 5 Kungl. Skogs- och lantbruksakademien (Royal Swedish Academy of Agriculture and Forestry) *Maten i Genteknikens Tidevarv.* Paper based on the conference report "Transgenic Animals and Food Production." KSLAT nr 20-1997. Kungl. Skogs- och Lantbruksakademiens tidskift Årg. 136 Nr 20.

Kates, R. W. & Haarmann, V. (1992) "Where the Poor Live." *Environment*, Vol. 34, No. 4.

Kennedy, P 1993: *Preparing for the Twenty-first Century*, London, Harper Collins Publishers.

Kenny, M & Meadowcraft, J. 1999: Planning Sustainability, London, Routledge.

Kramer, P.J. & Boyer, J.S. 1995: *Water Relations of Plants and Soils*, San Diego, Academic Press.

Kumm, K-I. 1998: "Kyckling, biff eller gröt?" *Kungl. Skogs- och Lantbruksakademiens tidskift* Årg. 137 Nr 5 Kungl. Skogs- och lantbruksakademien (Royal Swedish Academy of Agriculture and Forestry). In *Maten i Genteknikens Tidevarv.* Paper based on the conference report "Transgenic Animals and Food Production". KSLAT nr 20-1997.

Lafferty, W.M & Meadowcroft, J. 1996: 'Democracy and the environment: congruence and conflict – preliminary reflections.' In Lafferty, W.M & Meadowcroft, J. (eds). *Democracy and the Environment: Problems and Prospects.* Cheltenham, Edward Elgar.

Lang, T. 1999: "Local sustainability in a sea of globalisation? The case of food policy." In Kenny, M & Meadowcraft, J. 1999: *Planning Sustainability.* London, Routledge.

Langhelle, O. 2000a: *Fra ideer til politikk: Baerekraftig utvickling – svade eller rettesnor for samfunnsutvicklingen*, Institutt for statsvitenskap, Oslo University.

Langhelle, O. 2000b: "Why Ecological Modernisation and Sustainable Development should not be Conflated." *Journal of Environmental Policy and Planning* vol. 2 no: 4

Langhelle, O. 2000c: "Sustainable Development and Social Justice – Expanding the Rawlsian Framework of Global Justice." *Environmental Values* vol. 9 no: 3

Leach, G. 1995: *Global Land and Food in the 21st Century: Trends & Issues for Sustainability.* Stockholm, SEI (Stockholm Environmental Institute).

Lélé, S.M. 1991: "Sustainable Development: A Critical Review." *World Development*, vol 19, no 6.

Lindgren, S. 1996: "Mikroorganismer och genteknik: Effektivare livsmedelsproduktion – men politisk enighet krävs." *Vår Föda* 5/96.

Livsmedelsverket 1996: *Kost och hälsa – riskuppfattningar och attityder. Resultat av en enkätundersökning.* Swedish national food administration Report 1/96.

Low, N. & Gleeson, B. 1998: *Justice, Society and Nature. An Exploration of Political Ecology.* London, Routledge.

Lu, Y-C. & Kelly, T. C. 1995: "Implications of Sustainable Agriculture for the World Food Situation." *Food Review International,* 11(2).

Luc, J. & Jeffrey, R. 1997 "Sustainable agriculture and global institutions: Emerging institutions and mixed incentives." *Society & Natural Resources.* May/June, Vol. 10, no. 3.

Lukes, S. 1973: *Individualism.* Oxford, Blackwell.

Lukes, S. 1991: "Equality and Liberty Must They Conflict?" In Held, D. (ed) *Political Theory Today.* Cambridge, Polity press.

MacCallum, G. 1967: "Negative and Positive Freedom". *Philosophical Review,* 76,

Macpherson, C.B. 1977: *The Life and Times of Liberal Democracy.* Oxford, Oxford University Press.

Manning, D.J. 1976: *Liberalism.* London, Dent.

Martell, L. 1994: *Ecology and Society.* Cambridge, Polity Press.

Martinez-Alier, J. 1987: *Ecological Economics. Energy, Environment and Society.* Oxford, Blackwell.

Maslow, A. 1943: "A theory of human motivation." *Psychology Review*, 50.

Mason, A. 1998: *Ideals of Equality.* Oxford, Blackwell.

Mason, M. 1999: *Environmental Democracy*, London, Earthscan

Mathews, F. 1995a: "Introduction". *Environmental Politics*, volume 4, no 4

Mathews, F. 1995b: "Community and the Ecological Self." *Environmental Politics*, volume 4, no 4

Mautner, T. 1996: *A Dictionary of Philosophy.* Oxford, Blackwell.

Max-Neef, M. 1991: *Human scale development.* New York, Apex Press.

Meadows, D., Randers, J. And Brehens, W. 1972: *The Limits to Growth: A Report for the Club of Rome's Project on the Predicament of Mankind.* New York, Universe.

Meredith, T.C. 1992: "Environmental Impact Assessment, Cultural Diversity, and Sustainable Rural Development." *Environmental Impact Assessment Review* 12:1/2 (March/June).

Milio, N. 1990: *Nutritional Policy for Food-Rich Countries: A Strategic Analysis.* Baltimore: The Johns Hopkins University press.

Milio, N. 1991: "Toward health longevity." *Scandinavian Journal of Social Medicine* 19, No. 2.

Mill, J.S. 1848: "Principles of Political Economy." Reprinted in Eccleshall, R. (ed) 1986: *British Liberalism. Liberal thought from the 1640s to 1980s.* London, Longman.

Mill, J.S. 1982: *On Liberty.* (orig.1859) Reprinted by Penguin books, Harmondsworth

Miller, D. 1991: *Liberty.* Oxford, Oxford University Press.

Montesquieu, C.L. 1952: *The Spirit of Laws,* Chicago, William Benton.

Mooney, P. 1993: "The law of the seed: another development and plant genetic resources." *Development Dialogue* 1-2.

Morris, J & Bate, R. 1999: *Fearing Food. Risk, Health & Environment* (eds.). Woburn, MA, Butterworth Heinemann.

Munasinghe, M. & McNeely, J. 1995: "Key Concepts and Terminology of Sustainable Development." In Munasinghe, M. & Shearer, W. *Defining and measuring sustainability: the biogeophysical foundations.* The International Bank for Reconstruction and Development/The World Bank, Washington.

Naess, A. 1989: *Community, Ecology and Lifestyle.* Cambridge, Cambridge University Press.

Nagpal, T. 1995: 'Voices from the Developing World: Progress Toward Sustainable Development." *Environment* 37 no 8

Nozick, R. 1974: *Anarchy, State, and Utopia.* Oxford, Basil Blackwell.

Nussbaum, M. 1990: "Aristotelian Social Democracy." In Douglas, R.B. & Gerald, M.M. & Richardsson, H.S. (eds.) *Liberalism and the Good.* New York, Routledge.

O'Neill, J. 1993: *Ecology, Policy and Politics. Human Well-being and the Natural World.* London, Routledge.

O'Neill, O. 2000: *Bounds of Justice.* Cambridge, Cambridge University Press.

O'Riordan, T. 1996: "Democracy and the sustainability transition." In Lafferty, W.M. & Meadowcroft, J. *Democracy and the Environment. Problems and Prospects.* Cheltenham, Edward Elgar

Ohlsson, L. 1997: "Miljörelaterad resursknapphet." In Jervas G. M fl. *2000-talets stora utmaningar. Aktuella resurs- och miljöproblem i ett konfliktperspektiv.* Stockholm, SNS förlag.

Ohlsson, L. 1999: *Environmental Scarcity and Conflict. A study of Malthusian concerns.* PhD Thesis at the Department of Peace and Development Research, Göteborg University.

Oksanen, M. 2001: "Privatising Genetic Resources: Biodiversity Preservation and intellectual Property Rights." In Barry, J & Wissenburg, M. 2001: *Sustainable liberal democracy. Ecological Challenges and Opportunities.* Basington, Palgrave

Olson, M. 1965: *The Logic of Collective Action.* Cambridge, Harvard University Press.

Ophuls, W. 1977: *Ecology and the Politics of Scarcity.* San Francisco, Freeman.

Ophuls, W. & Boyan, A. Jr. 1992: *Ecology and the Politics of Scarcity Revisited. The Unraveling of the American Dream.* San Francisco, Freeman.

Ostrom, E. 1990: *Governing the Commons.* Cambridge University Press, Cambridge.

Ostrom, E. Burger, E., Field, C.B., Norgaard, R.B. & Polansky, D. 1999: "Revisiting the Commons: Local Lessons, Global Challenges." *Science,* 9 April, vol 284.

Ostrom, E., Gardner, R. & Walker, J. 1994: *Rules, Games, & Common-Pool Resources.* Ann Abor, The University of Michigan Press.

Paelke, R. 1995: "Environmental values for a sustainable society: the democratic challenge." In Lafferty, W.M. & Meadowcroft, J. *Democracy and the Environment. Problems and Prospects.* Cheltenham, Edward Elgar

Paelke, R. 1996: "Environmental challenges to democratic practice." In Fischer, F. & Black, M. *Greening Environmental Policy. The Politics of a Sustainable Future.* London, Paul Chapman Publishing

Passmore, J. 1974: *Man's Responsibility for Nature*, London: Duckworth.

Patton, C.V. & Sawichi, D. S. 1993: *Basic Methods of Policy Analysis and Planning.* Englewood Cliffs, Prentice Hall

Pearce, D.W. & Turner, K.R. 1990: *Economics of Natural Resources and the Environment,* London, Harvester-Wheatsheaf

Peczenic, A. 1995: *Vad är rätt? Om demokrati, rättssäkerhet, etik och juridisk argumentation.* Institutet för rättsvetenskaplig forskning (CLVI). Stockholm, Nordstedts juridik

Perrings, C. 1991: *Ecological Sustainability and Environmental Control.* Center for Resource and Environmental Studies, Australian National University.

Plamenatz J. 1963: *Man and Society.* Vol 1. London, Longman.

Plant, R. 1991: *Modern Political Thinking.* Oxford, Blackwell.

Popkin, B. M. (1993) "Nutritional Patterns and Transition." *Population and Development Review.* 19 No. 1 (March)

Postel, S. 1998: "Water for Food Production: Will There be Enough in 2025?". *BioScience Vol. 48 No. 8*

Postel, S. 1997: *Last Oasis. Facing Water Scarcity.* New York, W.W. Norton & Company

Postel, S., Daily, G.C., Ehrlich, P.R. 1996: "Human appropriation of renewable freshwater". *Science* 271: 785-788

PRB 1995: *1995 World Population Data Sheet.* (Population Reference Bureau) Washington (D.C)

Premfors, R. 1989: *Policyanalys.* Lund, Studentlitteratur.

RSAAF 1997: *Transgenetic Animals and Food Production,*(Royal Swedish Academy of Agriculture and Forestry) Kungl. Skogs- och Lantbruksakademiens tidskift Årg. 136 Nr 20

Radcliffe, J. 2000: *Green Politics: Dictatorship or Democracy?* Basingstoke, Macmillan

Ramsay, M. 1992: *Human needs and the market.* Avebury (England), Aldershot.

Raskin, P. & Margolis, R. 1995: *Global energy in the 21st Century: Patterns, Projections and Problems.* Boston, SEI (Stockholm Environmental Institute)

Rawls , J. 1972: *A Theory of Justice.* Oxford, Oxford University Press. *Studies,* 7

Rawls, J. 1982: "Social Unity and Primary Goods." In Sen, A. & Williams, B. (eds.) *Utilitarianism and Beyond.* Cambridge, Rawls, J. 1993: *Political Liberalism.* New York, Columbia University Press.

Rawls, J. 1987: "The Idea of an Overlapping Consensus." *Oxford Journal of Legal* Studies 7 Cambridge university Press

Raz, J. 1986: *The Morality of Freedom.* Oxford, Clarendon Press.

Rifkin, J. 1992: *Beyond Beef. The Rise and Fall of the Cattle Culture.* New York, Penguin Group (Plume).

Rifkin, J. 1998: *The Biotech Century. The Coming Age of Genetic Commerce.* Suffolk, St Edmundsbury Press.

Robinson, J.B. 1990: "Future Under Glass. A recipe for people who hate to predict." *Future.*

Robinson, J.B. 1988: "Unlearning and Backcasting: Rethinking Some of the Questions We Ask about the Future." *Technological Forecasting and Social Change,* 33

Rosegrant, M.W. 1997: *Water Resources in the Twenty-First Century: Challenges and Implications for Action.* Washington, International Food Policy Research Institute.

Rothstein, B. 1996: *Vad bör staten göra? Om välfärdsstatens moraliska och politiska logik.* Stockholm, SNS förlag.

Routley, R. & Routley, V. 1982: "Nuclear power – some ethical and social dimensions." In Regan, T. & Van De Veer (eds) *And Justice for all.* Totowa, N. J. Rowman & Littlefield.

Russell, B. 1945: *A history of western philosophy and its connection with political and social circumstances from the earliest times to the present day.* New York, Simon and Schuster

Rönnfeldt, C. 1997a: "Linking Research on the Environment, Poverty and Conflict." In Smith, D. & Öngstreng, W. *Research on Environment, Poverty and Conflict. A Proposal.* FNI/PRI Report (PRI REPORT 3/97)

Rönnfeldt, C. 1997b: "Three Generations of Environmental and Security Research." *Journal of Peace Research,* vol 34, no 4

Sachs, W. 1999: "Sustainable Development and the Crisis of Nature: On the Political Anatomy of an Oxymoron." In Fischer, F. & Hajer, M.A. (eds.) *Living with nature: environmental politics as cultural discourse,* New York, Oxford University Press.

Sagoff, M. 1988: *The Economy of the Earth. Philosophy, Law, and the Environment,* Cambridge, Cambridge University Press.

Sahlins, M. 1968: *Stone Age economics.* London, Tavistock

Samuel, H. L. 1902: "Liberalism: an attempt to state the principles and proposals of contemporary liberalism in England." Reprinted in Eccleshall, R. 1986 *British Liberalism. Liberal Thought from the 1640s to 1980s.* London, Longman.

Sanchez, P.A. & Leakey, R.B. 1997: "Land use transfomation in Africa: three determinants for balancing food security with natural resource utilisation.". *European Journal of Agronomy, 7*

Sausouney, R. 1995: "Livestock: A driving force for food security and sustainable development." *World Animal Review* 84/85

Saward, M. 1993: "Green Democracy?" In Dobson, A. & Lucardie, P. *The Politics of Nature. Explorations in green political theory,* London, Routledge.

Schroten, E. 1997: "Animal Biotechnology, Public Perception and Public Policy from a Moral Point of View." In *Transgenetic Animals and Food Production,*(Royal Swedish Academy of Agriculture and Forestry) Kungl. Skogs- och Lantbruksakademiens tidskift Årg. 136 Nr 20

Scitovsky, T. 1992: *The loyless economy: an inquiry into human satisfaction and consumer dissatisfaction.* (2nd edition.). Oxford, Oxford University Press.

Sen, A.K. 1993a: "The Economics of Life and Death." *Scientific American,* May.

Sen, A. K. 1993b: "Capability and Well-being." In Nussbaum, M. & Sen, A. K. *The Quality of Life,* Oxford, Clarendon Press.

Sen, A. K 1992: *Inequality reexamined.* Oxford, Oxford University Press.

Sen, A. K. 1988: "Freedom of choice: concept and content." European Economic Review 32, 269-94

Sen, A. K. 1982: *Choice, Welfare and Measurement.* Cambridge, Mass., MIT Press.

Sen, A. K. 1981: *Poverty and famines: an essay on entitlement and deprivation.* Oxford, Oxford University Press.

SEPA 1996: *Biff och bil?* – *Om hushållens miljöval* (Swedish Environmental Protection Agency/Naturvårdsverket) 1996: 4542

SEPA 1997a: *Omvärlden år 2021.* (Swedish Environmental Protection Agency/Naturvårdsverket) 1997:4726

SEPA 1997b: *Fosfor* – *livsnödvändigt, ändligt och ett miljöproblem* (Swedish Environmental Protection Agency/Naturvårdsverket) 1997:4730

SEPA 1997c: *Förluster av fosfor från jordbruksmark.* (Swedish Environmental Protection Agency/Naturvårdsverket) 1997:4731

SEPA 1997d: *Att äta för en bättre miljö. Slutrapport från systemstudie Livsmedel* (Swedish Environmental Protection Agency/Naturvårdsverket) 1997:4971

SEPA 1997e: *Det framtida Jordbruket. Slutrapport från systemstudien för ett miljöanpassat och uthålligt jordbruk.* (Swedish Environmental Protection Agency/Naturvårdsverket) 1997:4755

Shiva, V. 1998: *Biopiracy: The Plunder of Nature and Knowledge.* Totnes, Green Books

SIDA 1998: *Opinion –98. En sammanfattning av Sidas basundersökning.* Sida Informationsavdelningen.

Smil, V. 1990: "Nitrogen and phosphorus". In Turner, B.L., Clark, W.C., Kates, R.W., mfl.(eds) *The Earth as Transformed by Human Action – Global and Regional Changes in the Biosphere over the past 300 Years.* Cambridge, Cambridge University Press.

Smil, V. 1994: "How Many People can the Earth Feed?" *Population And Development Review* 20. No 2 (June)

Smil, V. 2000: "Phosphorus in the environment: Natural flows of human interferences." *Annu. Rev. Energy Environ.* 25

Smith, P. B., Okoye, S.E. et al. (eds) 1994: *The World at the Crossroads. Towards a Sustainable, Equitable and Liveable World.* London, Earthscan.

SOU 1997: *EU:s jordbrukspolitik och den globala livsmedels-försörjningen. Rapport till Kommittén för reformering av EU:s gemensamma jordbrukspolitik (komiCAP)* Jordbruksdepartementet. Statens offentliga utredningar SOU 1997:26. Stockholm, Fritzes

Sparks, P., Shepherd, R. & Frewer, L.J. 1995: "Assessing and Structuring attitudes towards the use of gene technology in food production: the role of perceived ethical obligation". *Journal of Basic and Applied Social Psychology,* 16

Steen, P. *et al.* 1997: *Färder i framtiden. Transporter i ett bärkraftigt samhälle.* Preliminär version från FMS (Forskningsgruppen för Miljöstrategiska Studier) fms 58, Stockholm.

Steen, P. & Åkerman, J. 1994: *Syntes av studier över omställningen av energi- och transportsystemeen i Sverige.* Supplement 6 in report from K-delegationen 1994, SOU 1994:138. Fritzes, Stockholm.

Steiner, H. 1974: "Individual Liberty", *Proceedings of the Aristotelian Society*

Stålgren, P. & Swain, A. 2000: "Managing the Zambezi: Need to Build Water Institutions" In Dan Tevera, D. & Moyo, S. (eds.) *Environmental Security in Southern Africa.* Harare, SAPES

Tawney, R.H. 1931: *Equality.* London, George Allen & Unwin

Thompson, J. 1995: "Towards a Green World Order: Environment and World Politics". *Environmental Politics,* 4, no 4

Thompson, P. B. 1997: "Public Understanding and Acceptance: Ethical Aspects." In *Transgenetic Animals and Food Production,*(Royal Swedish Academy of Agriculture and Forestry) Kungl. Skogs- och Lantbruksakademiens tidskift Årg. 136 Nr 20

Tietenberg, T. 1994: *Environmental Economics and Policy.* New York, Harper Collins Collegue Publishers.

Timmer, P. (ed) 1991: *Agriculture and the State: Growth, Employment, and Poverty in Developing Countries,* Ithaca, Cornell University Press.

Timmer,P. C. & Falcon, W. P. & Pearson, S. R. 1984: *Food Policy Analysis.* Baltimore, John Hopkins University Press.

Tims, W. 1995: "Response to section A & B." In Bouma, J, Kuyvenhoven, A & Zandstra, H.G. *Eco-regional approaches for sustainable land use and food production. Proceedings of a symposium on eco-regional approaches in agricultural research.*12-16 December 1994, ISNAR, The Hague. Dordrecht, Kluwer Academic Publishers

Toman, M.A. 1992: "The Difficulty in Defining Sustainability." *Resources* (Winter issue)

Torgerson, D. 1994: "Strategy and Ideology in Environmentalism: A Decentered Approach to Sustainability." *Industrial and Environmental Crisis Quarterly*, 8

U.S. Congress (Office of Technology Assessment) 1992: *A New Technological Era for American Agriculture.* OTA-F-474. Washington (DC), Government Printing Office, August.

UNDP 1992: *Human Development Report.* New York, Oxford University Press (for the United Nations Development Program).

Uno, K. 1995: *Environmental Options: Accounting for Sustainability.* Dordrecht, Kluwer Academic Publishers

USDA (United States Department of Agriculture.) 1997: *Production, supply, and contribution.* (electronic database)

Waever, O. 1995: "Securitization and Desecuritization." In Lipschutz, R. D. (ed) *On Security.* New York, Columbia University Press

Waggoner, P. E. 1994: *How Much Land Can Ten Billion People Spare for Nature?* City Ames, Council for Agriculture Sciences and Technology (CAST). Taskforce report 121

Wagner, H-G. & Hammond, K. 1997: "Animal Production Improvement in Developing Countries: Issues Concerning the Application of Biotechnology." In *Transgenetic Animals and Food Production,*(Royal Swedish Academy of Agriculture and Forestry) Kungl. Skogs- och Lantbruksakademiens tidskift Årg. 136 Nr 20

Walzer, M. 1983: *Spheres of Justice; A Defence of Pluralism & Equality.* Oxford, Blackwell

Van Parijs, P. 1992: *Real Freedom for All. What (if anything) can justify capitalism?* Oxford, Clarendon

WCED 1987: *Our Common Future* (United Nations World Commission On Environment and Development). Oxford, Oxford University Press.

Weale, A. 1999: *Democracy.* London, Macmillan

Webster, A.J.F. 1994: "Meat and Right: the Ethical Dilemma." *Proceedings of the Nutrion Society*, 53

Wichelns, D. 2001: " The role of 'virtual water' in efforts to achieve food security and other national goals, with an example from Egypt." *Agricultural Water Management* 49

Wilson, M.A & Hillman, J.R & Robinson, D.R. 1999: "Genetic Modification in Context and Perspective." In Morris, J & Bate, R. (eds.) *Fearing Food. Risk, Health & Environment*, Woburn, MA, Butterworth Heinemann

Wirsenius, S. 2000: *Human Use of Land and Organic Materials. Modeling the Turnover of Biomass in the Global Food System.* Göteborg, Department of Physical Resource Theory, Chalmers University of Technology.

Wirsenius, S. 2002: "Scenarios of Global Food and Agriculture to the Year 2050." Working paper. Göteborg, Department of Physical Resource Theory, Chalmers University of Technology.

Wissenburg, M. 1998: *Green liberalism. The free and the green society,* London, UCL Press.

Wolff, J. 1998: "John Rawls: Liberal Democracy Restated." In Carter, A. & Stokes, G. *Liberal Democracy and its Critics.* Cambridge, Polity Press.

Wolff, J. 1991: *Robert Nozick. Property, Justice and the Minimal State,* Cambridge, Polity Press.

WRI (World Resource Institute) 1986: *World Resources 1986-87.* A report by the World Resources Institute in collaboration with The United Nations Environment Programme and The United Nations Development Programme. New York, Oxford University Press.

WRI (World Resources Institute) 1992: *World Resources 1992-93.* A report by the World Resources Institute in collaboration with The United Nations Environment Programme and The United Nations Development Programme. New York, Oxford University Press.

WRI (World Resources Institute) 1994: *World Resources 1994-95.* A report by the World Resources Institute in collaboration with The United Nations Environment Programme and The United Nations Development Programme. New York, Oxford University Press.

Zechendorf, B. 1994: "What the Public Thinks About Biotechnology. Better than synthetic food but worse than organ transplantation: A survey of opinion polls." *Bio-Technology* Vol. 12